DRINK IN 1914-1922 : A LESSON IN CONTROL

DRINK IN 1914-1922 : A LESSON IN CONTROL

Arthur Shadwell

www.General-Books.net

Publication Data:

Title: Drink in 1914-1922 : a Lesson in Control
Author: Shadwell, Arthur, 1854-1936
Publisher: London : Longmans
Publication date: 1923
Subjects: Liquor laws – Great Britain
Liquor traffic – Great Britain

DRINK IN 1914-1922 : A LESSON IN CONTROL

PREFACE

This book was written for the Carnegie Endowment Fund for International Peace, as one of the war monographs the directors are issuing, and consequently its scope was limited by editorial requirements to the war experience of Great Britain. But that experience throws much light on the wider question, which is always with us, of the hquor trade and its control in general. It is an instructive addition to our knowledge of the problem, and as such it has a permanent value and a more than historical interest. It furnishes fresh proofs of the need of control in the public interest, demonstrates the possibilities and the limitations of control, and indicates the most effective means of control. As an old student of the subject I have had that aspect constantly before my mind, and hope the book will be read in the same sense. I know of no field of legislation in which the teaching of experience is more needed yet more often subordinated to fancy, prejudice, and interest; whence its unfortunately controversial character.

The book was withdrawn, after completion, from the Carnegie Endowment Fund in order to secure speedier publication than the arrangements of that institution would permit, because the state of my health necessitated its passage through the press without delay. I am happy to have placed it in the experienced hands of Messrs. Longmans,

Green Co., who pubhshed an earher work on temperance and liquor legislation for me some years ago.

I have to acknowledge indebtedness to Lord D'Abernon and Sir John Pedder, of the Home Office, for invaluable assistance in the collection and verification of facts. I have also to thank the Brewers' Society, the United Kingdom Alliance, and other organisations for particular information, and I am under obligations to the Eev. Henry Carter's book on the

Control of the Drink Trade," published in 1918, for certain details in the early part of the period covered. For the arrangement of the material, the interpretation of facts, and the conclusions drawn, I am solely responsible.

The official documents contained in the Appendix are reproduced by the kind permission of the Controller of H. M. Stationery Office, for which my thanks are due.

A. SHADWELL. September 1923.

INTRODUCTION

The war affected the production and consumption of alcoholic liquors in every country by the withdrawal of materials for manufacture in order to make good the deficiency of food, by interference with transport, and by increase of prices. These changes caused a general, though unequal, diminution of production and consumption. The civilian population was further affected in belhgerent countries by the withdrawal of varying quantities from ordinary consumption for the use of the armies. But in addition to these general effects of the war, specific measures of inteiference were enacted by Government in certain countries. In France the manufacture and sale of absinthe were prohibited, and spirits in general were excluded from the war zone, with an exception in favour of home-distillation from fruits; in Kussia the manufacture of vodka, which was a Government monopoly, was stopped; in Sweden the serving of spirits for consumption on the premises was allowed only with meals above a certain price, and the sale for off consumption was rationed; in Great Britain a system of control was instituted which placed the trade in all its branches on a wholly different legal footing, changed its practice in many important respects, and introduced far-reaching experiments. In this procedure Great Britain stood quite alone. Prohibition, adopted in Norway in 1916, was rather the culmination of a long-standing campaign than a war measure; and the same may be said of its adoption during the war in the Canadian provinces and Newfoundland. The war no doubt stimulated a movement already in progress, as it did in the United States, where national prohibition came into force in 1919; but the action in Great Britain was quite new and totally different.

In April 1919 an international conference, of an informal character, was held in Paris on the invitation of the French Ligm Nationale contre VAlcoolisme, at which representatives of the leading temperance organisations in many European countries and the United States were present. One of the declared objects of the meeting, which lasted for several days, was to collate information about the measures taken during the war and their results." But the only countries about which any precise information was presented were Great Britain and Sweden. For the former Lord D'Abernon, chairman of the official Control Board, read a paper on ' The Effects of War-time Control of the Liquor Traffic in England," with full statistics, and for Sweden M. Bratt, chairman of the Stockholm Bolag, presented a mass of detailed information. Some general statements were made about the experience of France and Belgium; but from other countries no information at all was forthcoming. It was decided to establish an office for collecting international statistics under the direction of the Bureau International Anti-alcoolique of Lausanne, and the Anti-Saloon League of the United States, which was represented at the meeting by Bishop Cannon and Mr. W. Johnson, undertook to defray the expense. But nothing has yet been published by the Bureau. The only countries, therefore, for which sufficient data are to hand for a study of liquor control in war time are Great Britain and Sweden.

The present volume deals with the former, but a reference will be made to the experience of Sweden, which is of considerable interest. Much is to be learnt from the extensive and many-sided British experiments in control. They have conjBrmed old lessons and taught new ones, and have left a permanent impress upon the whole system. The emergency of the war forced the country to adopt changes which would not have been accepted in other circumstances; and though no conclusion remains unchallenged in this most controversial domain of social life, the complete restoration of the former state of things is desired by no responsible person.

For the information of readers unfamiliar with the conditions in the British Isles and to enable them to understand the war-time changes, it is necessary to explain that the retail sale of intoxicating hquor for consumption on the premises that is, the ordinary public-house trade has been subject to statutory control in England since the year 1495, and under a system of hcensing since 1551. The sale was then prohibited except under a licence granted by the local justices; and this system, apphed later to Scotland and Ireland, and extended to other forms of sale, has continued ever since with innumerable changes in detail. It has become exceedingly complicated through successive enactments; but the main point is that justices' hcences, which must be distinguished from excise or revenue Hcences, are granted for a year only on conditions laid down by Acts of Parhament for regulating the conduct of the trade. The most important of these is the limitation of the hours of sale, but there are many others. Except for such conditions the trade was free when war broke out.

At the very outset of war the bearing of intoxicating drink Military on mihtary efficiency was recognised, and among the earhest ' g" '-measures taken to meet the national emergency were two relating to the sale of drink. The first Defence of the Eealm Act was passed on August 8, 1914, empowering the Government to make regulations by Order in Council; and the first regulations under it were issued on August 12; No. 7 ran thus:

The competent naval or military authority may by order require all premises licensed for the sale of intoxicating liquor within or in the neighbourhood of any defended harbour to be closed except during such hours as may be specified in the order."

No. 17 forbade the giving or supplying of liquor to any member of the Forces in certain circumstances:

No person shall with the intent of eliciting information for the purpose of communicating it to the enemy or for any purpose calculated to assist the enemy, give or sell to a member of any of His Majesty's Forces any intoxicating liquor; and no person shall give or sell to a member of His Majesty's Forces employed in the defence of any railway, dock or harbour, any intoxicating liquor when not on duty, in the intent to make him drunk, or when on sentry or other duty, either with or without any such intent."

These provisions were extended by regulations issued under an Amending Act (August 28), which gave power to the control.

2 DEINK IN 1914-1922

Admiralty or Army Comicil to proclaim ' any area ' to be an area which it is necessary to safeguard in the interests of the training or concentration of any of His Majesty's Forces." By virtue of this Act proclaimed areas were brought under the same control as ' defended harbours ' in Regulation 7 quoted above, and as railways, docks and harbours in Regulation 17.

So far the control contemplated was of a purely military character. The Acts gave the naval and military authorities power to over-ride the ordinary law in specified areas under their jurisdiction; and this power was subsequently extended. But civihan interference with the normal trade followed very quickly. Civilian The question of giving the civil authorities the licensing magistrates and the pohce, under the supreme jurisdiction of the Home Office, power to reduce the facilities for obtaining intoxicating liquor during the war was raised in the House of Commons as early as August 10; and on August 31 an Act was passed, entitled Intoxicating Liquor (Temporary Restriction) Act, to be valid for the duration of the war and for one month afterwards. The following was the main provision:

The licensing justices for any licensing district may, if they think fit, upon the recommendation of the chief officer of police that it is desirable for the maintenance of order or the suppression of drunkenness in any area, by order direct that the sale or consumption of intoxicating liquor on the premises of any persons holding any retailers' licence in the area, and the supply or consumption of intoxicating liquor in any registered club in the area, shall be suspended while the order is in operation, during such hours and subject to such conditions or exceptions (if any) as may be specified in the order."

In effect, the licensing magistrates and the pohce were empowered to alter the hours of sale at their discretion, with the limitation that an order to close before 9 p. m. must be approved by the Home Secretary before being applied. The Bill, as originally introduced by the Government, did not contain the last provision, and was more drastic in other respects; but it met with considerable opposition, though strongly urged by naval and military authorities, at whose instance it had been introduced. The fact that it was opposed and modified in consequence is strong evidence of the regard for liberty in this matter and of the suspicion aroused by any encroachment even in a great emergency, in which the competent authorities declared a curtailment of facilities to be necessary for the national safety. The object was to protect soldiers and sailors from their civilian friends, as Major Morrison-Bell explained in the House of Commons: ' The trouble comes not so much from the soldiers as from civilians, and I wish it were possible for some kind of authoritative warning to be given to civilians that every time they see on the notice boards that there has been some large victory is not the occasion to stand treat all round to every soldier they meet. Soldiers are under great temptation from well-meaning and patriotic civilians, but these civilians are not doing their country or the soldiers any good by treating them in this way."

The practice of making soldiers drunk in war time is one Treating that the most ardent advocates of liberty cannot defend, and soldiers, experience proves that it cannot be left to the good sense either of soldiers or their friends. That was demonstrated over and over again in the South African war, when disgraceful scenes frequently occurred on the embarkation of troops at certain ports where laxity prevailed. At others, where strict regulations were enforced, there were no such scenes. The need and the effectiveness of control were convincingly shown, and this is the broad lesson of war-time experience. It is particularly instructive in the case of soldiers and treating, because the motives of comradeship and good-fellowship, which led to the practice, are in themselves wholly laudable, and yet the results of abuse are so mischievous as to constitute a real national danger. But it was not very long before the same lesson was taught in civil life, and treating in general had to be prohibited, as we shall see in due course. One of the catch-words of the day is ' Trust the people," but the truth is that there are too many people who cannot be trusted. If ever they might be expected to exercise self-restraint it would be in such a common danger as that which threatened the nation in 1914; but they did not, and their failure necessitated compulsory restriction.

Use was promptly made of the Temporary Kestriction Act by local authorities. In the first two months following its enactment the hours of sale were curtailed in 259 out of 1000 licensing districts in England and Wales, and by the end of the year the number had been increased to 427, apart from places in which a military order alone was in operation. In some cases, where public-houses were already under restraint by the military authority, the licensing justices, as empowered by the Act, extended the same restrictions to clubs. The hours of sale were shortened at both ends; in the morning by fixing the time for opening at 8 a. m. or 9 a. m. instead of 6 a. m., and in the evening by closing an hour or two hours earlier. In London the closing time was shortened on September 4 from 12.30 a. m. to 11 p. m., and on October 19 to 10 p. m. In Scotland, where the hours were already shorter, little action was taken by the authorities, and the same may be said of Ireland, which formed an exception to most war measures almost from the first.

It is clear that many of the licensing authorities were fully alive to the need of action and ready to take advantage of the new Act. Indeed the Government seem to have apprehended an excess of zeal on their part, for the Home Office issued a circular on September 4, informing them that ' The powers are intended not for immediate or universal use, but for the purpose of meeting the special conditions which may prevail in any locality from time to time during the war." Here we see again the influence of the jealously guarded principle of Hberty asserting itself. And the Home Office exercised its own powers under the Act in the same sense by refusing, in certain cases, to sanction orders for closing earher than 9 P. M. and to ratify restrictions imposed by justices on their own initiative without any recommendation from the pohce, as provided in the Act. But the pressure of circumstances,

The normal hours of sale on week-days allowed by the law were in London from 5 a. m. to 12.30 midnight; in other towns from 6 a. m. to 11 p. m.; in country districts from 6 a. m. to 10 p. m.; in Scotland from 10 a. m. to 9-11 p. m.

and doubtless representations from the naval and military-authorities, presently effected a change of attitude; and by November the Home Office was urging a fuller use of the Act, not only on account of the soldiers but also for the benefit of other classes, particularly women, and suggesting systematic action by the chief constables in consultation with the local military authorities.

In the early months of the war these restrictions on personal liberty were accepted cheerfully and without protest by the public, as all war measures were. But later, when the Central Control Board had fully estabhshed its regulations, and, still more, when the supply of drink was cut down, a good deal of grumbling arose, and the Board became the object of much criticism, most of which had nothing to do with its operations. The origin of control was completely forgotten and erroneous ideas gained currency. It is therefore necessary, in order that the lessons of war-time experience may be rightly understood and remembered, to recall the facts. They prove that control was originally demanded and exercised by the naval and military authorities as a measure necessary for the conduct of war and the safety of the country; that it was increased and extended at their request; that it was apphed to civil life on the same grounds, and forced upon the Government by the conduct of the people; that its application was at first permissive and tentative and in the discretion of the standing administrative authorities, guarded by statutory Hmitations and the higher authority of the Home Office. In short, restriction of the ordinary trade was found to be necessary and was introduced by degrees, with careful regard for the principle of hberty, which was over-ridden only on proved necessity. Neither love of interference nor hostility to the trade nor fanatical influences played any part in the procedure, which was dictated solely by national needs and adopted on grounds of expediency.

Unimpeachable testimony to the effect of restricted hours Benefits of was forthcoming at an early date. The following passage J J"gj g is quoted by Mr. Carter from the Brewers Gazette of September 24, 1914, on the effect of changing the hour of closing in London from 12.30 a. m. to 11 p. m.:

A transformation of the night scenes of London has followed from the closing of the public-houses at 11. Great trajffic centres, like the Elephant and Castle, at which immense crowds usually lounge about until 1 o'clock in the morning, have suddenly become peaceful and respectable. The police, instead of having to " move on " numbers of people who have been dislodged from the bars at 12.30 at night, found very little intoxication to deal with, the last hour and a half being responsible for much of the excess of which complaint is made. Many of the public-houses were half empty some time before closing time. Journalists, who are necessarily out late, have quickly noticed the effects of the change upon public conduct and have been spared the sounds of ribald songs, dancing and quarrelling which hitherto have marked " closing time " since the war began."

This testimony from an organ of the trade to the effect of earlier closing is convincing. It exphcitly endorses a conclusion of my own stated in my book on ' Drink, Temperance and Legislation ' ' The last hour before closing is the drunkard's hour ' op. cit, p. 146). And being one of those referred to who were necessarily often late in returning home from work, I can confirm the Brewers' Gazette from my own experience. I had to use Waterloo Station late at night a great deal in the war; and no place offered a better test because of the constant departure of troops. Under the restrictions it became quite orderly, in spite of the throng and bustle, and entirely free from the greatest nuisance that late travellers suffered from under the old hours. This was not only ' ribald songs, dancing and quarrelling ' in the streets though these were bad enough but drunken men in the railway carriages, where one cannot escape from them. They are sometimes affectionate, sometimes quarrelsome, sometimes sick, sometimes asleep, but always a nuisance. And this nuisance disappeared entirely when the hour of closing was fixed at 10 p. m.

Further testimony is quoted by Mr. Carter from the Chairman of the London Sessions, Mr. Robert Wallace, K. C., who observed on December 1, 1914, in reference to crimes of violence and charges of wounding that came before the Court:

In the first nine months of this year 103 of these charges were heard here, an average of nearly twelve per month. In September the number rose to seventeen. Then the 11 p. m. closing order was introduced, and the result was that in October the number fell to five. The 10 p. m. order brought about a further improvement, there being only two cases during November. And to-day, for almost the first time in the history of the country, there is not a single " wounding " case for us to deal with."

Further experiences at the same Court confirmed this conclusion. In charging the Grand Jury on April 6, 1915, the Chairman said: ' The calendar is the lightest in the history of the country. The main cause has been the shortening of the hours during which drink could be obtained. The last two hours of the day are the most fatal in connection with crime in London, and the closing of the public-houses at 10 o'clock has undoubtedly produced a wonderful result."

While the measures enumerated above were being applied Moral in the early months of the war, moral suasion was at the same suasion, time actively brought to bear not only by temperance organisations and religious bodies, but by men of note in the form of public appeals. Lord Kitchener, besides providing every member of the British Expeditionary Force with a warning against drink, issued on October 24 an appeal to the public to abstain from treating soldiers: ' The men who have recently joined the Colours are doing their utmost to prepare themselves for Active Service with the least possible delay. This result can only be achieved if by hard work and strict sobriety they keep themselves thoroughly fit and healthy.

Lord Kitchener appeals to the public, both men and women, to help the soldiers in their task. Ho begs everyone to avoid treating the men to drink, and to give them every assistance in resisting the temptations which are often placed before them. Lord Kitchener suggests that in the neighbourhoods where soldiers are stationed, committees should be formed to educate public opinion on this subject, and bring home its importance to those who prevent our soldiers from being able to do their duty to their country in a thoroughly eflcient manner."

The Archbishop of Canterbury and Lord Roberts followed with pubhc appeals to the same effect. They all had in view the welfare and efficiency of the Forces, which were the great objects of concern in the first autumn and winter of the war. At the same time the connection between these two objects and the use or abuse of intoxicating drink was realised by two other voluntary agencies. On the one hand the temperance societies found in the occasion an opportunity and a reason for quickening their usual activities into an intensive campaign, which took two forms propaganda for individual abstinence and pohtical pressure in favour of drastic legislation. The latter was particularly strong in Scotland, where total prohibition during the war was urged by several bodies, including the Corporation and the School Board of Glasgow. On the other hand the social work of various rehgious bodies, being directed to the welfare of the troops, became automatically an anti-alcohol influence through the provision of institutes, reading-rooms, shelters, meals and refreshments, which offered counter-attractions to the pubhc-houses. The taxa One other influence first brought to bear in this period tion of remains to be mentioned, though its main object was not to promote temperance, but to raise revenue. This was a war tax on beer imposed on November 18, 1914. The duty per standard barrel was raised from 7s. 9d. to 23s., with further advances of Is., to follow in April 1916 and April 1917. The immediate effect was to raise the retail price by d. a glass and to cause a large drop in consumption. The number of barrels charged with duty which had been rising, instead of falling, after the commencement of war, and had reached 8,121,000 in October, fell to 2,629,000 in November, and to 1,922,000 in December, a decline of 37 4 per cent, from the quantity recorded for December 1913. This enactment, made by the Government for revenue purposes, was the beginning of the upward movement of prices for alcoholic liquor, which afterwards became a current grievance against the Control Board, though that institution had nothing to do with it.

The whole subject of taxation and price is fully treated in Chapter VI; the foregoing details are only introduced here to make the narrative complete.

This brings us down to the close of the year 1914 and what may be called the first phase of the problem of drink in war time. The measures and influences brought into operation and described above may be classified thus: (1) Compulsory: (a) Hours of sale in licensed houses curtailed by naval and military authorities in places under their jurisdiction.

(h) Treating members of the Forces prohibited in the same areas.

(c) Hours of sale in pubhc-houses and clubs curtailed in other areas by the licensing justices.

(d) Duty on beer raised involving a higher price.

(2) Voluntary: (a) Appeals to the public to refrain from treating soldiers. () An active temperance campaign, (c) The provision of counter-attractions for soldiers by religious and philanthropic agencies.

Except the temperance campaign, which aimed at more general restriction in accordance with the standing policy of the societies, and the beer tax, all these efforts were directed to protecting members of the Forces from temptation. The effect of the compulsory measures has already been noted, and there is no doubt that the provision of counter-attractions afterwards greatly extended was very beneficial, though results cannot be calculated. But appeals to the pubhc produced no perceptible effects; treating went on as before unless forcibly suppressed. This was in keeping with the general experience of such appeals, of which there were many during the war. The offenders, to whom they were addressed, paid no attention to them; those who did pay attention had no need of such exhortations. Again and again voluntary action failed and compulsion had to be apphed, proving once more that men themselves create their own social ills, and that they cannot be trusted to do the right thing even in their own interest.

This was pre-eminently the case with the abuse of liquor, which proved a real national danger, not only in the Forces but in civil life, and drove a reluctant Government to increasingly stringent measures of control as will appear in what follows.

During the winter of 1914-15 interest in the Hquor problem Drink and increased rather than diminished, and notwithstanding the i ustrial improvement effected by the measures enumerated in the previous chapter, their inadequacy and the need of more comprehensive treatment gradually became apparent as the strain of war grew more intense. The question assumed a far larger scope with the discovery, made early in 1915, that efficiency at home and in the workshops was hardly less necessary than abroad and in the Forces, and that it was seriously impaired by the abuse of drink. The truth, which afterwards became a commonplace, that this war demanded the whole national strength and the utmost possible effort, was not realised all at once; but it was perceived that the naval and military operations required an immensely increased output of war material of all kinds subsequently called munitions ' and that to supply them, work must proceed at the highest pressure.

The need was urgent and continually increasing in urgency, though for months neither the general public nor the workmen concerned understood the position, which was known only to the naval and mihtary authorities, the Government, and the armament makers, who were overwhelmed by an ever-rising demand for increased and speedier output, which they were unable to satisfy. They were in a state of feverish activity, combing the country for labour and extending their works; but they failed to execute orders at the promised dates, and among the reasons given by them to the Government departments, lost time and slackness due to the intemperate habits of a section of workmen took a prominent place. The public were jrst openly enlightened on the subject by a speech delivered at Bangor on February 28, 1915, by Mr. Lloyd George, then Chancellor of the Exchequer, in which he took the country into his confidence on the output of munitions.

Mr. Lloyd Most of OUT workmen are putting every ounce of strength
George on into this urgent work for their comitry, loyally and patriotically.
intemperance-g j- jj rpj gj g j, g j j g g y among,"
workmen. who shirk their duty m this great emergency. 1 hear of workmen in armament works who refuse to work a full week's work for the nation's need. What is the reason? They are a minority. But, you must remember, a small minority of workmen can throw a whole works out of gear. What is the reason? Sometimes it is one thing, sometimes it is another, but let us be perfectly candid. It is mostly the lure of the drink. They refuse to work full time, and when they return their strength and efficiency are impaired by the way in which they have spent their leisure. Drink is doing us more damage in I the war than all the German submarines put together.

What has Eussia done? Eussia, knowing her deficiency, knowing how unprepared she was, said: " I must pull myself together. I am not going to be trampled on, unready as I am. I will use all my resources." What is the first thing she does? She stops the drink. I was talking to M. Barck, the Eussian Minister of Finance, a singularly able man, and I asked " What has been the result? " He said, "The productivity of labour, the amount of work which is put out by the workmen has gone up between 30 and 50 per cent." I said, "How do they stand it without their Hquor? " and he replied, "Stand it? I have lost revenue over it up to 65,000,000 a year, and we certainly cannot afford it, but if I proposed to put it back there would be a revolution in Eussia." That is what the Minister of Finance told me. He told me that it is entirely attributable to the act of the Czar himself. It was a bold and courageous step one of the most heroic things in the war. One afternoon we had to postpone our conference in Paris, and the French Minister of Finance said, "I have got to go to the Chamber of Deputies because I am proposing a Bill to abohsh absinthe! " Absinthe plays the same part in France that whiskey plays in this country. It is really the worst form of drink used, not only among workmen but among other classes as well. Its ravages are terrible, and they abolished it by a majority of 10 to 1 that afternoon.

' That is how those great countries are facing their respon-sibihties. We do not propose anything so drastic as that. We are essentially moderate men, but we are armed with full powers for the Defence of the Eealm. We are approaching it, I do not mind telling you, for the moment, not from the point of view of people who have been considering this as a social problem; we are approaching it purely from the point of view of these works. We have got great powers to deal with drink and we mean to use them. We shall use them in a spirit of moderation, we shall use them discreetly, we shall use them wisely, but we shall use them fearlessly; and I have no doubt that as the country's needs demand it, the country will support our action and will allow no indulgence of that kind to interfere with its prospects in this terrible war which has been thrust upon us."

This highly characteristic speech, which at the same time let the country into the secret of a source of national weakness and indicated the intention of the Government to deal with it, was evidently meant to prepare the public for further interference with their habits. The Government were feeling their way. It had the intended effect of arousing opinion in favour of control, and the lesson was driven home by Lord Kitchener in the House of Lords a few days later. He made the same points, but with characteristic brevity: ' We have unfortunately found that the output is not only Lord not equal to our necessities, but does not fulfil our expectations, for a very large number of our orders have not been output of completed by the dates on which they were promised. munitions There have, I regret to say, been instances where absence, irregular timekeeping and slack work have led to a marked diminution in the output of our factories. In some cases the temptations of drink account for this failure to work up to the high standard expected."

This was in anticipation of a Government conference with representatives of trade unions to be held two days later on the question of speeding up war work. At the meeting, held on March 17, 1915, Mr. Lloyd George raised the subject of

Kitchener on the drink among other causes of low production, and told the deputation that reports from both the Admiralty and the War Office concurred in emphasising the evil of excessive drinking, which was interfering not only with output but also with the transport of mmiitions and even of necessaries for the troops. The trade union representatives signified their acquiescence in whatever measures were necessary provided that there was evidence to justify restrictions and that it was applied equally to all classes. The Transport Workers' Federation went much farther than this rather guarded support, and in a letter to Mr. Lloyd George urged the Government to ' take immediate and decisive action to reduce the results of intemperance to a minimum." The executive of this organisation were highly patriotic and had had some trouble with their own members in connection with excessive drinking. At the same time they made a valuable suggestion which was eventually carried out upon a large scale and occupied an important place in the development of war work. This was that for night-work in shipyards, docks and other places, canteens should be provided for the workers. Thn ship The Conference with trade union representatives was builders followed by One with the Shipbuilding Employers' Federation on March 29,1915, when a deputation representing the principal shipbuilding firms on the Clyde and the Tyne, at Birkenhead, Barrow, Sunderland and Hartlepool, explained their views to Mr. Lloyd George, who was so impressed that he made an impetuous remark which was quoted everywhere: We are, fighting Germany, Austria and Drink, and as far as I can see, f the greatest of these three deadly foes is Drink." The statement was rhetorical and out of perspective, but it caught the public ear as it was probably intended to do, and helped to create an atmosphere ' favourable to more drastic measures, which the Government then had under consideration. The shipbuilders, who included a strong ' temperance ' element in their ranks, urged total prohibition during the war, and Mr. Lloyd George, impressed by their views, confessed to a growing conviction that nothing but root-and-branch methods would be of the shghtest avail in dealing with the evil." He also intimated that the King was deeply concerned on the question.

The interview with the shipbuilders and Mr. Lloyd The King's George's statement aroused great resentment in Labour circles ' and caused a general sensation, which was increased by the publication, two days later, on March 31, of the following letter to Mr. Lloyd George from Lord Stamfordham, the King's private secretary: ' Dear Chancellor of the Exchequer, ' The King thanks you for so promptly letting him have a full report of the proceedings at yesterday's meeting of the deputation of employers.

' His Majesty has read it with interest but also with the deepest concern. He feels that nothing but the most vigorous measures will successfully cope with the grave situation now existing in our armament factories. We have before us the statements not merely of the employers, but of the Admiralty and War Office officials responsible for the supply of munitions of war, for the transport of troops, their food and ammunition. From this evidence it is without doubt largely due to drink that we are unable to secure the output of war material indispensable to meet the requirements of our Army in the field, and that there has been such serious delay in the conveyance of the necessary reinforcements and supplies to aid our gallant troops at the front.

The continuance of such a state of things must inevitably result in the prolongation of the horrors and burdens of this terrible war.

I am to add that if it be deemed advisable the King will be prepared to set the example by giving up all alcoholic liquor himself and issuing orders against its consumption in the Eoyal Household, so that no difference shall be made, so far as His Majesty is concerned, between the treatment of rich and poor in this question."

On April 5, 1915, this pledge was made good and the use of wine, beer and spirits totally given up in the Eoyal Households. Lord Kitchener and other prominent persons followed the King's example, and showed that they were wilhng to share any sacrifices that might be demanded of the working classes. This produced a good effect, though the practice of voluntary abstention was not generally adopted; opposition legislation.

16 DEINK IN 1914-1922 to stricter control gradually receded and opinion in favour of it gathered momentum. Proposed In the meantime a Bill had been prepared by the Church

Temperance Societies and was to have been introduced into the House of Lords; its chief provision was earlier closing at night. Another was drafted at the instance of Mr. Balfour, containing several proposals which were afterwards applied in some measure by the Control Board; they included the general prohibition of treating, of serving drink without meals, and of strong liquors. But in view of the Government's intention of dealing with the matter, private efforts were dropped. Discussion of the problem, however, continued and became extremely animated. It was coloured by the excitement in which every subject connected with the war was at that time approached, and many people lost their heads about it. They raised the whole question of alcoholic drink, forgetting that the real end was the supply of munitions and that the control of drink was only a means to it. Total prohibition throughout the kingdom was urged, not only by its regular advocates, but from many quarters in which it had previously always been opposed, without any adequate reason for the change of view or serious consideration of what prohibition would involve. Subsequent events and the resentment aroused by the inadequate supply of beer, which forced the War Cabinet to permit more to be brewed, showed how ill-considered the campaign for prohibition was and how dangerous that step would have been to internal peace and industrial activity.

A leading article in The Times of April 3, 1915, recalled the pubhc to a more sober view of the problem, and put the question of drink in its right place. It is worth quoting because it reveals the excited state of opinion at the time, and shows how the country moved towards the system soon after adopted.

' The question of drink in connection with the production of war material is getting a little out of perspective. There is a problem to solve, and the only way to solve it is to look at it as a whole, keep it steadily in view and adjust the means to it on a reasoned plan. To magnify a single point until it assumes monstrous proportions and blocks out everything else is the certain road to failure. The problem is to increase the production of war material, but it is in danger of disappearing from view in a cloud of controversial dust about the age-long subject of drink. Mr. Lloyd George's striking remark about fighting three enemies of whom the worst is drink, may have led to a certain confusion. It puts drink, which can only be fought in a metaphorical sense, on the same plane with the enemy whom we are really fighting and makes the conquest of drink an object in itself co-ordinate with the defeat of the enemy. If that were literally the case no measure for dealing with drink would be disproportionate to the end in view, provided that it were assured of success. But the case is really rather different. We are engaged in a war a real, not a metaphorical, war which we must win or go down for ever, and in order to prosecute it with vigour and success our forces need a better supply of material. The supply can be improved by various means, some positive others negative. The negative means are the removal of hindrances to production, among which are the drinking habits of a certain number of men in certain localities. The evil is serious enough; but it is only one point among many others. Its conquest, so far from being an end in itself, is only a means towards the real end. It is highly desirable, and may even be necessary to stop the evil where it is, but its influence is localised and its sphere of operations confined within definite limits.

' To identify this limited evil with the whole question of the liquor traffic, which has been for centuries the object of incessant attention and innumerable efforts of every kind, is to view it out of perspective. Total prohibition, which has been proposed, is in our opinion out of proportion to the object. That might not be a conclusive objection if the measure were certain of success; but when success is uncertain it is a very serious objection because it means that there will be other effects which are not intended or desired, and that the net result may be to do more harm than good to the real object in view. Those who propose total abolition have evidently no conception of what it would involve. This comprehensive and uniform veto on the liquor trafc would affect many millions of people and carry its influence far beyond the licensed trade. It would affect other countries, and this is a weighty point, which has been overlooked. A very heavy economic blow would be inflicted on France. it would hit our ally in a sore spot where she can ill stand a blow. Another country which is also forgotten is Australia, which has gradually-developed a large traffic with the United Kingdom. At home not only would all the people engaged in the traffic be thrown out of work, but those who are occupied in growing and handling the materials and in making the plant, with innumerable subsidiary trades, would be ruined. The disturbance that would be thus caused is disproportionate to the evil to be cured, and the resentment to be aroused would probably do more harm to the real object in view than cutting off the drink of these particular workmen would do good."

The correctness of these views was shown when the Control Board was established with ample powers for imposing any restrictions thought expedient. On a closer examination of the problem, the Board did not think it advisable even to prohibit the sale of spirits only. This had been recommended as more feasible than general prohibition and better suited to the case on the ground that the evil complained of in the shipyards and workshops of the North was mainly due to the concentrated form of alcohol. Spirits might, indeed, have Workmen's been prohibited, though not without a risk of exciting acute attitude. discontent among workmen, particularly on the Clyde, where discontent was already rife. The charges of drunkenness made by the employers w ere deeply resented as a slur on British workmen in general, the ' industrial truce ' had been broken and a dangerous feeling of suspicion and antagonism was gathering way. It is not that the men were indifferent about the war. They were thoroughly patriotic and heart and soul for the national cause; but they had no conception of the magnitude of the struggle or of the effort it demanded. Their mood was one of complacent confidence, sedulously fostered by ultra-patriotic but exceedingly mischievous journals, which in 1915, and long afterwards, regularly gave out the pleasing intelligence that the enemy were virtually beaten, and that the war would be over in a few weeks. The consequence was that every encroachment on their liberty was regarded by workmen with suspicion as quite unnecessary and therefore proof of the hostile intentions of the Government and of Capitalism ' against Labour, of which they were continually warned by Socialist speakers and journals.

I can testify to this from my own knowledge, having made direct investigations among the workmen on Clyde and Tyne, in order to learn their real thoughts and feelings at first hand. General prohibition, which would have penalised innumerable sober and good workers and, in their opinion at least, have reduced their efficiency, would not have been borne and would have done far more harm than good. Its advocates knew nothing of the mind of the men; but the trade union leaders, Trade who did, were against it. They denied that the lost time and "g Jj 3 slackness complained of were caused mainly by drink, and views, maintained that the chief causes were over-work and sickness. These undeniably important causes had been completely overlooked in the excited chase after drink; and there were several others. One was the fact that men were earning very high pay, particularly in the shipyards and the transport services, in which absenteeism was most marked, and when that is the case a certain proportion of men always take it easy, quite apart from drink, though high earnings conduce to excessive drinking also.

It gradually became clear that the shipbuilding employers, and Mr. Lloyd George after them, had overstated the case against drink; and the Government wisely dropped the extreme measures that had been urged. Others, of a more moderate character, advocated at the same time, were a uniform restriction of facilities, the substitution of light for heavier alcoholic liquors. State purchase of the trade and the systematic provision of canteens in works. All these were eventually adopted in whole or in part. The imposition of uniform restrictions was called for by the defective administration of the Act described in the previous chapter and the variable practice of the local authorities, which had resulted in producing widely different conditions in contiguous areas. The use of light in preference to heavy drinks was suggested by the proposal to prohibit spirits on the ground of their injurious influence; but it was thought that the end might be secured by dilution, without the risk of exciting resistance which would be entailed by prohibition. State purchase was, of course, favoured by Socialists, and at one time took the fancy of Mr. Lloyd George, who was always open to the latest impression. It received support from other quarters usually

The Government's proposals.

adverse to State control, but was opposed by temperance societies on moral grounds and by financial experts on technical grounds; but it was not wholly dropped, and later found expression in the Carhsle scheme, which was one of the most interesting features of the system of control to be presently described. The provision of works' canteens has already been mentioned as a measure urged by the Transport Workers' Federation. It was called for by the conditions of war work independently of the liquor question; but was rendered the more necessary by the restrictions imposed on the licensed trade. Its merits were obvious, and it commanded universal approval.

Under the influence of all this discussion the Government tentatively formulated their proposals, which were outlined by Mr. Lloyd George in the House of Commons on April 29. They embraced two principles: (1) the higher taxation of drink; (2) complete State control of defined areas. The first was a fiscal measure, to be included in the Budget, the second required fresh legislation in the shape of an amending Defence of the Eealm Act. These proposals were obviously in the nature of a compromise. They excluded both prohibition and State ownership as general measures, but went some way towards both.

The proposed taxation was on a scale that would have amounted to partial prohibition through the high prices of drink entailed. The duty on spirits which stood at 145. 9d. a gallon imposed in 1909 and then thought to be extreme was to be doubled and raised to 29s. 6d. The duty on beer was to apply only to the higher grades, beginning at the level of forty-three specific gravity and being graduated upwards. There was to be a surtax of 12s. a barrel on specific gravities 43-48; 24s. on 48-53 s. g., and 36s. over 63 s. g. The duty on still wine was to be increased fourfold, and on sparkling wine sixfold. And in addition to the prohibitory effect of these duties, the proposed State control included power to prohibit in particular areas. And in like manner it included the power of local State purchase. There was thus a good deal of both of these drastic measures themselves incompatible, for general prohibition obviously excludes State purchase in the Government scheme.

In order to convince the public of its necessity and to The indict-strengthen their case, the Government pubhshed on May 1 j-ink." a White Paper containing the evidence on which it was based. It included reports from the Admiralty, a despatch from Sir John Jellicoe, statements by the shipbuilding employers' deputation referred to above, reports from firms engaged on war work, from the naval transport service, from a number of special investigators sent down by the Home Office, and from factory inspectors. Though there was little in this formal indictment that had not been already brought forward in general terms, it was more comprehensive, detailed and precise than previous utterances on the subject, and it made a great impression. It proved beyond all possibility of denial the prevalence of drinking habits in certain districts, chiefly in the Northern shipyards and in naval transport areas, both North and South; and at the same time it established the fact that work on shipbuilding, ship-repairing, munitions of war and transport was much impaired by avoidable delays and hindrances, which brought the standard of efficiency not only below a possible maximum, but below the normal level.

The document has a permanent value, not only as the most complete statement of the grounds on which the system of control described in this volume was set up, but also as a contribution to the general study of alcoholic drink in relation to national efficiency. It is therefore given in full in the Appendix.

The weak point in the argument or indictment, as critics were not slow to perceive (see the leading article in The Times, May 3, 1915), was that though it estabhshed both drinking and delay, it did not prove the connection between them with any certainty or precision. The general tendency of the reports was to assume a relation of cause and effect, which made the two things virtually co-extensive, and it was this assumption that gave an opening for criticism. In particular, Labour Members of Parliament, while not denying the evil of excessive drinking, complained that the evidence was one-sided, and did not take into account the other causes of lost time and absenteeism mentioned above. In short overdra'ttti.

22 DEINK IN 1914-1922 the official statement of the case in the White Paper provoked a more formal counter-statement in the House of Commons. The reply

to this was that the special investigators sent down by the Home Office had been instructed to take other factors into account, including industrial fatigue, and their reports did in fact mention other causes besides drink. Nevertheless the defence put up by Labour loaders made an impression, and received outside support. The reports by the special investigators hardly bore out the sweeping indictment of the shipbuilding employers, except perhaps in regard to the Tyne. Elsewhere drink assumes a more modest position as one cause among several and not always the most important. The indict " question is of sufficient general interest to justify ment an attempt to weigh the evidence. I went into it myself on different occasions by personal observation and investigation in and about the shipyards, and tried to estimate the relative importance of the several causes of lost time with a view to judging whether the gain that might be expected from the prohibition of spirits would warrant the risk of upsetting the men. I came to the conclusion that the indictment against drink, though only too well founded and true up to a point, had been overdrawn, and that the Labour leaders were right in maintaining that insufficient weight was allowed to other factors. The whole controversy had been coloured by class feeling. Friction between employers and employed was acute and growing at the time. As already stated, the industrial truce had been broken, and there was irritation on both sides. Employers were at their wits' end to carry out the orders rained upon them and to complete delivery by the scheduled dates; while the naval and military authorities, chaffiag at delay, grew more and more insistent. Realising the urgency and working themselves to their utmost capacity, the employers and responsible works' officials were continually baffled by delays in the yards and shops; and inquiry, filtering downwards, always arrived at the workmen and put the blame on them. Drink, being a real weakness and only too familiar, was the simplest reason to give and became the stereotyped charge. The employers did put a stigma on the men, and this was passed on from them to the Government, the naval and military authorities, and the investigators, who derived their information mainly from the same sources.

The reports themselves show that drink had become an idee fixe in the minds of those who were responsible for getting the work done but could not get the men to do it. The trouble was most acute in the transport service, and in this branch of work drunkenness was most fully proved, because firemen came on board drunk and incapable of getting up steam, and ' coahes ' men engaged in coahng ships returned to work on Saturdays, after getting their pay, in the same condition," so that they had to be dismissed. What proportion of the men behaved in this way was not indicated, but the fact that work was hindered by excessive drinking was proved by such cases beyond all possibility of denial. The officials jumped to the conclusion that drink was the cause of all other lapses, such as crews deserting ships, or missing ships, men leaving work early and not turning up. Thus the Director of Transports wrote that the root cause of congestion at the docks was not shortage of labour, ' but the fact that the men could earn in two or three days what would keep them in drink for the rest of the week."

The words ' in drink ' are a gratuitous assumption. It is Dislike a commonplace of experience that some men will not work longer than is necessary to earn a certain amount of money per week, and that if they can reach that standard which they fix for themselves in three days or two days or one day, they stay away the rest of the week and enjoy themselves. They may drink or not; some do, some do not; some merely rest, some indulge in sport or other amusements. What they do is immaterial; the essential point is that they prefer a minimum of work to a maximum of pay. Nor is this a new phenomenon. Writing of them more than 250 years ago Sir Josiah Child remarked: ' In a cheap year they will not work above two days in a week; their humour being such that they will not provide for a hard time, but just work so much and no more as may maintain them in that mean condition to which they have been accustomed."

I remember an occasion during the South African war when men employed in sweeping out the transport sheds at the Albert Docks refused to work because it began to rain shghtly. They were being paid 2s. an hour, and had made enough to indulge in a httle relaxation; the rain was merely an excuse. There was not so much talk about drink then, and their defection was put down, more simply, to laziness. There is such a thing, and it did not disappear during the late war, or at any rate in the period under consideration, for, as explained above, the men did not behve in the urgency or see why they should work harder and longer than they chose to please an employer and put money in his pocket. What may be called the minimum wage habit prevails chiefly among imskilled workers such as those employed at docks, and in the shipyards among the ' black squad '; and the complaints of the war departments applied chiefly to these and to the firemen in the transport service, not to men in the workshops, with certain exceptions. The causes My own investigations into the causes of lost time led me to the conclusion that, though drink was one of them, and a serious one in particular districts, there were several others much more important than the official reports allowed, and that no matter what was done with the drink, there would always be some lost time in large establishments. In addition to the minimum wage habit, I found that men stayed away because they were unwell, over-tired and really in need of rest, or unable to face exposure in bad weather; in short, suffering from temporary indisposition, as we all do at times, short of going formally on the sick list. Another occasional cause common to all classes is trouble at home from illness or death. All these things mount up and cause an irreducible minimum of absenteeism, which was higher than usual in the conditions then prevailing because of the extreme pressure. Another exceptional circumstance was the great influx of labour into particular centres, which compelled many men to lodge at a distance through lack of accommodation and overtaxed the existing means of conveying them to work. The result was an unusual amount of lateness and lost mornings. I notice that Dr. H. M. Vernon, who is the highest authority of lost time.

we possess on the causes of inefqciency in workmen, lays hardly any stress on drink as a cause of lost time in his admirably thorough study of the subject.

To return to the course of events. The results of the criticism levelled at the Government's scheme in the early part of May was that the taxation proposals were dropped, but the plan of control was adopted and embodied in a Defence of the Eealm (Amendment) Bill, which became law on May 19. The text of this unprecedented measure is as follows:

State Control of Liquor Trade in Certain Areas (1) Whereas it appears to His Majesty that it is expedient The Control for the purpose of the successful prosecution of the present war,–that the sale and supply of intoxicating liquor in any area should be controlled by the State on the ground that war material is being made or loaded or unloaded or dealt with in transit in the area, or that men belonging to His Majesty's naval or military forces are assembled in the area. His Majesty has power by Order in Council, to define the area and to apply to the area the regulations issued in pursuance of this Act under the Defence of the Realm Consolidation Act 1914, and the regulations so applied shall, subject to any provisions of the Order or any amending order, take effect in that area during the continuance of the present war and such period not exceeding twelve months thereafter as may be declared by Order in Council to be necessary in view of the conditions connected with the termination of the present war.

(2) His Majesty in Council has power to issue regulations under the Defence of the Realm Consolidation Act 1914, to take effect in any area to which they are applied under this Act (a) for giving the prescribed Government authority, to the exclusion of any other person, the power of selling or supplying or controlling the sale or supply of intoxicating liquor in the area, subject to any exceptions contained in the regulations; and (h) for giving the prescribed Government authority power to acquire, compulsorily or by agreement, and either for the

Industrial Fatigue and Efficiency. By H. M. Vernon, M. A., M. D., Investigator for the Industrial Fatigue Research Board. (Chapter viii, on ' Lost Time and Its Causation.") period during which the regulations take effect, or permanently, any licensed or other premises or business in the area, or any interest therein, so far as it appears necessary or expedient to do so for the purpose of giving proper effect to the control of the liquor supply in the area; and (c) for enabling the prescribed Government authority, without any licence, to establish and maintain refreshment rooms for the supply of refreshments (including, if thought fit, the supply of intoxicating liquor) to the general public or to any particular class of persons or to persons employed on any particular industry in the area; and (d) for making any modification or adjustment of the relations between persons interested in licensed premises in the area which appears necessary or expedient in consequence of the regulations, and (e) generally, for giving effect to the transfer of control of the liquor traffic in the area to the prescribed Government authority, and for modifying, so far as it appears necessary or expedient, the provisions of the Acts relating to licensing or the sale of intoxicating liquor in their application to the area.

(3) Any regulations made before the passing of this Act under the powers conferred by any Act dealing with the Defence of the Realm as respects the restriction of the sale of intoxicating liquor are hereby declared to have been duly made in accordance with those powers.

Effect of This statute completely superseded the ordinary law the Act. within the defined limits and transferred the control of the trade from the local authorities to the Government, to be administered through a special organ called ' the prescribed authority." At the same time, it conferred on this authority far wider powers of action than those previously possessed by the local magistrates. The power of ' selling or supplying or controlling the sale of supply' may obviously cover any interference except general prohibition; and, as shown by the regulations subsequently issued, it did cover local prohibition by the exclusion of particular kinds of drink. It also included the compulsory acquisition of premises that is. State ownership all minor restrictions thought expedient, and various other novel measures, which will be described in due course. The one limitation, other than the exclusion of general prohibition, was geographical. The Act applied only to defined areas, which were to be those involved in the production and conveyance of war material and those where military or naval forces were located. That is to say, it was essentially a war measure having for its object, as stated in the first clause, ' the successful prosecution of the present war."

This extremely drastic Act, which in its appucation furnished Favourable one of the most remarkable examples of legislation by adminis- ortl Tct. trative order produced by the war, met with singularly little opposition in Parliament and the Press. What criticism there was came chiefly from temperance societies and had reference to the provision for State purchase, to which some of them objected. There was practically no opposition from the trade, and on May 19, 1915, the Bill became law. This easy passage was due to several reasons (1) patriotism; the successful prosecution of the war had become for all classes the supreme object to which everything else was secondary, and the conviction had been hardening all round that the hindrance caused by drink called for strong measures; (2) the preceding campaign for prohibition made the Bill seem mild by comparison; (3) the proposed high taxes on drink, which were the other part of the Government's scheme and had met with a storm of criticism, were dropped, and this concession conduced to a favourable reception of the administrative part of the scheme. Another circumstance tending to the ready acceptance of the Bill was the fact that while it was before Parliament great excitement was caused by a sensational revelation of the deficiency of high explosive ammunition at the front, which switched public attention on to the production of shells, without diminishing the urgency of liquor control, and so facihtated the speedy disposal of that question.

But the general acceptance of so great an inroad on jealously The moral guarded Hberties, affecting the personal habits of millions, of the Act. at so early a stage of the war is a most remarkable fact, of which the significance was not appreciated at the time. It amounts to a national admission (1) of the prevalence of excessive drinking; (2) of the injury to national efficiency so caused; (3) of the need and efficacy of compulsory restriction. Of course all these propositions are in a sense truisms; the case of temperance reformers is built on them. But they have never been so clearly demonstrated and so fully admitted before. There has always been a strong counter-current of opinion disposed to deny them, or at least to resist the logical inference; and it is by no means confined to the trade. It has been to a great extent provoked by the exaggerations of intemperate reformers, who do not distinguish between use and abuse, and regard alcoholised liquor in any and every form as the chief enemy of mankind and the cause of nearly all social ills vice, crime, disease, insanity, and poverty. But in addition to the sober-minded people who are driven to defend the use of alcohol by this over-done indictment and the proposed extreme measures based upon it, there have always been persons who advocate the abohtion of all restrictions and profess to believe that it could be done in this country without injury and even with benefit to the community. To these is recommended a study of the facts given in this chapter.

The ' prescribed Government authority' mentioned in the Act was set up within a few days and announced before the end of May as The Central Control Board (Liquor Traffic). It consisted of the following:

Lord D'Abernon (Chairman).

Major the Hon. Waldorf Astor, M. P.

Mr. Neville Chamberlain.

Mr. G. Eichard Cross.

Colonel J. M. Denny, M. P.

Mr. John Hodge, M. P.

Sir William Lever (afterwards Lord Leverhulme).

Sir George Newman, M. D.

Mr. John Pedder, C. B. (now Sir John Pedder, K. B. E.)

Mr. E. Eussell Scott, C. S. I.

Mr. Philip Snowden, M. P.

Mr. W. Towle.

Of these gentlemen Mr. Chamberlain, Colonel Denny, and Sir William Lever represented industrial interests; Mr. Hodge and Mr. Snowden represented Labour; Mr. Pedder was from the Home Office; Mr. Eussell Scott from the Admiralty; Sir George Newman from the Board of Education; Mr. Eichard Cross, formerly President of the Justices' Clerks Society, brought to the Board expert knowledge of licensing; and Mr. Towle brought great experience in hotel management.

The Secretary to the Board was Mr. J. C. G. Sykes, C. B.; Mr. E. C. Sanders, Clerk to the Liverpool Justices, was appointed Assessor for England and Wales, and Sir Thomas Munro, Clerk to the Lanark County Council, Assessor for Scotland.

Functions and powers of the Control Board.

Ireland was not represented on the Board, because it was not intended to apply its operations in Ireland; and, as a matter of fact, they never were.

Some changes subsequently took place. Mr. W. Waters Butler, member of the Birmingham brewing firm of Mitchells and Butler, and the Eev. Henry Carter, of the Wesley an Temperance Society, joined the Board in January 1916; Mr. E. S. Meiklejohn, C. B., from the Treasury, in May 1916; and Mr. S. 0. Nevile, member of a brewing firm, in July 1917.

Mr. Chamberlain resigned in February 1916 on account of his duties as Lord Mayor of Birmingham; Mr. Hodge resigned in January 1917 on becoming Minister of Labour; Mr. Scott resigned on returning to the Admiralty in May 1917; Mr. Eichard Cross was drowned while bathing in August 1916.

So much for the personnel of this new type of Government department, called into being to perform an entirely novel function of extreme delicacy and one involving highly controversial issues. A heavy responsibility rested on it, and particularly upon the Chairman, of whom it should be added here that he brought to the task great experience in finance and a wide knowledge of public affairs with an open mind on the controversial aspects of the liquor problem. As Sir Edgar Vincent he had been successively Financial Adviser to the Egyptian Government and Governor of the Imperial Ottoman Bank for several years, and had then entered Parliament. In 1912 he had been appointed Chairman of the Eoyal Commission set up to inquire into the industrial resources of the British Overseas Dominions. His experience and the diplomatic ability he has since exhibited as British Ambassador in Berlin, fitted him in an eminent degree to guide the policy of the Board.

On June 10, 1915, the Government issued a set of Statutory Eules and Orders under the Act described in the previous chapter, defining the functions, constitution, and powers of the Board. This document is given in full in the Appendix. It begins by reasserting the geographical limitation of the new control to defined areas, and its purpose, which was to ' increase directly or indirectly the efficiency of labour in such areas ' and prevent its impairment ' by drunkenness, alcoholism or powers.

THE CONTKOL BOAED 31 excess." With regard to the constitution of the Board, it was so far under the jurisdiction of the Government that the Ministry of Munitions appointed the Chairman and members, and the size of the official staff was subject to the approval of the Treasury; but otherwise it was an autonomous body, possessed of legal entity, capable of suing and being sued and of acquiring property, to be vested in trustees appointed by the Board from its own membership. It had not power, however, to schedule any area for control at its own discretion. This required an Order in Council; and it was stated in the House of Commons in a debate on the subject that the Board was responsible to the Minister who submitted any such order. As a matter of fact no trouble arose; nor was the action of the Board in this respect seriously called in question during the war.

The powers conferred on the Board for the purpose of Extra-carrying out its functions, and specified in the Statutory J J", Rules and Orders, were wide and varied. The more important provisions included power to (1) close any licensed premises or club; (2) regulate hours of sale; (3) prohibit the sale of any particular liquor; (4) impose conditions of sale; (5) regulate the supply and transport of liquor; (6) establish supervision of hcensed premises; (7) prohibit the sale and supply of liquor by any person other than the Board that is, create a monopoly; (8) prohibit treating; (9) estabhsh refreshment rooms; (10) acquire licensed or other premises compulsorily or by agreement, or alternatively take temporary possession of premises and plant; (11) acquire businesses, including stock-in-trade; (12) carry on business independent of the licensing laws; (13) provide any entertainment or recreation at their discretion and subject to no restriction on any premises in which they carried on business; (14) provide postal and banking facihties on or near premises in which they carried on business; (15) modify the Sale of Food and Drugs Act in regard to the dilution of spirits; (16) grant excise Hcences; (17) exercise the right of inspecting hcensed premises and clubs.

In short, the Board were made complete masters. They could, in effect, do anything they pleased within the limits already defined; their agents were exempt from the licensing

The need of discretion.

Procedure of the Board.

laws, and the police were placed at their disposal with instructions to carry out their orders and enforce the regulations. Nor was there any appeal from their decisions, which were not subject to public revision.

It is obvious that the exercise of such extensive and drastic powers was attended with considerable risk. A too severe and sudden application might have excited general resentment and led to a dangerous crisis. The British people are extremely law-abiding and amenable to restraint which they consider reasonable; but no people are so tenacious of hberty and so resentful of any interference with their personal habits and customs which they consider unwarranted. The Control Board might easily have gone too far and too fast in several directions, and have seriously antagonised popular sentiment. The fact that this did not happen, in spite of the inevitable grumbling, is proof of the discretion and circumspection with which the powers enumerated above were brought to bear on the problem. The Board did nothing in haste, but proceeded step by step on a regular plan.

The first step was to schedule the areas to be controlled, and this was done by degrees. No area could be scheduled without an Order in Council, which did not lie within the competence of the Board, but required ministerial sanction. The initiative in the selection of areas was generally taken by one of the several authorities concerned with the maintenance of eficiency namely, in naval areas, the Admiralty; in military ones, the Army Council or General Officer Commanding; in industrial ones, the Ministry of Munitions. There was no arbitrary imposition of the control system. Application was first received from one or other of the authorities mentioned, requesting an area to be scheduled; but this was not immediately done. The procedure of the Board, on receipt of such a request, was to hold a local inquiry into the conditions prevailing in the area and to confer with representatives of all the local authorities concerned naval, military, municipal and judicial (the police and licensing justices) with employers of labour and trade union officials, with temperance organisations, if they desired it, and licensed traders; in short, with representatives of all interests and with any other persons able to furnish useful information. The result was reported to the Board, and on their recommendation, approved by the Minister of Mimitions, an Order in Council was made.

These inquiries were no mere formahty. They had three Local objects (1) to ascertain whether the conditions were such '" " '7-as to require the imposition of control; (2) to decide what restrictions were best suited to the needs of the case; and (3) to fix the geographical limits of their application. With regard to the first point, the Board did not assume as a matter of course that an application for control proved the need of it, but satisfied themselves of the need by independent investigation in the manner indicated, before deciding to recommend an area to be scheduled. As a rule inquiry confirmed the application, but some exceptions occurred. With regard to restrictions, of which there was a wide choice, they were for the most part framed on the same general lines, but with variations adapted to local wishes or requirements, and subject to subsequent modifications. With regard to defining the areas, the Board began by fixing small ones, based on the principle of a radius from a central point, and confining the restrictions within rather narrow limits, but experience soon showed that it was often necessary to extend the boundaries so as to include a wider surrounding fringe and places in close proximity to the principal one.

It will be seen from all this that the Board proceeded in a very cautious and tentative manner; and it is desirable to emphasise the fact because complaint was made later that they had acted in an arbitrary and unreasonable way in imposing restrictions where they were unnecessary. The truth is that the demand for larger areas and more uniform regulations came chiefly from the police and other local authorities, who were embarrassed by different legal conditions in contiguous places under their jurisdiction. But no order was Licence-made without due consideration of the rights of licence-holders attitude, and the convenience of the public. The former for the most part accepted the interference with good will. Opportunity was always given to them to state their case, and in many instances the Board had the active co-operation of the recognised local representatives of the Hquor interest. I can bear

The issue of regulations.

First districts controlled.

witness from my own investigations in some important centres, both to the care taken by the Board to consult the trade and to the readiness with which the local trade defence associations complied with the requirements made of them. Some of the restrictions were, in truth, welcomed by pubhcans, if not by brewers and distillers.

The next step after scheduling an area was to issue an order specifying the regulations to be applied. Copies of this were supphed to all the authorities concerned and to the central organisation of the trade, and were distributed to Hcensed premises and clubs through the pohce. Each order was also pubhshed in the official journal known as the London Gazette, and thence copied by the local newspapers. A circular letter, explaining the provisions and sent out with the order, contained the following appeal:

After careful consideration of the representations made in the district, the Board have made the Order with the desire to meet local opinion, so far as is consistent with an effective result and with the necessity of treating the various areas over which their powers extend with some degree of uniformity. The Board have taken steps to ascertain local opinion on the questions involved, but they are conscious that in some respects the provisions which they have found it desirable to make may cause some inconvenience and impose some sacrifice. They trust, however, that this will not diminish that hearty cooperation in the locality, which is essential to the proper administration of the Order.

' They confidently hope that all in whose locality the Order is in force, will use their influence in attaining this result, both by making the terms of the Order as widely known as possible, to all classes, and also by endeavouring, as far as in them lies, to secure adherence to its terms. They will thus contribute in the present emergency to the object which the Board's Orders are intended to promote, viz. the successful prosecution of the War."

A period of ten days was allowed after the issue of an Order before its provisions were enforced, to enable the authorities, the trade, and the consumers to prepare for the change.

The first batch of Orders in Council was obtained on July 6, 1915, and the first Order issued by the Board was dated July 15, 1915. It came into force on July 26, and applied to New-haven. During the month of August the following districts were placed under control in the order given: Southampton and Barrow (August 2); Dartford Thames (August 6); Bristol and Avonmouth, North-East Coast (August 10); Liverpool and Mersey district (August 16); Newport, Cardiff and Barry (August 18); Scotland West Central and East Central (August 23). The two last named were extensive areas, including not only the Clyde and the Forth, but also adjacent manufacturing centres and coal-fields.

It will be observed that the areas first taken under control, and therefore presumably the most urgent cases, were seaports, and that they iucluded the chief shipbuilding centres and commercial ports, as well as Channel ports directly engaged in war transport. The obvious inference is that the most pressing requests for control came from the Admiralty and had their origin in the urgent demands of naval ojbficers responsible for the transport of men and goods, the production of the shipyards and the safety of shipping. The first inland industrial areas dealt with were the Midlands and the West Eiding of Yorkshire, both on November 22, on which date Portsmouth, Plymouth, Falmouth, Pembroke and the Western Border country of Scotland also came under control. London, London, which had been subjected to partial control (no treating and dilution of spirits) on October 11, was placed under a full Order on November 29.

By the end of 1915 about half the population of Great Gradual Britain were hving under the new conditions, and during 1916 f conjrol. large additions and extensions of scheduled areas were made. In February control was extended from the previous small Mersey area over the whole of Lancashire and Cheshire. The Humber region was added to the Hst of ports, and the isolated districts on the Southern coast were expanded into a large tract embracing several counties and stretching northwards to Bristol. Later, the same process of extension was applied to the South-Eastern counties, the Midlands, Wales, and Scotland. By the end of 1916 control was complete over the Southern and South-Eastern, Midland and North-Western counties of England, over the whole of Wales, and nearly the whole of Scotland, including the Orkney and Shetland Isles. It was estimated that a population of 38 millions out of a total of 41 millions were living under control. A few more extensions took place in 1917, and eventually the whole of Great Britain was scheduled with the exception of some purely agricultural areas, chiefly on the East coast, the Midlands, and the South-Western counties of England. The accompanying map shows the distribution of controlled and non-controlled areas.

This process of extension was necessitated mainly by the gradual establishment of new munition factories, aerodromes, camps and naval bases, spread all over the country, but also by the administrative considerations previously mentioned. The two together left few areas untouched by war needs. But the fact that some were never scheduled shows that the principle of necessity was maintained to the end. It would have been much simpler to put the whole country under control when it became clear, as it did in 1916, that large areas in all directions were becoming involved.

Eegulations of the Board rpjjg As the areas were subject to extension, so the regulations regulations, were Open to improvement and modification in the light of experience; and the tendency was towards uniformity in the one case as in the other. A few particular areas were subjected to exceptional measures, which will be described presently; but for the most part the conditions imposed were broadly the same with only minor variations. A specimen Order of the Board, issued in February 1916, is given in full in the Appendix, with the explanatory notes accompanying it. A summary of the chief points will be sufficient here to give the reader a grasp of the conditions imposed and the changes made in the preceding practice.

Hours of Sale. The greatest change introduced was a drastic reduction in the hours of sale. Previously these had been on week-days in London 19 hours, namely from 5 a. m. to 12.30 midnight (Saturdays 12 midnight); in other Enghsh towns 17 hours, namely from 6 a. m. to 11 p. m.; in country districts 16 hours, namely from 6 a. m. to 10 p. m.; in Scotland 11 to 13 hours, namely from 10 a. m. to 9 p. m. (earliest) or 11 P. M. (latest). The Board reduced these hours at one stroke to 5 in all districts, namely 2 hours at midday (12 to 2.30 p. m.) and 3 in the evening (6 p. m. to 9 p. m., or 6.30 p. m. to 9.30 p. m.). Except during these hours the sale of alcohohc liquor for consumption on the premises was prohibited, and this applied to clubs as well as to licensed houses of all kinds. The hours of sale for consumption off the premises that is, for drink bought and taken away to be drunk at home or elsewhere which had been the same as for on consumption, were still further curtailed by one hour in the evening and so reduced to 4 hours; the latest time at which drink could be obtained for this purpose was fixed at 8 p. m. or 8.30 p. m. instead of 9 p. m. or 9.30 p. m. The object of this distinction between on and off consumption was to prevent the practice of drinking in a public-house up to the closing time and then taking away more liquor to continue drinking at home. Objects of Three great changes were effected by this curtailment of jumr hours. (1) Public-house drinking in the forenoon was completely stopped; (2) drinking in the evening ceased much earlier; (3) an interval of several hours was interposed in the afternoon between the morning and the evening periods of sale, so that the consumption of liquor coincided broadly with meal-times, and ceased in the intervening period. All these changes were directed to the prevention of particular evils, which varied in importance in different localities. The prohibition of morning drinking had special reference to the industrial centres in the North, and particularly the shipyards, where the practice prevailed of calhng at the public-house first thing in the morning on the way to work for a glass or two of spirits; but drinking during the forenoon was injurious in other ways and contributed a good deal to intemperance among women living at home, who used to shp out to the public-house half-way through the morning. The closed interval in the afternoon was similarly aimed at irregular drinking between meals, and the habit of soaking ' or continuous drinking for many hours together. But the change most generally operative was undoubtedly the curtail- ment of hours at night, when the greatest amount of drinking takes place everywhere.

This great reduction in the hours of opening was a very Sunday bold step, but one justified by the results. In effect, it assimi- ' lated the weekday hours to those previously obtaining on Sunday in England, but went a little further. The Sunday hours had been seven in London and six in other parts of England namely, two at midday and five or four after 6 P. M., with a long interval in the afternoon. These were reduced to a uniform five hours by advancing the evening hour of closing to 9 p. m. In Scotland and Wales there had been fo many years complete closing on

Sunday, except to bona fide travellers ' (persons who had travelled three miles from the place where they had passed the previous night). This permission for the sale of drink during prohibited hours, which applied to weekdays as well as to Sundays, was abolished by the Board, and at the same time clubs, which had been quite free, were placed under the same restrictions as licensed houses. The treatment of clubs on the same footing as public-houses was one of the greatest innovations introduced by the Board; but it was obviously an unavoidable corollary of the reduction of hours, which would otherwise have resulted in the transference of custom during prohibited hours from the licensed trade to clubs and so have proved nugatory.

Modifications of the standard hours to suit particular cases Local mo-should be mentioned here. They were not numerous, but they show the care taken to adjust restrictions to varying conditions. The most important concerned Saturday in the central areas of Scotland. Here it was thought advisable, largely at the instance of the trade union leaders consulted, to keep the public-houses closed until 4 p. m. on Saturday and to let them open continuously from that hour to 9 p. m. The object was to prevent men from visiting the public-house before returning home from work on pay-day, as they were accustomed to do, but to allow in compensation more time after 4 p. m. This measure had less to do with the efficiency of men at work than with the welfare of the home, on which it had an excellent effect. In other parts of Scotland a number of minor variations were introduced mainly at the instance

Saving provisions.

Meals and hotel residents.

of the naval or military authorities. In the Northern and North-Western coast areas and the Orkney and Shetland Islands, the evening hours of opening were reduced to two, from 6 P. M. to 8 p. m.; in other districts the closing hour was fixed at 7 p. m. (Perth, Peterhead, Nairn, Eoss and Cromarty), with opening at 2 p. m., 4 p. m., or 5 p. m., and no afternoon break; in the Inverness district the hours were 12.30 to 6 P. M., without a break. These and other small variations appear to have been determined by military requirements and topographical conditions.

A notable relaxation of the general rule was the permission given to a limited number of houses (about 300) near docks and wharves and the large food markets in the London area to open at certain hours in the early morning for the benefit of men employed on night work. So far as the markets were concerned this was a continuation of the old arrangement whereby certain houses used by men attending the wholesale markets, which begin very early in the morning, were permitted to open during prohibited hours. A condition imposed by the Board was that the exempted houses should make suitable provision for the supply of refreshments other than intoxicating liquor.

Another relaxation, which will be found under the heading of ' Saving Provisions ' in the specimen Order given in the Appendix, was important because it differentiated between drinking bars, eating places, and hotels. This practical distinction, forced into recognition by the exigencies of situation, touched one of the standing defects of the licensing system in this country, which puts places that provide food and lodging as well as drink on precisely the same legal footing as those which provide drink only by subjecting them all to the same licence and the same restrictions. This practice, which has come down from remote times when conditions were quite different, is not only contrary to common sense and the cause of great inconvenience, but it stands in the way of various desirable reforms. The distinction was recognised under the Control Board by permitting the consumption of drink supplied with meals to continue for half an hour after closing time, and in the case of persons residing on the premises to take place at any time. In both cases the relaxation applied to consumption only; the liquor had to be ordered and supplied within the legal hours. What it amounted to in the working was this. Persons drinking at a bar, as in an ordinary public-house, had to stop abruptly at the appointed closing hour; persons consuming liquor with a meal, as in a restaurant or club, need not stop at closing time, but were allowed time to finish their drink though they could order no more; persons living on the premises, as in a hotel or club, could consume drink at any time, though they could order it only at the permitted hours. Persons in hotels requiring drink at other times generally kept it in the bedrooms and had it brought down at meals.

The restrictions did not apply to the supply of food and non-intoxicating liquor, for which licensed houses might open at any time from 5.30 a. m. to the closing hour at night.

Special Restrictions on Spirits. The supply of spirits for Spirits, consumption off the premises, whether obtained from licensed dealers or clubs, was prohibited on Saturday and Sunday and permitted on other days only in the midday period 12 to 2.30 P. M. The object was to discourage the home-drinking of spirits, especially at the week-end, which was the cause of much absenteeism in works on Monday morning. Further, the supply of spirits in less quantities than a quart was prohibited, bottles of spirits were to be sealed up and to bear a label showing where they came from, and the sale of spirits in railway refreshment-rooms was totally prohibited. The quart bottle regulation, which was borrowed from an Act of 1861, or, perhaps, from Sweden, gave rise to much controversy. Its object was to prevent the practice of carrying small flasks on the person into works, railway carriages, ships, and elsewhere. It was contended on the other hand that the effect was to compel people to buy much larger quantities than they otherwise would have done, and so to conduce to drinking. The same criticism was raised against the same provision in Sweden, and there is undoubtedly force in it. The Control Board did not deny it and admitted the need of carefully watching the working of the large bottle regulation. It was not enforced everywhere; but since it was not withdrawn

Dilution of spirits.

Canvassing.

Treating. Credit.

the inference is that the balance of advantages was held to be in its favour, and that was my own conclusion after inquiry, though I attach little value to the measure as a general aid to sobriety. Its chief value in the war lay in preventing soldiers from carrying spirits on railway journeys and sailors from taking them on board ship.

For naval purposes the sale of spirits was totally prohibited in the north of Scotland.

Another measure of a different kind relating to spirits was a change in the law governing their alcoholic strength. By the Sale of Food and Drugs Acts sellers were compelled for the protection of the public from fraud to supply spirits of a certain standard strength, unless customers were informed beforehand to the contrary. Gin might not be watered down to more than 35 degrees ' under proof," and for other spirits the limit was 25 degrees. ' Proof ' spirit is as nearly as possible half the strength of pure alcohol. The Board began by extending these limits and permitting gin to be diluted to 45 degrees u. p., and other spirits to 35 degrees u. p. Then permission was given to dilute all kinds to 50 degrees u. p., and dilution to 25 degrees u. p. subsequently increased to 30 degrees was made compulsory. That is to say, spirits were not to be stronger than 30 degrees u. p., and might be as weak as 50 degrees u. p.

The supply of spirits for strictly medical purposes was safeguarded by a ' saving provision," which permitted the sale at any time and in less quantity than the prescribed quart on the production of a medical certificate stating the quantity as immediately required for medicinal use.

Minor Restrictions. To meet evasion of the restrictions placed on licensed premises by increased trading at customers' houses, it was forbidden to canvass for orders, to deliver liquor not previously ordered of a dealer in accordance with the regulations and to take money at customers' houses for liquor delivered.

' Treating ' was prohibited, except in conjunction with a meal.

The supply of Hquor on credit was prohibited. This was directed against public-house ' scores," but it necessarily applied all round to the great advantage of wine merchants, who received cash payment with orders.

The so-called ' long pull' was prohibited. This is the Long pull, practice of drawing rather more beer, generally into a jug, than the quantity ordered by measure, in order to attract custom.

A health measure.

Feeding the worker.

THE PROVISION OF MEALS PUBLIC-HOUSES AND CANTEENS

In the previous chapter the restrictive measures imposed by the Control Board on the sale and consumption of drink through the regular channels have been enumerated. These may be called the negative part of its functions; and since they came to be applied to nearly the whole population of Great Britain (38 miuions out of 41 milhons), as described in Chapter III, they form the largest and most important part. But the Board was also entrusted with power to carry out positive or constructive measures namely, the provision of refreshment rooms, the acquisition of premises or businesses and their conduct, with some accessory matters. The present chapter will deal with the first of these.

The provision of refreshments had only an indirect bearing on the liquor trade; it was really a measure of general health and efficiency among war-workers. If the reader will refer to the Statutory Rules and Orders printed in the Appendix it will be seen that Clause 5 gives the Board power to establish refreshment-rooms either for the use of the general public or for any particular classes of persons, which meant, in effect, transport and munition workers.

In commenting on this clause the Second Report of the Board, issued in May 1916, observed: ' It is a matter of common knowledge and experience that the absence of proper facilities for obtaining wholesome and sufficient nourishment frequently leads, directly or indirectly, to drinking habits with all their resultant evils. It devolved, therefore, upon the Board to secure the supply of sufficient and proper nourishment for the worker in order to maintain his health, increase his energy and output, and to diminish or prevent fatigue and exhaustion. The circumstances of the moment emphasised the desirability of vigorous action. The enormous and rapid increase in the number of munition workers, their concentration in well-defined districts, the local difficulty in obtaining food at reasonable prices, the distance from the factory at which many of them lived, all these were conditions which made more acute and pressing the whole problem of the food supply of the workers.

' Stated shortly, the problem is how to feed the worker sufficiently well to keep him physically fit and at full capacity of working power and to prevent or postpone the onset of disease or disability arising from the strain or stress of his work. It must be admitted that the circumstances and conditions of his life, both at home and in the factory, have not infrequently combined to prevent him from obtaining such a food supply. He has had to depend on food brought with him from home in some cases to be warmed up at the factory, and in other cases to be consumed cold or upon food, un-suited to his needs, obtained near his place of work. Both these methods are unsatisfactory. The real requirement is to supply for large numbers of persons at specified times a suitable dietary containing a sufficient proportion and quantity of nutritive material, suitably mixed and easily digestible, appetising and attractive, and obtainable at a reasonable cost."

The stress here laid upon nutrition and dietetic considerations goes beyond the idea, indicated in the opening sentence, of food as a counter-attraction or a safeguard against drink, and suggests the assumption by the Board of the function of supervising the feeding of munition workers, quite apart from the question of liquor. The two things are distinct and should not be confused, as they were in consequence of the emphasis laid on the drinking habits of workmen. One of the reasons given for injurious drinking was the lack of proper facilities for meals, and this was associated with the old complaint against public-houses for not supplying food as well as drink. But had there been no liquor question at all the need of providing food must have forced itself upon the attention of all concerned. In ordinary times it has long been recognised by intelligent employers, who have provided facilities of various kinds, and the practice has been steadily growing for many-years. In the exceptional circumstances created by the war the need was greatly enhanced by the prolonged and continuous work involved and by the employment of much larger numbers of workpeople than usual, of whom many were necessarily housed at a distance; and in addition to the enlargement of existing establishments, new factories were being built, many at some distance from towns. Inadequate The question of providing meals was therefore urgent on provision. j s own accoimt; and this had been recognised, before the Board took it up, by voluntary organisations and commercial caterers, as well as by employers. But the provision made by these agencies was scattered, partial and quite inadequate to the need. A more systematic and comprehensive effort was called for, and this the Board undertook to organise and assist. At first two lines of action were contemplated: (1) The increased supply of food by public-houses and licensed restaurants; (2) the establishment of canteens. The first was directly connected with the functions of the

Board as the special authority placed in control of the liquor trade; the second was not so connected except in so far as canteens are regarded as alternatives or counter-attractions to the public-house. Public-houses The Supply of food in public-houses is an old question and the which has often been discussed in connection with temperance Bupply of. ".

food. reform, and particularly in connection with the principle of ' disinterested management," whether on the lines of the Scandinavian (Gothenburg) system, which involves a sort of municipal control, or by means of philanthropic organisations (pubhc-house trusts) which run public-houses for use, not for profit. The theory underlying these systems and the general principle of reform by converting drinking into eating houses, which is advocated by many besides professed reformers, is that if publicans supplied food and non-alcoholic drinks, a good many of their customers would prefer them to alcoholic liquor, which they take because there is nothing else. This theory is supported by two arguments. One is that public-houses are primarily and properly places of refreshment, where travellers should obtain food as well as drink, and that ' licensed victuallers' the legal term for publicans are persons privileged to sell drink on condition that they supply victuals. The second is that in some parts of the Continent, which are more sober than this country, the place of the public-house is taken by the cafe or general refreshment establishment, where food and other things are provided; from which the inference is drawn that if our public-houses were conducted in like manner a like sobriety would follow.

These ideas were put to the test of experiment by the views of Board. The Second Eeport (1916) devoted some space to the Control subject. Under the head of Facilities for Meals at Public-houses," the policy and action of the Board are explained. After referring to the fact, noted in the previous chapter, that the curtailment of hours applied only to the sale of alcoholic liquor, and that houses might be open all day from 5 A. M. or 5.30 A. M. for the sale of food and non-intoxicants, the Eeport proceeds:

Due credit should be given to those public-houses near works and in the business centres of towns which make a practice of supplying food and other refreshments. It will generally be found that in such cases the. food is excellent in quality and very reasonable in price. But the Board found that a very large proportion of public-houses were not fulfilling their traditional function of victualling-houses. In some cases the circumstances of the neighbourhood were such that it would be unreasonable to expect them to do so. But in others want of enterprise on the part of the licence-holder, or the fact that the object of the owner was simply to push the sale of liquor, has prevented him from developing an important and potentially remunerative side of his business.

' Under the English licensing system, the provision of food Food and in public-houses is stimulated in two ways. First, the common-law throws on the innkeeper i. e. on the man who professes to provide accommodation for travellers) the obligation of providing food for travellers who come to his house. The obligation may be enforced by action. But this is obviously a clumsy and imperfect remedy, and in any event it is inapplicable to cases where the publican makes no pretence of providing for travellers. Secondly, the Justices have always had the power of closing or withdrawing the licences of inns which neglected to provide properly for the requirements of travellers. The Licensing Act of 1904, while it restricted in many respects the power of Justices to refuse the renewal of licences, preserved and extended their disciplinary powers with regard to the provision of refreshments. It was made a ground for refusing renewal without compensation that the holder of an alehouse licence, whether an innkeeper or not, had persistently and um-easonably refused to supply reasonable refreshment, other than intoxicating liquor, at a reasonable price.

' The Board realise that there are many licensed houses which, from their position and circumstances, it would be unreasonable to expect to supply food, no actual or potential Failure of demand for it being conceivable. But when all allowances pubhc-houses jjave been made, there is still a very large number of houses the needs of which ought to, but do not, make an effort to supply the needs of the public in this respect. The Board in December last, addressed a circular to Licensing Justices in all the scheduled areas, reminding them of their powers in this matter, while pointing out that the extreme penalty of refusal would in most cases be neither just nor practicable. They also suggested to them that the practice, obtaining in some districts, of systematic personal visitation of licensed houses, and the preparation of tabulated information as to their situation, structural arrangements and conditions, particularly with reference to the question of food supply, should receive a wide and immediate extension owing to the needs of persons engaged in war work. The Board in the same circular advised the licensing authorities to give sympathetic consideration to proposals for the extension of licensed premises for catering purposes under proper safeguards. The reports of the Brewster Sessions just concluded show that these suggestions for increasing national efficiency have been favourably received by licensing authorities, who are, in many cases, taking active steps to give effect to them."

the public.

The Board and the Justices.

Disappointing results.

The results of this attempt to foster the supply of food in pubhc-houses were disappointing. The Third Eeport of the Board (1917) makes only a very brief reference to the question, to the effect that pubhc-houses and restaurants had been found inadequate and that canteens were the prime necessity. The Fourth Eeport said still less and concentrated entirely on canteens. We shall deal with them presently; but the provision of food in public-houses is a question of so much general interest that the experience of the Board calls for further comment, which can be most conveniently given here. The supply of meals formed a prominent feature of their own administration of the hquor trade in the Carlisle area, which is dealt with in the next chapter; but that stands on a different footing. We have here, as part of the general policy of the Board in relation to the supply of food, a systematic and comprehensive attempt to utilise ordinary pubhc-houses for that purpose, and the result of the experiment throws hght on the whole problem.

The extract given above begins by recognising the existence Public-houses of pubhc-houses near works and in the business centres of towns which make a practice of supplying food and other refreshments, and credit is given them for doing it well. The fact is well known to everyone acquainted with the actual conditions, and it may be added that the practice has been growing for many years. The Keport quoted goes on to admit, after a reference to the ' traditional function of victualling," which most houses do not fulfil, that some are so circumstanced that it would be unreasonable to expect them to do so. We may therefore eliminate two classes those that already provide food and those that carmot be expected to do so. There remains a third class, which might do so but does not. The reasons suggested are want of enterprise on the part of the licence-holder or pressure exercised on him by an owner, whose object is simply to ' push the sale of hquor," whereby he is ' prevented from developing an important and potentially remunerative side of his business." The Board sought to bring pressure to bear on these houses through the licensing benches in the manner described, and their representations were favourably received and acted upon. In some places, notably Cardiff, the licensed victuallers, who are as patriotic as any other class, made a united and determined attempt to develop the victualling branch of their business, not altogether without success." But the net result was so small as to be negligible.

Henry Carter, The Control of the Drink Trade, p. 178.

No demand for food.

Inns and ale-houses.

fourteenth century.

The supply of food a growing practice.

It would be foolish to ascribe this to mere perversity on the part of some Ucence-holders or owners. The thing was given a trial and failed, for the sufficient reason that the great bulk of the people who frequent the pubhc-house go there for drink and not for food, and they know perfectly well what they want. Moreover they always have done so, ever since the drink trade became the object of legislation, and long before that. The legal term ' licensed victualler ' appears to rest on a misreading of history by lawyers. There were in the Middle Ages victuallers and innkeepers, and they were regulated, like other tradesmen, by their respective guilds. But there were also ale-houses, which were distinct from both; and the earhest statutory regulation, which was introduced in 1495, had particular reference to them. The Act then passed empowered justices of the peace to put away common ale-selling ' at their discretion and to ' take sureties of ale-house keepers in their good behaviour." So, too, the first Licensing Act, passed in 1551, was directed against common ale-houses and ' tippling houses." The reason was that they were the resort of disorderly characters. But we have a much earlier picture of the ale-house in ' Piers Plowman," which was written about 1360. All the villagers were there, including the parson, the squire, and some of the women, and also some strangers. The company sat till the evening; there was much drinking, talking and singing, and some quarrelling. Glutton," who was treated by some of those present, got drunk, fell down in the doorway and had to be carried home and put to bed. It is clear that the ale-house was then already the common resort of the inhabitants of the place, who went there for drink and company. That, and not victualling, is the traditional occupation of such houses; the functions are different, and the belief that the drinking house was once an eating house, which has degenerated in modern times, is a traditional delusion. The change that has been taking place in our time is rather in the opposite direction. Food is supphed at some public-houses, as the Report acknowledges; it is supplied, in fact, where there is a demand for it. Both demand and supply are growing with a change of habit, but such changes proceed slowly. They can be encouraged and assisted, but they cannot be forced; and this is the lesson taught by the Board's experience. Whether the mere drink-shop will ever die out is a matter of conjecture, but it will certainly take a long time. It exists, contrary to popular belief, in those continental countries in which the cafe system is held up to us for imitation. English tourists and travellers see the cafe or the beer-garden, because these are conspicuous objects lying in the beaten track; they do not see the cabaret and the drinking-bar, which are more obscurely placed; but they are there all the same.

I have dwelt at some length on this point because of its Canteens, bearing on the general question of temperance; and I shall return to it in connection with the Carlisle scheme, which presents it in a different form. But enough has been said about it for the present. We will pass on to the second line of action taken by the Board for providing meals for war-workers namely, by direct supply in the form of canteens. As already pointed out, this was necessary on its own account without reference to drink, and it formed an important part of the Board's work. Its connection with the liquor trade, however, was only indirect and too indefinite to justify any decided conclusion as to its influence in promoting sobriety; though the Board claimed that it did promote sobriety. But it had a direct and permanent connection with the welfare and efficiency of workers, which was the final object in view, and consequently it deserves some notice.

In the Second Eeport of the Board three methods of establishing canteens were stated: (1) by employers; (2) by voluntary agencies; (3) by the Board itself, in default of the other two. In the Third Keport (1917) the operations of these agencies were described:

In the first enthusiasm of the great movement to develop Voluntary the manufacture of munitions a number of voluntary societies provision, made successful appeals for public subscriptions for the establishment of canteens for munition workers. The advantages of this method of meeting the recognised need were considerable, as the societies were able to recruit large numbers of voluntary workers for service in the canteens and were thus able to set them going more speedily than would have been

Employers.

Financial assistance.

possible under any other system. At first sight it appeared that the voluntary system was susceptible of practically unlimited development provided that the necessary funds were forthcoming, and in order to ease the situation in this respect the Board obtained Treasury authority to pay grants-in-aid to approved voluntary societies up to one-half of their capital expenditure on canteens for munition and transport workers.

' It was not long, however, before the flow of public subscriptions for the provision of canteens for munition workers became exhausted. The public, on whom numerous demands were being made in other directions, evidently considered that these canteens should be provided by those who jointly with the workers reaped the benefit of their establishment. The conclusion forced itself upon the Board that the services of the voluntary societies could best be utilised by employing them to manage canteens erected and equipped by employers, and that these services would be rendered more readily available if the societies were freed from the necessity of finding the funds required to establish the canteens. It was obvious, however, that some special stimulus would be necessary to induce employers to incur the capital expenditure involved in finding canteen accommodation. The Munitions of War Act, 1915, provides that " controlled " employers, in which category are included practically all manufacturers of munitions, in the wide meaning that modern warfare has imparted to the term, are to receive only their standard pre-war profits plus one-fifth, the remainder being paid to the Exchequer. It seemed hardly reasonable to expect them to sacrifice profits so rigidly limited in order to provide canteens for their workers, and it could fairly be argued that, as the advantages of the increased output anticipated from the establishment of canteens would accrue to the State, the State should find the money. On the initiative of the Board it was therefore decided that controlled employers should be allowed to charge to revenue the expenditure they might incur with the approval of the Board on the establishment of canteens at their works; in other words, that the cost of establishing canteens should be borne from funds which would otherwise accrue to the Exchequer. At the same time the Minister gave instructions for the provision, where necessary, at all Government munition establishments (royal arsenals, national factories, etc.) of adequate canteen accommodation at the expense of the State, and entrusted the Board with the general responsibihty for the organisation of the canteens at these estabhshments.

The Board have thus for some eighteen months been The Board a the responsible authority for the organisation of industrial organiser, canteens in munition works throughout the country. They have established the necessary departmental and expert staff for the effective performance of this duty, and in its execution have through their representatives visited all the larger and many of the smaller munition works, and have urged the provision of canteens wherever a real and undoubted need was found to exist, whether that need arose on grounds of liquor control or of nutrition. The Board have made it their duty to do all that is possible to assist employers in the design, equipment and management of canteens. The services of their expert staff have been placed freely at the disposal of employers, and they have published a handy compendium of information on these subjects in the form of a pamphlet entitled " Feeding the Munition Worker," to the usefulness of which they have received numerous testimonies."

There were at that time (March 1917) 570 canteens in works and 60 at docks, as against less than 100 in the middle of 1915. Of the 570 works' canteens, 420 were in controlled establishments and 150 in national factories. A year later (1918) these numbers had been raised to 600 and 180 respectively; the number of persons employed in the 780 establishments thus provided with canteens exclusive of docks was 990,000 out of a total of 2,299,000 employed on munition work, including the naval department. At this juncture (February Ministry of 1918) the Ministry of Munitions took over the responsibility 'i itioiis-for the canteen system from the Control Board and placed it in charge of a special department, mainly on account of the general shortage of food, which made close co-operation with the Food Controller desirable. This step may be regarded as a testimony to the importance of the canteen system in maintaining efficiency of production. At the same time it emphasises the distinction between the provision of food and the hquor question. The services of the Canteen Committee of the Board, who had become experts in organisation, were retained in an advisory capacity by the new authority, and their pohcy was continued. New canteens were then still being provided. The total amount of allowances from the profits of controlled establishments assigned by the Board to the provision of canteens was 1,505,980, and the grants-in-aid to voluntary societies totalled 15,237. These figures do not include the 180 national factories, in which the canteens were directly financed by the Ministry of Munitions. Results. The results of the canteen system were highly satisfactory.

It was one of the most important items in the welfare work ' which was stimulated to such rapid development by the industrial needs of the great national emergency. Dr. H. M. Vernon, writing on the subject, observes:

The physical efficiency and health of the workers can only be maintained if they get an adequate supply of nutritious food, and there can be no doubt that in the past many industrial workers suffered from malnutrition. This held especially for badly paid women workers, who often could not afford to spend sufficient on their food, and who likewise were apt to spend injudiciously on unsatisfying food, such as tea and pastry, instead of a more substantial and digestible dietary. The splendid achievements of most munition workers during the war, and especially of the women, has frequently been attributed in large part to the better food they could afford to buy because of their good wages."

He goes on to quote a report made by the Health of Munition Workers' Committee, who had collected opinions from all parts of the country as to the benefit of these canteens, and were impressed by the substantial advantages they conferred. There was ' a marked improvement in the health, nutrition and physical condition of the workers, a reduction in fatigue and sickness, less absence and broken time, less tendency to alcoholism, and an increased efficiency and output. Moreover such of the workers as had formerly gone home for meals now benefited by getting increased opportunity for rest and recreation, whilst those who had been accustomed to eat the food they had brought with them in the workshops got a salutary change of venue and the shops got a better midday ventilation."

Industrial Fatigue and Efficiency, p. 246.

The Committee were ' satisfied that the evidence of these results was substantial, indisputable and widespread."

With regard to the influence on sobriety, the Committee Canteens emphasised among other results a ' lessened tendency to exces- gobriety sive consumption of alcohol," and probably such eli'ect as meals in the works had upon drinking would be in that direction; but no evidence was offered, and the theory that excessive drinking in general is caused by lack of food has no foundation. When wages are high and food plentiful the consumption of drink is high too; and the consumption of both went down together in the war. The canteens were ' dry ' to use the current slang term and sold no intoxicants, with the exception of a few, which were registered as clubs for special reasons and allowed to sell beer. In some cases the usual tendency to expansion in welfare work was exhibited, and canteens developed into centres for recreation, amusement, and sport. They were, no doubt, alternatives to the public-house, but experience shows that alternatives appeal for the most part to different classes. There was nothing intrinsically new either in canteens or other forms of welfare work in the war; there was only a very extensive and special development necessitated by exceptional circumstances. It will leave a lasting impression, but to expect too much from it can lead only to disappointment, as all experienced observers know.

Among the powers conferred on the Control Board and enumerated in Chapter III were those of purchasing and carrying on licensed premises and businesses, which meant in effect State purchase. The Board made a sparing use of this power, and only took over the trade in three districts, in which special conditions prevailed; but one of these was sufficiently large to furnish a fair experiment in State ownership and management, which were novel methods of dealing with the problem in this country, though they have been tried elsewhere. This lends exceptional interest to the experiment, which was, and still is, the subject of much controversy; and since the plan has been continued under a Government Department the interest is permanent.

The areas The three areas were: (1) Enfield Lock, near London; osierehr (2) Gretna and Carlisle on the West Scottish border; (3) Inver-gordon and Cromarty on the North-East coast of Scotland. The first and second of these areas contained large Government factories for the manufacture of explosives; the third was an important naval base and dockyard. In each case the action of the Board was taken at the instance of the Government Department concerned, namely the Admiralty in the last-mentioned case and the Ministry of Munitions in the others. Of the three schemes, only one involved State purchase on such a scale and in such circumstances as to furnish material for testing this method of deahng with the problem and its applicabihty to ordinary life; and accordingly attention will be directed mainly to it. The other two cases were too exceptional and isolated to throw much light on the question, and can be briefly dismissed; but a preliminary account of the circumstances that led up to State purchase is necessary to a proper understanding of its bearing.

The question was first broached in the autumn of 1915, Reasons for when the Admiralty and the Munitions Ministry approached?" the Control Board; the former with reference to the Cromarty Firth area, the latter with reference to Gretna and Enfield. The Admiralty suggested that the Board should take over the licensed premises in the villages of Invergordon and Cromarty on the ground that ' notwithstanding the special measures that had been taken by the Naval authorities and by the police, a state of drunkenness existed which required remedy in the interests of the Naval service." The first move, therefore, came from the Admiralty on the declared ground that the existing authorities had failed to grapple with an evil detrimental to the service. The premises, which were taken over in 1916, numbered thirteen in all and included four inns.

In the other cases the question arose in a somewhat different manner. The problem at Enfield was to supply the needs of a greatly increased number of workmen at an isolated Government factory, and it was originally raised on behalf of men employed on night-work, for whose benefit a readjustment of the opening hours was suggested. A deputation from the men themselves urged the need. On inquiry it was found that a canteen inside the works and the supplementary accommodation provided by adjacent public-houses were quite inadequate, especially in regard to meals; and since these houses four in number were close to the factory and almost exclusively used by the men employed there, it was thought that the best solution would be a unified system of management and the equipment of some of them with canteen facilities, which could be most speedily and effectively accomplished by taking them over. They were, therefore, compulsorily acquired under the provisions of the empowering Act (p. 25), and came into the possession of the Board on January 2, 1916. This was the earliest practical application of State ownership. An adjacent house holding an off-licence was subsequently taken over, making five in all.

The origin of the third scheme, embracing Gretna and The problem Carhsle, was similar. The Munitions Ministry had decided at Gretna.

Failure of ordinary restrictions.

Increased drunkenness.

to erect a very large explosives factory occupying a strip of land nine miles in length, in the thoroughly rural parish of Gretna on the Scottish border north of Carlisle, and adjacent to the Solway Firth. It was estimated that 10,000 persons would eventually be employed in the factory, representing an additional population of from 20,000 to 30,000, and that during construction many thousands of navvies and other workmen would have to be provided for in the immediate neighbourhood. The Ministry requested the Control Board to consider the problem that would arise from the influx of all these persons into a rural neighbourhood, where the surrounding villages and Carlisle itself but a small town offered the only accommodation.

The Board at first placed the whole area under a restriction order on the lines explained in Chapter III. This was in November 1915; but as the number of workmen, and particularly of navvies gathered from all parts of the country, increased with the progress of construction they eventually reached 22,000 the restrictions proved quite inadequate. The men, who were very highly paid, had nowhere to go and nothing to do in the evening, and they poured into Carhsle and the smaller places near the factory. They naturally resorted to the public-houses, which were wholly unsuited to serve such large numbers and were habitually overcrowded. Effective supervision, whether by the publicans or the police, became impossible and increasing disorder ensued. Sufficient evidence of the state of things is the enormous increase in the convictions for drunkenness which took place at this time. In Carlisle they rose during the autumn of 1915 from the former average of 5 to 13 per week, and in 1916 continued to rise till they reached 33 per week in June, before the Board took over the trade. The aggregate for six months, January to June, rose from 72 in 1915 to 564 in 1916; in Annan, over the Scottish border, the corresponding rise was from 6 to 146. The police figures were fully confirmed by descriptions of street scenes of disorder by eye-witnesses.

These facts prove that it was imperative to adopt stronger measures and explain the action of the Board, who decided to take over the trade in preference to prohibition, which was also suggested. A further decision arrived at after full consideration was of great importance. This was that the licensed premises and other businesses which were to be taken over should be purchased outright and acquired permanently, not merely for the duration of the war. The process was accomplished by degrees. The Board began by purchasing the houses in villages nearest to the factory in January 1916, and then gradually extended operations, as the situation developed in the manner indicated above.

Such were the circumstances leading up to the introduction of State ownership in this country at the beginning of 1916. The subsequent conduct of the trade under the system varied somewhat in the three areas, being adjusted to particular conditions.

At Enfield the main question was the supply of food, as Action at already explained, and consequently the chief change effected " fi '-was the reconstruction of two out of the four public-houses acquired, and the provision of large dining-rooms with facilities?

for the supply of meals. It was really a canteen case, rather than one of excessive drinking, and no licence was suppressed; but the hours of opening were limited to four and a half, adjusted to suit the workmen's meal times. The dining-rooms were greatly appreciated by the men, who formally expressed their thanks to the Control Board.

On the Cromarty Firth, on the other hand, the problem Action at that presented itself was the prevalent intemperance, and it-pl took a somewhat special form determined by naval requirements. Consequently the measures taken were of a special character to suit the conditions. The licensed premises were situated in two villages Invergordon and Cromarty on the Cromarty Firth, at a considerable distance from each other, and included, in both places, inns and grocers' hcences (off-sale) as well as pubuc-houses. Having a perfectly free hand by virtue of purchase the Board were in a position to rearrange the business at pleasure. Five out of the thirteen hcences were extinguished as redundant; the sale for off-consumption, which had been carried on by the inns and public-houses as well as by the four grocers' shops, was separated from the on-sale and confined to two of the shops, which were entirely given up to that business and ceased to sell groceries.

In this way the liquor trade was divided up into two distinct compartments, on- and off-sale, carried on in distinct establishments and separated from other forms of retail trade. At the same time the off-sale was confined to residents. The hours of opening for on-sale were limited to four and a half. In 1917 one of the inns at Invergordon was partly reconstructed and opened as a workmen's restaurant; and in 1918 the Board, at the request of the Admiralty, extended the scheme to include Alness and nine additional licensed houses, making twenty-two in all, of which eleven were closed. The interest of these details lies in the evidence they afford of the extent to which the trade can be reorganised under pubhc ownership. But whether such a free use of authority would be tolerated or prove beneficial, if generally apphed, is a different question. In this particular instance the Admiralty were well satisfied with the results of State purchase and administration. We pass on to the principal case of State management which calls for more extended examination, because the conditions, though exceptional, were less so and included many ordinary elements, and because the principle was applied on a scale large enough to furnish an object-lesson, from which some general conclusions can be drawn. Extent and It has already been said, in explaining the initiation of ' f p ' v 'f this scheme commonly and conveniently called the Carlisle area. Scheme that from a small and tentative beginning it was gradually extended to cover a considerable area on both sides of the Scottish border, from Ecclefechan in Dumfriesshire to Maryport in Cumberland. This area was estimated at about 500 square miles and its population at 140,000. It is a rural district containing only one considerable town, namely Carlisle, which has a population of about 52,000 and is a great railway, market and shopping centre and the seat of a few manufactures. It is a town which is generally very quiet, but to which large numbers resort on market-days, Saturdays, and special occasions. The next largest town is Maryport, a small port on the Cumberland coast about thirty miles from Carhsle at the southern extremity of the controlled area, and having a population of 10,000. The only other place that can be called a town is Annan on the Scottish side, about half the size of Maryport and chiefly known to fame as the place where Thomas Carlyle went to school. It is filled with people from the country-side on market-days. Numerous villages scattered about on both sides of the border account for the rest of the population. But to these standing elements must be added two new residential settlements built for the factory population at Gretna.

The gradual extension of State control just indicated was Gradual not undertaken arbitrarily or for its own sake, but for definite f (foq rol. reasons. During the construction of the factory and the settlements the workmen employed were living wherever they could find lodgings, and not only filled all the available space in Carlisle, Annan, and the villages nearest to the factory, but had to go much farther afield. They were widely scattered in adjacent parishes and all along the railways, and it became necessary to push out the zone. The largest and latest extension, which brought in Maryport, was due to the fact that many of the licences acquired in Carlisle and in the intervening area were owned by the Maryport brewery, and it was found desirable to acquire the brewery also, as in the case of the Carhsle breweries, and to round off the whole area. That the Board's motive was not extension for its own sake is shown by the fact that a request made by the local authorities of Dumfries and other burghs in Dumfriesshire, for the inclusion of the whole county in the scheme of purchase and control, was declined, after inquiry, on the ground that ' the problem of drink in the county, apart from the Gretna district, was not of such large dimensions or instant urgency as to justify the special action recommended."

The accompanying map shows the initiation and extension of purchase in successive zones.

With regard to the trading interests involved in the transfer Trading from private to pubhc ownership I have been unable to find ' any summary statement for the whole area. Though topographically continuous, it was divided for convenience into two administrative districts, one north and the other south of the Border, because the English and Scottish hcensing laws

Lockerbie
Cockermourh
Penrihhi
Inner factory area taken over January-March 1916.
: V; v:'–'-."i First extension taken over July 1916.
Carlisle area taken over July-December 1916.
Maryport area taken over 1917.-. Border between England and Scotland.

differ somewhat in detail; and there are also differences of custom. It appears from the Third Eeport of the Board that the number of licences in the northern section was twenty-eight, of which eight were grocers' off-licences. In the southern section, which is by far the larger of the two, there were, including the final extension to Maryport, 340 licensed premises of all kinds and five breweries. This makes a total of 368 licensed premises; but all of these were not taken over. At the date of the General Manager's last report there still remained forty-seven that had not been acquired. In Carlisle itself, which was the heart of the whole scheme, there were at the outset 119 licensed premises and four breweries. As already stated, the Board began operations in January 1916 in a restricted zone round about the works at Gretna. By the end of March all the licences had been acquired in this inner area, which was then extended. In Carlisle the process of acquisition was begun in July 1916, after a series of conferences with the town and county authorities and with representatives of the trade. By the end of that year the bulk of the properties in the town had been taken over; but in consequence of the later extension to Maryport the process was continued during the succeeding years.

I have been unable to find any classified Hst of the premises and businesses acquired, which included property of several kinds. In addition to the ordinary pubhc-houses there were hotels, breweries, maltings, blending and botthng stores, wine and spirit merchants' estabhshments, shops and offices, cottage property and land. The total payments made in Payment respect of all the properties acquired by the Board inclusive peng ation. of Enfield and Cromarty down to March 1921 was 883,265. The table on next page shows the payments made in each of " ""'-, the five years, 1916-21.

It will be seen from this table that the financial transactions were of considerable magnitude and extended over the whole period. The settlement of claims took a very long time in some Delayed cases, and was not completed at the date of the last report payments. October 1921; properties acquired at the begirming of 1916 were still being paid for in 1921. The delay, which caused much dissatisfaction, was due in a large measure to the method

Methods of assessment.

Bearing on the policy of nationalisation.

of deciding claims for compensation. Acquisition was compulsory, and at first the method was adopted of endeavouring to come to a provisional agreement, which was then referred to the Defence of the Eealm Losses Commission for endorsement. Some cases were settled in this way without difficulty and within a reasonable time, as is shown by the substantial payments completed in 1916-17; but in others there was delay and friction, which is reflected in the small total for the year 1917-18. This procedure was indirectly brought to an end in 1918 by the Cannon Brewery case, in which it was decided that the above-mentioned Commission had no jurisdiction in the matter. After that a system of direct agreement between the Board and claimants, subject to Treasury sanction, was adopted with much greater success, as shown in the large payment made in 1918-19.

But the history of the process of State purchase in this very limited area, with its delays and difficulties despite the patriotic spirit prevailing in the national emergency and the local feeling in favour of the step, is a lesson to be remembered in considering the policy of general State purchase of the trade, which is advocated in some quarters. The Control Board gave a marked impetus to this movement by a Memorandum submitted to the Government in December 1916, definitely recommending the pohcy of State purchase. It was a conclusion prematurely arrived at in the enthusiasm of the initial success. Later on, after a more extended experience, the chairman of the Board, in pubhcly referring to the question.

adopted a guarded attitude and carefully refrained from expressing an opinion on the expediency of State purchase as a national policy.

To return to the Carlisle scheme, we take the Board as Administra-having purchased the properties mentioned above and having,. thereby become brewers, hotel-keepers, publicans, wine and ' spirit dealers wholesale and retail, caterers, blenders and bottlers. The administration of these undertakings was entrusted to a resident general manager with the aid of a local advisory committee of twenty-four persons, representing the civic authorities of Carlisle and the adjoining county areas affected. The Committee included three ladies, four members of the Control Board, and a representative of the Carhsle Trades and Labour Council. The president was the Earl of Lonsdale, and the chairman Mr. F. W. Chance. The Committee met regularly once a month for the discussion of matters involved in the conduct of the trade and affecting public interest.

It has already been said that the whole area associated with the Gretna factory was divided for administrative purposes into two sections, one on each side of the Border. The foregoing details relate more particularly to the English section, which was much the larger and more important. The general manager appointed there was Mr. E. C. Sanders (later Sir Edgar Sanders), who had previously been Clerk to the Liver-j)Ool Justices. He furnished annual reports to the Boards until his retirement in 1921; these were published, and form a full and authoritative official narrative of the proceedings in the area in addition to the Board's own reports. No corresponding reports were published for the Scottish section, officially called Gretna-without-the-Township; but the administration was carried on in the same way by a general manager with a local advisory Committee, and the policy pursued was in all respects similar. Such particulars as seem to call for notice in regard to the Scottish area will be given in due course, but the main interest pertains to the Carlisle section.

The General Manager's Report for the year 1920 contains The a summary statement of the pohcy pursued, which may be po L regarded as a retrospective survey of his experience during the first four and a half years of administration. It runs: ' While always keeping principally in view the sobriety of the district and the improvement of the conditions under which the trade is carried on, the undertaking is managed as far as possible as a business proposition; the most detailed accounts and statistics are kept, and no effort is spared to eliminate waste and overlapping. The results are seen in the strong financial position which has been established in so short a time.

' The Board's policy in the area can be shortly summarised under the following heads: ' (a) Fewer and better houses.

' (b) The provision of food and non-intoxicants in those houses where there is likely to be demand for them.

' (c) The general improvement of the conditions under which the whole trade is carried on, and ' (d) The elimination of private interest in the sale of intoxicants.

' To these four considerations which, it is submitted, are fundamental to any comprehensive scheme of licensing reform, the Board have endeavoured to give due weight in their work in the Carlisle district."

A caveat must be entered here.

For these observations Sir Edgar Sanders is alone responsible. The Eeport is prefaced by a note, signed by the secretary to the Board, which says: It must not be understood that the Board, in approving the publication of this Report, necessarily endorse all the opinions which Sir Edgar Sanders expresses in it upon matters of general pohcy." His reference to licensing reform in general goes somewhat beyond the proper functions of the Board; but the foregoing statement conveniently sums up the objects aimed at by the changes effected in the trade under State ownership and control. These were:

Changes (1) A large reduction in the number of licensed houses effected. g j j businesses.

(2) Their re-arrangement.

(3) The improvement of premises.

(4) The provision of meals.

(5) Salaried managers of pubhc-houses.

(6) Minor changes.

(1) Beduction.

Two out of the five breweries were permanently closed and Brewing brewing was restricted to one brewery in Carlisle and one in concentrated. Maryport, which supplied all the beer sold in the Board's houses. The fifth brewery was converted into a beer and spirit store. The main object of these changes was economy, in which they were successful.

In the whole area there were, in July 1916, 340 licences. Licensed By the end of 1920 the Board had acquired all but forty-seven J' J' and had suppressed 123. In Carhsle itself the number was reduced from 119 to sixty-nine. Here all the licensed premises had been acquired by the Board, except the two principal hotels and a restaurant, none of which had a bar. These were purposely left and have remained outside the scheme. The sixty-nine licences included two new ones granted by the Board, so that the total number of old ones suppressed was fifty-two. The process of reduction began with the entry of the Board into possession in July 1916, when six licences were suppressed simultaneously with the opening of the Gretna Tavern, to be described below.

Eeduction was continued by degrees, but in Carlisle and the immediate neighbourhood most of it had been accomplished by the end of 1917. Afterwards it naturally proceeded more slowly, and was not completed at the end of 1920. The numerical reduction was then 42 per cent, in Carhsle and 46 per cent, outside, ranging from 50 per cent, in the Longtown division nearest the factory to 25-6 per cent, in the Maryport division. It was calculated that to effect the same reduction under the Act of 1904 would have taken at least twenty-five years, which indicates the magnitude of the change.

The principles determining the selection of licences to be Grounds of suppressed were (1) redundancy, (2) unsuitability of premises ' 'i'i i-in regard to structure or position, (3) economy. The two first grounds have been familiar subjects of controversy for many years, and were recognised by the Legislature in the Act of 1904. The ground of economy, on the other hand, is peculiar to a monopoly ownership of the whole trade, and some stress was laid upon it in the General Manager's reports.

The amount of trade not a consideration.

Congested areas.

But in general the policy of the Board was guided by the considerations of redundancy and unsuitability. The Fourth Report of the Board (1918) says: ' As far as possible all houses have now been closed which from their structure or position were undesirable. In the older parts of the city many of the public-houses were situated in passages or narrow lanes. In other parts the licences were too numerous and the requirements of the public were fully met by those which were continued. In general it has been the aim of the Board in country districts to limit the number of licensed premises to the reasonable requirements of the villages and of travellers on the main roads. It has usually been found that one house is sufficient for a village, provided that it is of a structure suitable for the different types of customers who are likely to frequent it."

The General Manager's Report for 1919, referring to the question of the amount of trade done in particular houses, which is generally taken into account by licensing benches in selecting houses for suppression under the Licensing Act, observes that the Board were free to close those houses which were least suitable for their purpose regardless of the amount of trade they did.

' The houses in the side streets and in lanes and alleys were dislicensed if they were not suitable as licensed premises whether or not a large sale was done at them, and the better houses, and especially those in more open situations, were retained."

A plan of Carhsle, published in the Board's Fourth Report, shows the houses suppressed and those retained in the city. The great bulk of the former were in the central and older parts of the town and in small cross streets or passages. This is typical of ancient and quiet towns. The small pubhc-houses thick on the ground about the centre are relics of former days when there was little or no restriction on numbers and the houses were far more numerous in proportion to population than they are now. They have been spared for various reasons, often sentimental, in these more iconoclastic days; but the Board made a clean B reep of them. Unsuit- Unsuitable ability of premises is a more cogent gromid for suppression Premises. than mere redundancy, especially under State ownership and ' disinterested management," for the chief argument in regard to redundancy is that it leads to malpractices through excessive competition, but this automatically disappears under State ownership. The General Manager notices this point in his 1919 Report, but observes that ' a smaller number of public-houses means fewer temptations to drink to the large number of men and women who are not able to control their appetite for alcoholic liquor."

(2) He-arrangement.

This went with reduction and involved both concentration concentra-and diffusion. Brewing, bottling and the spirit trade were " concentrated. As already stated, one brewery in Carlisle of trade. was found sufficient in place of four; the bottling of beer, which had been carried on at a dozen places, was confined to a single estabhshment; the breaking-down, blending and wholesale distribution of spirits, which had been carried on at seventeen different premises, were similarly concentrated and conducted at a single store. The retail sale of spirits Off' sale for off-consumption, previously carried on in all the fully ' licensed houses, and by a number of wine merchants and grocers, was limited at first to eighteen and later to thirteen licensed houses, and to three or four stores wholly devoted to that trade and conducted by the Board. It was the pohcy Grocers' of the Board everywhere to abohsh the so-called grocers' '"' ' ' licences, which imply the sale of intoxicants on the same premises as other goods. In the Carlisle district there were ten such mixed shops, and eight in the Gretna district. They were all abolished by giving up one or the other trade. In the Carlisle district the licence was withdrawn from seven of the ten shops and the sale of groceries from the other three, which were then confined to intoxicants. In the Gretna district the same plan was followed; seven of the eight licences were withdrawn and one retained, without the groceries. The object of this re-arrangement was not merely to concentrate

Constructive measures.

the retail sale of bottled intoxicants in a few establishments, but to separate that trade from others. There is no evidence that inconvenience was caused by depriving customers of the facilities and the choice they had previously enjoyed, and this may be taken as proof that the redistribution was judiciously carried out; for it is obvious that much inconvenience might be caused by suppressing some shops and compelhng customers to resort to others, perhaps at a distance. This concentration is quite a different proposition from thinning out public-houses in a quarter where they are thick on the ground. The latter process, being accompanied by a certain amount of compensatory provision elsewhere, had the effect of rather diffusing than concentrating facilities topographically. The compensatory provision included the construction of new premises and the enlargement of old ones. These constructive measures, which formed the most interesting part of the Board's operations and the one that promises to have the most lasting influence, cannot be separated from the improvement of premises and the provision of meals. We will therefore take these points together.

The Gretna Tavern.

(3) Improvement of premises.

(4) Provision of meals.

The very first acts of the Board after coming into possession at Carhsle were to open a new pubhc-house and close six old ones in the town. The two measures were connected in time and purpose and marked a new departure. The new public-house was the Gretna Tavern, opened by Lord Lonsdale on July 12, 1916. The building was the former post-office of Carhsle, placed at the disposal of the Board by the Postmaster-General. The following account of the estabhshment appeared in The Times under date July 13, 1916;

A New Type of Public-house ' The Gretna Tavern is a converted post-office very skilfully adapted by Mr. Eedfern, the architect to the Control Board. The character of the building, both exterior and interior, in itself constitutes a new type of refreshment house. It is as far removed from a Gothenburg Bolag tavern or a German Bier Halle as from a British public-house of any type. IHs neither dingy like the old style of pothouse, nor garish like the new, nor "Quaint" like the still newer fancy imitations of antique architecture, nor gimcrack like most coffee taverns and temperance refresh-ment rooms. It is a solid stone building of dignified aspect, occupying a commanding position in a dignified street. Inside, the two principal rooms are a long open bar formed out of the old selhng counter, with very little alteration, and a large hall behind, which was the sorting room. The latter serves the new purpose admirably. It is spacious, lofty, and well lighted. There is a counter at which various things will be sold, several tables at which meals and minor refreshments will be served, a stand for newspapers, a piano, gramophone, and sundry conveniences.

Adjoining the hall is a well-equipped kitchen where all kinds of meals can be cooked, and a store-room. There are also some rooms for the attendants and the manageress, but no sleeping accommodation. No one will sleep on the premises. The only alcoholic liquor that will be served is beer. Customers must drink standing at the bar; in the hall beer will be brought to them seated at the tables. The idea is to encourage people to stop for rational recreation by making them comfortable, but not for mere drinking."

On the occasion of the opening. Lord D'Abernon explained that the policy of the Board was to replace small and unsuitable houses in back streets by others of a better character, where reasonable refreshments and non-alcoholic drinks could be obtained. At the same time he uttered some words of warning which may be recalled with advantage. He deprecated extravagant expectations. Changes of habit were slow, and alterations of premises would also take time. Management by the Board or the Government was no panacea for the evils of drink. He had gone carefully into the dangers and difficulties of direct management and was himself not inclined to underrate them. The present venture was an experiment, and the Board relied largely on local advice and help to make it successful.

The Gretna Tavern was the first of several similar ventures. A second new model estabhshment of the same type, but

Lord

D'Abernon's warning against extravagant expectations.

Other model taverns.

smaller and situated in another part of Carlisle, was opened in the following November. This was the London Tavern. The building, which had previously been occupied by a Unionist Club, was converted into a caf6-restaurant, with a bar for beer and wine on the ground floor and a dining-room upstairs. It was intended to serve the needs of a working-class quarter.

Outside Carlisle, new establishments were constructed at Annan, which lies at the Scottish end of the factory area, and at Longtown at the Cumberland end. The one at Annan was entirely new and built on a vacant site known as Grade's Banking, probably because someone named Gracie once constructed a bank there or did something of the sort. The building, which retained the name, was intended for the use of the navvies, many of whom lodged in and about Annan, where the public-houses were small, old-fashioned and quite inadequate to accommodate them, and where there was no other place to which they could resort after work. It comprised two large halls; one for food and drink, newspapers and games, and capable of seating 200 persons, the other fitted up as a cinema and available for other entertainments. There was no drinking bar in the restaurant, but beer and wine were served at the tables. This part of the establishment was greatly appreciated by the navvies, who resorted to it in large numbers for supper, but they showed httle interest in the cinema hall, which was used chiefly by the other inhabitants. Two bilhard tables were provided, besides draughts, dominoes, and newspapers, and out of doors a bowling green. This establishment was opened in November 1916.

The model tavern at Longtown, opened in June 1917, was erected on the site of an old public-house named the Globe," which had been demohshed. It was on similar lines to those described above in regard to uses and character, but aesthetically more ambitious. A special correspondent of The Times, writing of the model houses of the Board, said of it: ' The model tavern at Longtown, which is the most recently completed, seems thrown away in this little bleak old Border town. It is built of fine reddish stone, very solid and handsome, round two sides of a court, holding a bowling green, with a raised flagged walk all round and an Italian pergola down one side. The rooms are plain and strictly adapted to their purpose, but they are large and lofty, and they have an austere picturesqueness and refined dignity worthy of any one. If architecture can lift the public-house out of debasing associations it is done here."

Two other cases of a somewhat different character, but in line with the foregoing, deserve mention. At the village of Eockcliffe which lies between Longtown and Carhsle, there were two pubhc-houses and a village institute. The public-houses were closed and the institute converted into a sort of model tavern by adding the supply of food and beer to its other uses. The principal room here was furnished with books and newspapers, a piano and a billiard table. At Carleton, another village near Longtown, there were two licensed houses of a poor character. These were given up and a group of buildings was purchased and converted into a roomy and convenient iim with smoke-room and tea-room.

The five model houses just described stand somewhat apart as the most complete examples of the improvement pohcy, in that they were designed entirely for the purpose, and were not merely existing pubhc-houses enlarged and altered. But several of the last-named class were raised to pretty nearly the same status by reconstruction. There were Recon-five of these in Carlisle, opened at different dates in the summer ' of 1917. They were all of the same general type, and though naturally varying in detail had two essential features in common, as explained in the Board's Fourth Eeport:

In the first place they all contain spacious accommodation, both standing and sitting, for the consumption otliquid refreshments, intoxicating and non-intoxicating. Tha-Board have Seats and aimed at providing an alternative to the practice of standing at f f. ' the bar-counter to drink, and with this object the length of the bare, counter is greatly reduced, while the drinking-rooms are plenti-fullyprovided with seats, chairs and small tables. The drinking-roomsthemselves are arranged round an island or projecting bar-counter, and are large, airy, and bpen, forming a striking contrast to the innumerable small rooms and " snugs " in which the older public-houses abounded. In the second place, they 74 DRINK IN 1914-1922 all contain, as an integral part of their design, a kitchen well equipped to supply substantial meals and a comfortable dining-room in which meals, with or without drink, are served."

With reference to the first of these objects, the following passage in the General Manager's Eeport for 1918 is of interest:

Newar As regards the drinking portion of the premises, the rangements Board's aim at first was to have a large open hall with a small popular. service bar and tables with chairs and seats round for customers.

Standing at the bar to drink was to be discouraged and customers were to be urged to sit at the tables and have their drinks brought to them. This arrangement was not popular. The British drinker does not appear to like too large an open space. He prefers a room of moderate size where he can sit with his friends. Failing this he has become so accustomed to a long bar against which he can lean and on which he can put his glass, that it is contrary to his custom to remain seated. At the Irish Gate Tavern therefore (one of the latest houses to be reconstructed), the original plan was modified, and the open space was cut up into three or four spaces, each about the size of an ordinary bar parlour, separated by laced partitions. These partitions gave the space which they bounded a sense of privacy, and they were at the same time easy of supervision by the manager and his assistants. So far this type of house has proved more popular than the earlier pattern, although it is too soon to say that any settled opinion has yet developed on this point."

I have introduced this lesson from experience here because it was learnt and acted upon during the constructive transformation of the trade undertaken by the Board, and therefore belongs to that part of the subject. As a modification of plan forced upon the Board by experience, it shows very clearly that consumers must be reckoned with in re-modelling public-houses, and that ideal arrangements based more upon fancy than upon observation may fail of their purpose. It is a fallacy to assume that the public want what well-meaning persons think they ought to want, or that they can be readily induced to want it by forcing it upon them. Demand is very slow to follow supply. The State purchase scheme furnished other examples of the same truth, but this one is particularly clear and convincing. It could surprise no one really conversant with the public-house population and their habits.

One more point is to be noted here in connection with the A restaurant. model taverns. One of them the Citadel Tavern in Carlisle was of a superior order to the others, and served a different class of customers. It was, in fact, a restaurant of a good class, at which higher prices were charged. The obvious criticism that this lay outside the Board's proper functions of increasing the efqciency of the Gretna factory was made at the time, and elicited the equally obvious answer that since the Board had taken over the whole trade, with the exception of the two leading hotels and the railway refreshment-rooms, they were bound to cater for other classes than factory workers. The argument involves an admission that State purchase and control, though possibly the best solution of the immediate problem, did entail other measures which had nothing to do with the war; and there was a distinct and growing tendency, not indeed to forget the primary object, but to go beyond it and to make licensing reform in general the main object. This, however, was more open to objection from the trade than from the national point of view, provided that the war object was secured and the whole thing was not developed beyond the dimensions of an experiment. To have surreptitiously secured or promoted, under cover of war, such an immense change as the nationalisation of the liquor trade, without the full and explicit sanction of Parliament, would have been an indefensible abuse of the powers of the Board. It was not done, but some people tried to do it.

To return to the details of the Board's administration, the Food policy of providing food in public-houses was not confined to intoxicants.   the special class of new or improved houses we have been considering. The Fourth Eeport of the Board mentions another and larger class, in which ' a serious and sustained effort was made to encourage the supply of food." These houses were kept open on weekdays from 10 a. m. to 9 p. m. that is, during otherwise prohibited hours for the sale of food other than regular meals, such as sandwiches, meat pies, bread and cheese, biscuits, etc., and non-intoxicants, including

Little demand.

Tea-rooms.

Food for off-consumption.

tea, coffee, cocoa, etc.; and on Sundays they were opened for the same purpose from 12 to 2 p. m., and from 4 to 6 p. m. or 7 to 9 P. M., being thus exempted from the rule of complete Sunday closing which had been imposed on the district as part of the general restriction orders before the purchase scheme was put in hand. There were at one time twenty-eight of these houses; but the plan proved less successful than was hoped, and seven were given up before long for lack of demand. By 1918 only a few were left to continue the practice. The General Manager reported in that year that the provision of food in the ordinary public-house is not appreciated, and meets httle demand."

The experience is of great interest because the usual motive to which the non-supply of food, tea and coffee is ascribed, both by temperance reformers and other controversialists namely, the desire of the publican under orders to ' push the sale ' of drink was completely eliminated. As more fully explained under the next heading, the managers under the Board had no interest in the sale of drink, and were specially encouraged to sell the other things. Moreover, a catering superintendent was appointed to see that all the things sup-phed were good and fresh; but in vain. This confirms the conclusions reached in connection with the canteen movement (see p. 50), and reinforces the lesson noted above.

Tea-rooms in country inns, which were another experiment in the same direction, were more successful, at least in the summer. During the month of September 1918, light meals were served to the number of 4856 at the sixty-two licensed houses then under the Board's management in the district outside Carhsle. The bicycle and char-a-banc traffic, to which further reference will be made in a later chapter, accounts for a good deal of this.

One more form of food provision, which was quite novel, remains to be mentioned. This was the supply of hot cooked food to be taken away and consumed at home; it was arranged for at five of the improved houses. Separate entrances were provided for the messengers, who were generally children. The food supplied was chiefly soup and pudding, at very low prices. This departure had really nothing to do with the liquor trade, but it was very popular with the poorer classes during the shortage of food.

Nothing has hitherto been said about the hotels acquired Hotels. by the Board. They have a less important bearing on the general problem than the public-houses, but they also came into the scheme of improvement, though rather as a matter of business than of reform. The Board owned and managed two in Carlisle and eight outside in that district; two in Annan and others on the Scottish side, and in some cases ' it was found necessary to carry out large schemes of modernisation to bring the buildings into line with modern requirements in the way of heating, sanitary accommodation, furnishing and general equipment." The ' Graham Arms ' at Longtown was one of these. It had once been a favourite resort of fishermen, but being practically taken possession of by the navvies, it had deteriorated. The Board restored and improved it. Others, similarly treated, were the ' Golden Lion' at Maryport and the Grapes ' at Aspatria. At Wigton an old posting-house which had fallen into decay was replaced by converting a new building, constructed for a club, into a handsome modern hotel. All the Board's hotels were placed under salaried managers on the same principle as the public-houses.

(6) Disinterested Management.

This feature of the State scheme has just been mentioned in connection with the attempt to popularise the sale of food and non-intoxicants in ordinary public-houses. The question has long been a familiar subject of controversy, and great stress has been laid upon it in some quarters. In particular it is a Pushing leading feature in the Scandinavian or Gothenburg and the Pubhc-house Trust systems. The theory is that ordinary publicans promote excessive drinking by ' pushing the sale ' of intoxicants, in which they have a direct or indirect interest, at least in ' tied houses, owned by brewers or distillers, for whom they, in effect, act as managers. It is contended that sobriety would be greatly promoted by freeing the conduct of pubhc-houses from this element and placing it in the hands of salaried managers who have no such interest, but are rather

Managers under the Board.

No interest in the sale of intoxicants.

under a direct inducement to discourage excessive drinking beyond that of the penal law and also, per contra, to promote the sale of non-intoxicants. Under State ownership this principle was systematically applied on the lines indicated in the following passage from the Board's Fourth Eeport: ' It will be obvious that, while the enactment of measures such as many of those described in the foregoing paragraph is facilitated by the Board's status of ownership, their success must be largely dependent upon the character of the individual managers of the public-houses, and upon the manner in which they actually conduct the houses of which they are in charge. The Board expect their managers to prevent excessive drinking, and to conduct their houses as places where the public will find an efficient service of reasonable refreshments of all kinds; and the agreement entered into between the Board and their managers is framed so as to embody the principles to which the Board attach importance. The conduct of the houses upon these principles requires that the managers shall assist in securing their observance as a tradition of service, and during the past year much progress has been made towards the establishment of such a tradition. With but few exceptions the present managers of the Board's houses in the district are the same persons who were tenants two years ago, and the Board are glad to be able to record that, speaking generally, the Carlisle licensees have loyally accepted the change of status and have co-operated with the Board in the practical measures required to give effect to the general policy of the scheme of control."

The General Manager's Eeport for 1918 says: ' The decision to employ managers rather than tenants at the licensed houses was a deliberate one, and was only come to after the whole question had been carefully considered. It was decided that the intoxicants should be retailed by persons having no pecuniary interest at all in what they sold, and the terms on which the managers were appointed were such as to make it to their financial advantage to push anything else but the sale of intoxicants. In this way they differ from the manager appointed by the ordinary brewery company, whose duty it is to see that the trade of the house does not diminish, and who will not be overlooked when promotions occur if the trade at the house under his management is found to increase. In practice it has been found that in the great majority of cases where the former licensee has accepted the Board's offer to continue as manager, he has loyally accepted the new conditions, and has done his or her best to carry on the business according to the wishes of the Board."

At the end of 1918, out of 221 licensed premises in the Carlisle area owned by the Board and engaged in trade, 164 had been placed under management, and 57 were still in the hands of tied tenants.

(6) Minor Changes and Particular Bestrictions.

In addition to the structural improvements described above, Exteriors and it was the policy of the Board to improve the external appear- ub ic. ance and internal comfort of the ordinary public-houses, houses. Those remarkable advertisements which render so many public-houses an eyesore from the street were taken down, bottles and mirrors were removed from the windows and replaced by neat green curtains. The name of the house was inconspicuously painted over the door or on the wall. At the same time back entrances were closed. Inside, rooms were rendered more comfortable by the removal of partitions and the provision of seats, and more cheerful by better decoration. At least, these were the objects, but tastes differ in such matters.

Another change effected in Carlisle was the provision of a Spirits Trades Hall for the use of Trade Unions and Friendly Societies, l" ' ' by the conversion of a large, old-fashioned inn in the centre Saturdays. of the town. The licence was cancelled and the rooms let for meetings.

With regard to special restrictions, the most important was the prohibition of the sale of spirits on Saturdays in Carhsle and that part of the area which was under Sunday closing. This restriction, introduced in February 1917, was suggested by the results of prohibiting spirits on the Saturdays before Christmas Day and New Year's Day, and was justified by the effect. On the seven Saturdays before its introduction there had been forty-five arrests for drunkenness; on the seven succeeding Saturdays there were only seven, and they all occurred on one day, which happened to be the Feast of St. Patrick. On the forty-five following Saturdays the total number of arrests was only twenty-four.

A more drastic restriction was the total prohibition of the sale of spirits at Longtown and the district immediately adjoining the Gretna factory; but this was enforced only for about nine months in 1917. Persons In consequence of the number of girls employed in the erhteen factory, the Board prohibited the sale of spirits altogether to persons under eighteen, and permitted beer to be served to them only with a meal.

Before proceeding to discuss the effects of the Liquor Control Board's administration, it is necessary to deal here with another aspect of war-time control. The measures we have hitherto been considering had to do almost exclusively with the retail sale of drink and ancillary matters affecting the welfare of certain classes of war-workers. But other measures of a different character and quite apart from the Control Board were forced upon the Government by the exigencies of war, not with a view to promoting sobriety, but nevertheless forming a very important part of war-time experience, and exercising more influence upon sobriety than was commonly recognised. I refer to the diminution of supply through restricted production and the increase of price due to taxation. The former was a food, the latter a jfinance, measure; and both applied to the United Kingdom. Eeference was made to them in the opening sentence of the Introduction. Eestricted production was not peculiar to this country, like the measures previously described; but it was carried to greater lengths in Britain than in most other countries, and for definite reasons.

The chief of these was the exceptional dependence of The Great Britain on imported food. This condition has long national been a commonplace in the economics and pohtics of the supply, country, and its significance in connection with war was no new idea. But the ' optimism ' which refuses to recognise unpleasant facts prevented its being taken very seriously for a long time. It was not until the German submarine campaign brought possible starvation into view that the need of economising consumption as well as of increasing home production, was fully reahsed. Then the maintenance of the food supply began to take precedence of all other issues except

Need of economising by reduced production of drink.

Taxation.

Price and sobriety.

the actual fighting, and the drink question, which had previously been regarded solely in relation to efficiency, as explained in Chapters I and II, became also a food question. The conservation of food called for drastic curtailment of the production of drink. A second circumstance reinforcing this need and tending to differentiate Great Britain from some other countries notably France was the fact that the staple drink is beer, with whisky in the second line; and the manufacture of both, unlike that of wine, absorbs a large quantity of foodstuffs. The amount of grain consumed in the production of beer and spirits in 1913 was 1,358,000 tons, with a corresponding quantity of sugar. How much of this is really lost as food for men or animals in brewing and distilling is an intricate and controversial question, into which we need not enter, as we are here concerned only with the action taken and the reasons for it. The Government took the view that the materials used in this way could be otherwise consumed to greater advantage, and that consequently a substantial proportion should be diverted from the drink trade by a compulsory hmitation of production. Moreover, opinion in other countries, which supply us with food, had to be taken into account, and objections were raised in the United States and Canada, where the prohibition movement was rising in strength, to supplying us with food-stuffs when so much was being wasted and put to the worst possible use in the eyes of prohibitionists.

With regard to taxation, Great Britain was differentiated from other belligerent countries by the financial policy of defraying the cost of war as far as possible out of current revenue, which was accordingly raised to a maximum. And since excise duties are one of the principal sources, a large part of the increased taxation was placed upon them. At the same time it was thought that the raised prices entailed by higher duties would tend to check consumption and promote sobriety. The two objects of increased revenue and diminished consumption obviously tend in opposite directions, and if they are pursued together, a point is reached at which they become incompatible, when one or other must be sacrificed. The practical problem is to stop short of that point and so get the advantage of both.

Bestricted Production. The first step in the compulsory Government restriction of production was taken by the Government with action, the authority of Parhament in April 1916, when the Output of Beer (Restriction) Act was passed. It limited the aggregate quantity of beer brewed in the United Kingdom to 26 million barrels for the year ending March 1917. This was a reduction of 4 million gallons on the previous year's output, and less by 10 million gallons, or 28 per cent., than that of 1914. In December 1916 the Ministry of Food was set up, and the Minister, entitled Food Controller, was empowered to ' regulate The Food the supply and consumption of food as he thinks best for maintaining a proper supply of food." In March 1917 the powers which had been conferred on the Board of Trade by the Output of Beer Act were transferred by an Order in Council to the Food Controller; and subsequent restrictions were imposed by orders issued from his office.

In February 1917 orders were issued prohibiting the manu- Great facture and sale of malt except under licence from the Food f Q tput Controller. In March the output of beer for the ensuing twelve months was cut down to 10 milhon barrels, exclusive of that brewed for the Army and Navy, representing a reduction of 61 per cent, on the previous year and 72 per cent, on 1914. This drastic cut was not long maintained. It was so Popular widely and strongly resented, that within three months the resentment. Government were forced to give way, and from July onwards the reduction was modified and permission given by the Food Controller to increase the output by one-third. At the Strength same time the first restriction with regard to strength was reduced, imposed. Half the total amount of beer was to be brewed at a gravity not exceeding 1036 degrees, and encouragement was given to the production of light beer by the offer of allowing 20 per cent, increase of output for beer not exceeding that strength, the remaining 13 per cent, (making up the total concession of 33 per cent.) to be brewed under special licence for consumption in munition areas.

This order remained in force from July 1917 until April 1918, when the output was again reduced to 10 4 per cent, instead of 33 per cent, above the amount laid down in April 1917. Further steps were also taken towards lowering the strength. It was provided that the average gravity of all beer brewed should not exceed 1030 degrees for Great Britain and 1045 degrees for Ireland, a flagrant example of the favouritism shown towards Ireland throughout the war. No beer was to be brewed below 1010 degrees, an order apparently intended to prevent brewers from producing any strong beer by brewing some of very low gravity while keeping to the average strength ordained. Ketail prices were fixed according to specific gravity.

These conditions remained in force to the end of 1918, when the reverse process began. At the beginning of 1919 the barrelage was increased by 25 per cent., and the specific gravities raised by 2 degrees. In April 1919 the barrelage was again increased by 50 per cent., in May by a further 45 per cent., bringing the total up to 26 milhon barrels, and in July all restrictions on volume were removed, while the permitted gravity was raised to 1044 degrees in Great Britain and 1051 degrees in Ireland. In June 1921 all restriction on gravities was abolished.

Hops. A concomitant food measure in connection with beer was the reduction of the area of land under hops from 36,661 acres in 1914 to 15,626 acres in 1918.

Such is the history of the control of beer production in brief. The successive steps were essentially food measures taken by the Food Controller, and had nothing to do with

Spirits. the Control Board, as the public erroneously supposed. With - =- regard to spirits, in 1917 distilling for human consumption was prohibited, except under licence from the Ministry of Munitions; and when the great cut in beer output was made in that year, the quantity of spirits that might be cleared from bond for the year was limited to one-half the amount cleared in the previous year. This restriction was continued until February 1919, when the quantity was raised to 75 per cent, of the 1916 clearances. In the following November all limitation was ended. The clearances from bond in the year ending March 1920 were 24,393,000 gallons, as against 30,736,088 gallons in the pre-war year ending March 1914.

Details of the annual consumption are given in the table on p. 87.

With regard to strength, this was regulated for spirits by the Central Control Board, not by the Food Controller, as in brewing. The facts have already been given in Chapter III. The control took effect in the sale, not in the production. The Board imposed compulsory dilution down to a maximum strength of 30 degrees below proof, and permitted dilution down to a minimum strength of 50 degrees under proof.

Taxation and Prices. The duty on beer was first raised Taxation. in the autumn of 1914 from 7s. 9d. to 23s. a barrel, and afterwards by successive increments to 100s., or about thirteen times the pre-war rate, in 1920. The duty on spirits, which was 14s. 9d. a gallon in 1914, was raised to 30s. in 1918, to 50s. in 1919, and to 72s. 6d., or five times the pre-war rate, in 1920.

These changes necessarily affected prices; but there are Prices, so many grades and measures of drink, and so many local variations, that an exhaustive statement of the rise in prices is impossible; only some of the more salient facts can be given. From 1917 onwards the retail price of beer was controlled and a maximum fixed for different qualities, in accordance with their specific gravity. Previously prices had risen with increased taxation. Before the war the ordinary retail price of beer was 3d. a pint. When the duty was trebled in November 1914 this was raised to id., with corresponding changes for inferior qualities. The statutory restriction of output imposed in 1916 was followed by the addition of another Id. to the retail price of the pint. In October 1917 prices were fixed at id. a pint for beer under 1036 degrees gravity, and 5d. a pint under 1042 degrees. Six months later, in April 1918, the strength was lowered in relation to price: id. was fixed for beer under 1030 degrees, and 5d. for beer between 1030 degrees and 1034 degrees. The policy of fixing maximum retail prices in accordance with strength was carried farther in the following year, and seven grades were scheduled, ranging from under 1020 degrees to over 1054 degrees. The corresponding retail prices per pint for these grades were fixed in a rising scale, beginning with 2d. for the lowest grade and advancing to Sd. for the highest. When the duty was raised in 1920 to 100s. a barrel these prices were advanced by Id. a pint, bringing the lowest grade to Sd.

and the highest to 9d. These prices were for beer sold by the glass or jug in a public bar. For beer sold in the same way but not in a public bar they were Id. more that is, from 4d. to lod. a pint. The prices for bottled beer were higher. In August 1921 control of prices ceased.

With regard to spirits the retail price before the war was about Sd. per quartern, or from 2d. to 4d. per glass, according to size. During the earlier years of war small advances in price took place, but without any uniformity. When the clearances from bond were reduced by one-half in 1917 a much more decided rise followed, but it was too varied and irregular to be susceptible of precise statement. In 1918 prices were fixed by the Food Controller, varying from Is. Sd. to 2s. 6d. per quartern, according to strength. In 1920 these were raised to Is. lo d. and 2s. Q d. respectively. In effect, a glass had risen from 4d. to Is. 2d.

The following tables summarise chronologically the changes in production, taxation, revenue, and consumption:

BEER

Some details of retail prices have been given above; they are too complicated to be added to the foregoing table. But the general movement in respect of taxation and prices can be fairly summarised by saying that a glass of beer which before the war cost 3d. and paid d. in taxation, rose in price to Id. and paid 3 d. in taxation.

TAXATION

All Alcoholic Liquors.

CONSUMPTION AND EXPENDITURE Per head of Population Estimated).

These are estimates. The second column shows the amount consumed per head of all liquors, reduced to gallons of proof spirit. The third column shows the expenditure on the same, as calculated by the United Kingdom Alliance.

The preceding chapters have described the changes in regard to the hquor trade imposed by authority during the war. It Influences has been shown that they were very numerous and varied, and fn the war 3 affected not only the conditions of retail sale and consumption which are generally thought of in connection with control but also, and quite independently, the production, taxation, strength, and price of liquor. Nor do these exhaust the influences tending to modify normal conditions that were brought into play by the war. We must add to them the withdrawal from civil life of millions of men in the most active period of life, from 18 to 50, including members of the police force, the massing together of others by thousands in particular industrial centres, their disappearance from the countryside and replacement by women, the unlimited demand for labour, the general and unprecedented prosperity, due not only to extraordinarily high rates of wages, but to the employment at these rates of all members of the same family above school age.

In examining the state of the nation in regard to sobriety during this eventful period, and in endeavouring to assign consequences to their proper causes, it is necessary to bear all these factors in mind, for they all affect the drinking habits of the people. It is impossible to disentangle them all and measure their effects with precision. Some counteract others. For instance, the enrolment of men in the services was offset in particular places by their enrolment in factories, which greatly increased instead of diminishing the male population in those places; and, similarly, the enhanced price of liquor was offset by the increased command of money. These cross-currents greatly complicate the problem of tracing the connection between cause and effect. Nor must we forget the psychological influences which made the whole period abnormal the daily excitement and the domestic emotion aroused by leave-takings, news from men on active service, home-comings on leave or for good. It is impossible to separate all these factors; but nevertheless a careful examination of the evidence yields some definite and fairly certain conclusions.

We may start with the broad fact or net result that during the war a very large and progressive diminution of intemperance took place. The statistical evidence, both judicial and statistical medical, is quite conclusive and leaves no possible room " " for doubt. To state it in the most summary form: from Police 1914 to 1918 the convictions for drunkenness in England ' "-and Wales fell from 183,828 to 29,075; the deaths attributed to alcohousm from 1816 to 296; the deaths attributed to Mortality cirrhosis of the liver from 3999 to 1671; the cases of ' "-attempted suicide from 2385 to 666; the deaths from suffocation of infants under one year from 1233 to 557. The following table shows these remarkable figures at a glance:

ENGLAND AND WALES.

The several items are not of equal value. Cirrhosis of the liver, attempted suicide, and the suffocation of infants occur from other causes than intemperance; deaths from alcoholism and, still more, cirrhosis are the results of chronic intemperance and take longer to show change. But the simultaneous fall in all of them corroborates the more direct evidence of police drunkenness and adds to its value. The accompanying chart shows the movement graphically.

The general correspondence renders the proof irresistible. No such body of con-comitant evidence has ever been presented before. It is on such a scale and so decisive that there is no need to enter into any arguments about the precise vahdity of such statistics. The broad lesson is incontrovertible. But it may be observed that the general correspondence of the medical with the pohce returns furnishes a striking vindica- tion of the latter as a trustworthy index to the rising or falhng prevalence of intemperance. And this is further confirmed by another piece of evidence much more exact than either police figures or death certificates. I refer to the cases of delirium Delirium tremens occurring in institutions. There is none of the un- emens. certainty about this condition that attaches to the other items of evidence mentioned above. It is unmistakable, cannot be concealed or confused with anything else, and is due to nothing but excessive drinking. No comprehensive statistics about it are available, but returns were gathered for the Control Board from certain poor-law institutions, and they all went to confirm the other statistics. The experience of the poor-law infirmary at Liverpool is so remarkable as to be worth recording. During the twelve months immediately preceding the war there were 511 cases; in the three following years the number fell to 421, 205, and 99 successively; and women were as much affected as men. The experience was similar in East London and Woolwich, West Ham, Bradford, Glasgow and Govan. Some details are given in the Appendix.

The figures given above are for England and Wales. In Scotland. Scotland the movement was similar, but not of equal extent. The convictions for drunkenness fell from 35,252 in 1914 to 12,589 in 1919. If particular towns or areas are taken it is found that they shared, in varying degrees, in the diminution of intemperance, whatever criterion be applied. In the London, metropolitan area known as Greater London, with a population of about 7 millions, the convictions for drunkenness fell during the same period from 67,654 to 10,139.

It is unnecessary to multiply statistics to prove the general downward movement which took place during these years; and the evidence from observation furnished by police, naval and military authorities, local health authorities, employers of labour and special investigators, all goes to confirm the

I have elsewhere discussed this question at length. Police statistics must be used, like others, with common sense and due regard to circumstances. They are subject to local and temporary variations, and are therefore unsafe for minute comparisons. So are medical statistics. But when used in the mass and over sufficiently long periods of time they are a highly trustworthy index, not to the total amount of intemperance, but to its rising or falling prevalence, as reflected in public order, which is the primary and principal ground for statutory control.

Causes of diminished intemperance.

Effect of price.

Alcoholic strength of liquor.

same conclusion. There was a great improvment in the conduct of the people in this respect.

The question is to what was it due?

We may distinguish the following influences tending to diminish intemperance: (1) Absorption of men in the Services.

(2) Eestrictions on conditions of sale.

(3) Eeduced supply of drink.

(4) Eeduced strength.

(5) Increased price.

The problem is to estimate as far as possible their respective shares in the net result.

No. 5, the increased price of drink, is a very important factor in ordinary times, and its influence has become perceptible since the war, but during the time with which we are dealing it was more than offset in the great centres of population by the prevailing prosperity and abundance of money. It may therefore be classed as a minor factor.

No. 4, the diminished alcoholic strength of the liquor consumed, raises an interesting question from the general temperance point of view. It was, in regard to spirits a novel attempt to apply experimentally the well-established rule that the harmfulness of drink varies with the strength and concentration of the alcoholic content. This principle is illustrated chiefly by the comparison between distilled and fermented liquors. In countries in which spirits are the popular form of drink and these are the most drunken countries beer and wine are regarded as temperance drinks. Nor can there be any doubt that they are less conducive to excess and far less injurious to health, though rigid puritans decline to recognise any distinction between different forms of the accursed thing. Light beers and wines are on the same ground regarded as less injurious than heavy ones. Accordingly a systematic attempt was made by the Control Board to reduce the strength of spirits by the measures described in Chapter IV, and by the Food Controller to encourage the production of light beers. As a matter of fact, the liquor supplied, both distilled and fermented, did become very much weaker than it had previously been; and the change was at once noticed by consumers. It was one of the chief causes of discontent. That it contributed to sobriety cannot be proved, but that in conjunction with the reduced supply it must have had that effect is practically certain. The consumption of alcohol was doubly reduced, by the diminished volume of drink supplied and by its weaker content. The latter factor may therefore be regarded as accessory to the former, which was certainly the more important of the two; for consumers usually make up for what they consider deficient strength by increasing the quantity.

There remain the first three factors named above, and these were undoubtedly the chief causes of the increased national sobriety. It is not possible to assign to each its proper share with precision, but their action can be to a certain extent distinguished, and sufficiently perhaps to justify some positive conclusions. The first factor namely, the absorption of men Enrolment in in the Services operated from the outset and continuously Forces. during the greater part of the period, and one would expect a progressive decline of civilian intemperance in consequence. Some persons have attributed the whole movement to it, but that is a superficial view which will not bear examination. The influence of what we may call the active service factor can be checked in several ways; by comparing the movement before and after the other factors came into play; by comparing the rate of enlistment with the curve of drunkenness; by noting the course of events in places where the male population was not diminished but increased; by separating the movement among the female population from the whole; by observing what happened when active service came to an end and the return to civil life began, while the other two factors remained in operation. Such comparisons will enable us to distinguish the working of the several influences at least to a certain extent.

Immediately on the declaration of war on August 4, 1914, the Reserves were called up, the Territorial Force was embodied and recruiting actively carried on. The monthly The move-convictions for drunkenness in England and Wales, which J g poj e had been rising, fell from 17,410 in July to 16,332 in August, figures.

and 14,838 in September; in October they rose again to 15,362, but the fall was resumed in November and continued progressively until February 1915, when the number stood at 10,719. In March 1915 the convictions jumped up again to 12,392 and remained somewhere about that level until September, when a marked and progressive fall began. This continued until May 1916, when the figure had dropped to 6443. During the rest of that year it was considerably higher. At the beginning of 1917, however, another marked decline set in and continued, with minor fluctuations, until June 1918, when the low-water mark of 1992 was reached. During the rest of 1918 the figure remained steady at a little over 2000. In 1919 it began to rise in March and mounted rapidly till December when it reached 8730, or just about half the number at the outbreak of war. In 1920 it fluctuated about the same level for a time, but in the second half of the year it dropped irregularly and continued to drop until June 1921, when it stood at 5337, after which it rose again somewhat. For 1922 complete figures are not yet available.

The whole movement is full of meaning, which becomes plain when it is presented in graphic form month by month, as in the accompanying chart, and interpreted by the light of the following chronological table of the principal events bearing on the consumption of drink and detailed above:

Chronology op Chief Events affecting THE Liquor Trade 1914, August. War began. Naval and military authorities Events empowered to restrict hours of sale in or near harbours sobdet and in proclaimed areas. 1914, Septemher. Similsir power given to licensing justices in any district under Intoxicating Liquor (Temporary

Eestriction) Act.

1914, November. Beer duty raised from 7s. 9d. to 23s. a barrel.

1915, July-August. Control Board began restrictions.

1916, April. Beer Eestriction Act, limiting output to 26 million barrels for the ensuing twelve months.

1917, March. Beer output limited to 10 milhon barrels by Food Controller. Clearances of spirits from bond limited to one-half previous year's.

1918, April 'Duty on beer raised to 50s. Duty on spirits raised from 14s. 9d. to 30s. a gallon.

1918, November. Armistice.

1919, Ja7Mar?. Statutory barrelage of beer increased 25 per cent, and gravities raised 2 degrees.

1919, Feruar. Clearances of spirits raised from 50 per cent.

to 75 per cent, of 1916. 1919, March. Weekday evening hours of sale extended half an hour by Control Board generally to 9.30 p. m. 1919, April. Barrelage of beer increased by 50 per cent, and gravity raised. Duty raised to 10s. 1919, Mmj. Weekday evening hours further extended to 10 P. M. Statutory barrelage further increased up to 26 million barrels. 1919, July. Sunday evening hours of closing extended from 9 to 10 P. M. Restriction of output of beer removed and gravity raised.

1919, Nouember. Limitation of clearances of spirits removed.

1920, April Tntj on beer raised to 100s. a barrel and on spirits to 72s. 6d. a gallon.

1921, JMne. Restriction on gravities removed.

1921, w wsf. Official end of the war. Licensing Act with extension of hours. Control of prices abolished.

The table of events gives the key to the fluctuations of drunkenness shown in the chart, and the two together present a complete epitome of the whole story of the liquor trade as affected by the war. They are given for the whole period for the sake of continuity, but the present chapter is concerned only with the war years, during which the decline of drunkenness took place. The post-war period is the subject of Chapter IX. Good In 1914 the curve of drunkenness rises up to the corn- trade, mencement of the war. This movement is in keeping with the general experience that drunkenness rises with good trade and continues to rise after the boom has spent itself, because prices then begin to fall in advance of wages, just as they begin to rise before wages, when a depression is passing away and an upward movement is starting. The outbreak of war is followed by a sharp fall, which continues, but for one lapse in October, down to February 1915. This fall, from 17,410 to 10,719 or about 38 per cent, must be attributed Enrolment mainly to the enrolment of men in the Forces; but it was " assisted by the early restrictive measures described in Chapter I, Early which were clearly necessary to counteract certain special rictions. tendencies connected with naval and military mobilisation and were for that reason urgently demanded by the responsible authorities. Great excitement prevailed in the early months of the war and had a tendency to express itself in drinking in connection with leave-takings, the enrolment of men, the establishment of training camps, and the conveyance of troops, and the police also were inclined to turn a blind eye to excesses directly connected with the war. It is to this tendency that the relapse in October 1914, which was very widely diffused, must be attributed. The first shock of the war had worn off, enrolment and training were being actively pursued and extending all over the country, while the accompanying restrictions were still very capriciously and imperfectly applied. The effect of earher closing in London at this time has been noted in Chapter I (p. 6); and the fact that a second curtailment was found necessary towards the end of October shows what was happening and throws light on the set-back indicated in the chart. When the necessary safeguards were more completely adopted, the fall inaugurated by mobilisation was resumed and perhaps accelerated at the close of the year by the raised price of beer.

But in February 1915 the downward movement ceased The muni-and was succeeded by an upward one. This conclusively " shows that the subsequent decline of drunkenness cannot be attributed to enrolment, the influence of which was decisively outweighed by another and opposing factor during the first half of 1915, when the convictions rose from 10,719 in February to 12,642 in July. The new factor was the rapid growth of munitions work, which drew a constantly increasing stream of men into industrial centres and employed them on a rising scale of wages. This is clearly demonstrated by the fact that nearly all the increase of drunkenness occurred in ' Northern England," which includes the Midland industrial centres as well as Lancashire, Yorkshire, and the North-East coast. In Southern England and the London area the rise was comparatively shght.

The munitions rise, as we may call it, in the first half of 1915, is of a fluctuating character, though progressive as a

CONVICTIONS FOR DRUNKENNESS 1915 NEWCASTLE

CONVICTIONS FOR DRUNKENNESS 1915 MIDDLESBROUGH whole; and this is accounted for partly by the successive efforts to repress it in particular districts by the local authorities under the powers granted them in the autumn of 1914, and partly by the nature of the industrial migration, which proceeded in waves.

After July, when the upward movement reached its height, The Control we see a sudden and very striking change set in. The previous f fall is resumed and continues steadily for ten months. Between July 1915 and May 1916 the numbers dropped from 12,642 to 6,443. It is the most decided and clearly marked of all the movements recorded in the chart, and it can be attributed to nothing but the restrictions imposed by the Control Board. The two coincide exactly and no other new influence intervened. The rate of enlistment fell off markedly in the second half of 1915, when drunkenness was declining, and therefore that factor cannot be held to account for the reduction. The

Board began operations when the upward movment was still in progress, and reversal immediately set in. If particular towns are taken the case becomes still clearer, as the accompanying charts for Newcastle and Middlesbrough show. The progressive character of the fall for the country as a whole corresponds with the gradual extension of restrictions described in Chapter III.

But this decline comes to an end in May 1916 and is Reaction, succeeded by an upward tendency, small and rather fluctuating, but still constituting a distinct arrest of the downward movement. How is this to be accounted for? One explanation lies in the weakened influence of control. Eestrictions, when first imposed, act with great effect; but presently, when they have grown familiar and persons given to excess begin to find their way about in the new conditions, the hold is loosened. Evasion is practised here and there, and unless checked it gradually extends. Administration grows lax, and hard drinkers find new channels of gratification. The operation of this law was repeatedly exemplified by the experience of particular places, and sooner or later it took effect to a varying extent in all the large towns. In every case the introduction of control was followed by an immediate fall down to a certain point, after which the figures began to creep up again. The charts for Newcastle and Middlesbrough may serve as illustrations. The correctness of this diagnosis is confirmed by the prosperity factor.

Reduced supply of liquor.

fact that a tightening up of administration was always followed by cessation of the upward movement and resumption of the fall. A striking instance occurred in Glasgow, which was the most troublesome town in the kingdom. In 1916 the figures for drunkenness were rising, and the pohce reported growing evasion of the regulations. The Board made an example of five of the worst public-houses, which were summarily closed; the monthly convictions at once fell from 1,533 to 1,044.

A second factor tending to favour the reactionary movement was the increasing abundance of money, due both to the rising scales of pay and the expansion of munition industries, which absorbed a continually growing number of women, girls and boys, all earning more than a man's ordinary pay, not infrequently up to 5 or 6 a week, and making large additions to the family income. In view of the extraordinary abundance of money it is less a matter for surprise that there should have been some increase of drunkenness than that the increase should have been so small. There could be no better testimony to the general efficacy of the restrictions. They were assisted, no doubt, by the reduced output of beer ordered by the Food Controller in April 1916; but this did not take effect immediately. The limitation applied to the total output for the ensuing twelve months and its full effect was not felt until towards the end of this period, in the first quarter of 1917.

From the beginning of 1917 we see the downward movement resumed and thenceforward continued almost without interruption, except for the Christmas holidays, down to the low-water mark reached in the summer of 1918, at which it remained virtually stationary until the Armistice. In Northern England the lowest month of all was October 1918.

In the final stage of the dechne of drunkenness, extending over eighteen months, the fall proceeded naturally at a lower rate than in the earlier ones, when the room for improvement was so much greater; and it must be attributed to the combined working of several factors. The administration of the Control Board was in this period fully established and in complete working order. But its influence was reinforced by the restricted quantity of drink available, and particularly by the large reduction of both beer and spirits in 1917 which became a predominant factor. And lastly the heavy increase Prices. of duties imposed in the spring of 1918 with the accompanying rise of prices added a final touch. It is not possible to separate these factors when in simultaneous operation or to measure their respective values with precision; but the curves following the dates of entry point to some definite conclusions.

By far the most decisive fall of all is that which followed the commencement of the Control Board's operations in 1915. The change is abrupt, large, and progressive. The munitions rise, which was more than counteracting the enrolment of men, is suddenly arrested and converted into a continuous fall; and this change exactly coincides with the appearance of the Control Board on the scene by itself, without any other new factor. At the same time it is clear that its influence had limits, and would not have carried the decline of drunkenness so far as it actually went without the later supplementary factors of reduced quantities and raised prices. Of these two the reduction of quantity was undoubtedly the more important, because the high prices were offset by the greater abundance of money, particularly after the introduction of food rationing and fixed prices, which limited expenditure on food. There was always enough money to buy the depleted stocks on hand at public-houses, which were, in fact, often sold out in 1917 and 1918. In any case the theory that the whole decline of drunkenness was due to the enrolment of men in the army is incompatible with the record, and untenable. It exercised a marked influence at the outset of war; the number of men enrolled in August and September 1914 was 752,824, and the effect is visible in the chart. But this rate was never afterwards approached, and enrolment gradually declined when drunkenness was falling most. It took most effect in the rural districts which were denuded of young men, and it helps to account for the decline of drunkenness in areas which never came under control. But it must be remembered that enrolment in the army was not the only cause of rural denudation. It was accompanied by enrolment in mines and factories, whereby the consumption was merely transferred. A feature of the early enrolment was some depletion of the police forces and this tended to reduce the proceedings for drunkenness;

The value of the police returns.

Female intemperance.

Committee appointed.

Special Inquiry at Birmingham.

Decline of drunkenness, but the rise in 1915 showed that it was not an important factor.

Before leaving the chart for the present I would draw attention to the remarkable fidelity with which it reflects the operation of successive influences. As a particular illustration I may point out that in every year, except 1914 and 1915, it shows a rise in the month of December. That is the Christmas holidays.

I referred above to the question of female drunkenness as distinguished from the total that we have been considering. It affords another means of checking the operation of different causes by eliminating the active service factor. In the account of the Control Board's proceedings given in earher chapters, no mention was made of female drunkenness. It was purposely omitted in order to avoid confusion through the unnecessary multiplication of details, because it led to no special regulations. But it occupied the attention of the Board from an early date in their administration. In October 1915 a Committee of women, under the chairmanship of Mrs. Creighton, was appointed to inquire into the alleged excessive drinking among women, and to advise the Board on this subject. This Committee reported an increase of excessive drinking, but mainly among those who drank before; there was no evidence that women and girls who did not drink before had taken in any considerable numbers to drinking to excess because of the war. The remedies suggested were general ones, and the Committee expressly deprecated any restrictions dealing specially with women, ' both on account of their inherent injustice and because they are convinced that the evil of excessive drinking must be combated as a whole."

In June 1916 the Board received a petition from Birmingham signed b 37,155 women and girls, and supported by the Lord Mayor and the Chairman of the Licensing Bench, requesting the issue of an order to prohibit girls under twenty-one from being served with drink or being allowed on licensed premises. The Board appointed a special Committee of inquiry, under the chairmanship of Sir George Newman, to investigate the matter and advise on it. The Committee found a remarkable decline in the number of arrests and convictions in Birmingham. The arrests during the first six months of the year were: 1914, 511; 1915, 351; 1916, 182. A large number of women frequented pubhc-houses, but there was ' no evidence that any great number of these women were drinking to excess or that munition work was being materially delayed or interfered with on this account." The Committee concluded a reasoned examination of the conditions and the proposed measure by declining to recommend its adoption. It is clear that the promoters of the petition were shocked by the large number of women seen frequenting public-houses, but, as the Committee sagely remark, many of them had no previous experience of such investigations. They took an old practice to be a new and growing evil, because it was new to them.

This is one of the commonest and most persistent mistakes Women in made on the subject of intemperance, and particularly female P '- . nouses.

intemperance. Over and over agam the practice of women frequenting public-houses has been deplored as a new thing formerly unknown. The truth is that there is continuous evidence of its existence in this country right back to the Middle Ages, when public-houses were not only frequented by women as they are now, but were generally kept by them. The ale-wife was a standing subject for poets and satirists. John Skelton, poet-laureate to Henry VIII, has described in Eabelaisian verse the swarms of women who thronged the pot-house kept by Eleanor Eummin, and brought their wedding-rings, husband's clothes, and pots and pans to pay for drink. No doubt it was much more apparent in Birmingham during the war because there was a great influx of women into the munition works, which were chiefly operated by them; they had plenty of money of their own, and the restricted hours caused a visible concentration of numbers at particular times. But the investigation carried out on behalf of the Board showed that the inference of increasing intemperance was unfounded. On the contrary it furnished a particular proof of the general decline of female intemperance indicated by the consensus of different kinds of evidence for the whole country, as rendered in the preceding chart, which shows the parallel curves of police and medical returns.

A comparison of the male and female convictions throws further light on the causes of the decline. Between 1913 and 1918 the male convictions for England and Wales fell from 153,112 to 21,853, a reduction of 85 per cent.; the female convictions fell from 37,314 (1914) to 7,222, a reduction of 80 per cent. That is to say, the proportionate reduction of drunkenness among women approximated to that among men; and since the women enjoyed an unprecedented command of money, partly through munition earnings, and since they freely frequented the public-houses (for Birmingham was no exception), it is evident that the factors other than active service, which did not affect them, played the principal part in the general dechne.

This is brought out by a comparison of the rates of decline from year to year:
Percentage Fall of Convictions.

The figures in the second and third columns show the rates of reduction in each year as percentages of the convictions for the previous year.

In 1913-14 the male drunkenness fell slightly, while the female rose to about the same extent. The discrepancy shows the effect of enrolment in the second half of 1914; it affected men but not women. In 1914-15 we see a large reduction for men and a much smaller, but still appreciable one, for women. Here control has come in and begun to take effect, though not until the autumn, and in certain localities only. In 1915-16 the female rate of reduction rises rapidly and nearly equals the male; control in this period became general and was the dominant influence. In 1916-17 the rates are accelerated in both classes, showing the influence of reduced quantities and rising prices. In 1917-18 the rate on the female side exceeds that on the male, which is explained by the continued operation of these two factors; both affected women more than men, areas.

because men would be served first and had more money. In 1918 the publicans in Newcastle refused to serve women at all in the evening, with the result that male drunkenness rose, while female drunkenness fell heavily.

In short this comparison confirms the interpretation of the whole movement previously given.

The respective shares of the several factors contributing Uncontrolled to the general decline can be checked in another way by comparing the movement in controlled and uncontrolled areas. In the latter the element of control is eliminated. They represent, it is true, such a small proportion of the population that comparison is open to objection; but nevertheless it is not unfruitful when due allowance is made for the difference. A return made to the House of Commons in 1919 gave the number of convictions in (1) wholly controlled, (2) partly controlled, (3) uncontrolled pohce districts for the years 1915, 1916, 1917 and 1918. Leaving out the half-and-half districts and comparing the wholly controlled with the wholly uncontrolled we get the following figures:

CONVIOTIONS FOR DRUNKENNESS

The total reduction between 1915 and 1918 is 77 per cent. in the controlled and 72 per cent, in the uncontrolled. The difference is small and at first sight surprising; it looks as though control had exercised little influence and that the country would have done nearly as well without it. But that inference ignores the difference between the two classes of areas and assumes an equality of conditions which did not exist. The reduction in the uncontrolled areas proves that the factors other than control had a powerful influence, but it does not prove that they would have been equally effective by themselves in controlled areas. The former were sparsely populated rural areas, in which the removal of men of service age was not offset by any munitions influx and was more complete

Effect of reduced supply of drink.

than in industrial centres because, as already mentioned, the men went into mines and works as well as into the services, and were replaced by women. The conditions were entirely different in the great industrial towns which represented the bulk of the population and in which drunkenness was rising again in 1915 before the introduction of control, as already explained.

But apart from this difference two facts go to show that the uncontrolled areas would have done better than they did if they had been controlled. The first is that while convictions in controlled areas fell at once on the introduction of control in the middle of 1915, they rose in the uncontrolled areas, which had more drunkenness in the second half of that year than in the first. The second fact is that the Act of 1921 had the effect of lengthening the hours that is, diminishing the restrictions in controlled areas, but shortened them that is, imposed restrictions in the uncontrolled areas; and in the former drunkenness immediately rose, in the latter it fell. This remarkable fact is more fully dealt with in Chapter IX.

On the other hand the experience of the uncontrolled areas brings out clearly the importance of the reduced supply of drink, which took effect in 1917-18, for it was in these years that the uncontrolled areas, which had previously lagged behind the controlled, made their greatest advance and reduced the gap to the small dimensions indicated above. The following comparative table shows the respective rates of reduction in the controlled areas from year to year:

Conclusions. We Can now sum up the results of this statistical study, which will appear, I am afraid, rather tedious, but is essential to a thorough examination of the facts bearing on the causes of the great general decline of drunkenness which was the outstanding feature of the liquor trade during the war. The conclusions that emerge are that none of the three main causes enumerated above can be held solely responsible, but that they co-operated and that each played a predominant part at different periods enrolment in the first twelve months, control in the next two years, which may be called the munitions period, and the reduced supply in the last year and a half. These conclusions are not only in keeping with the facts, they also commend themselves to common sense as reasonable and probable, and, I may add in anticipation, they are confirmed by what happened later, as will appear in the chapter on after-war conditions. They were not perceived at the time because there was a tendency to stress the effect of control, which provoked a counter-tendency to stress the effect of enrolment, and between these rival views the third influence was rather overlooked. The tendency to stress control was perfectly natural because this was the one influence specifically brought to bear on the problem of drink, while the others were accidental, and the question of its success properly occupied public attention. One reason why enrolment exercised its greatest influence in the earlier period is that later on the men compulsorily enrolled were not of the class that is much affected by drink or comes into conflict with the police.

The last observations bring us to another view of the subject. I have devoted this chapter to the decline of drunkenness because, as I have just said, it was the outstanding feature of the liquor trade in war time and, as we have just seen, it affected the whole country. It is a bigger thing than the success or failure of control which has usually occupied the field of discussion in connection with drink and the war. But on the other hand the result of control goes beyond the decline of drunkenness. Its ultimate object was to increase the national efficiency, particularly in the production of war material of all kinds; the control of drink was only a means to this end. Now having examined its share in the general decline of drunkenness we can turn to the question of its success in promoting efiiciency, for which a different kind of evidence is available. The two things are of course very intimately connected, but they are not identical, and in any case it is desirable to know if the statistical evidence already dealt with is confirmed by evidence from observation. Were the measures introduced by the Control Board followed by actual improvement in the workshops and the homes of the workers? It will be convenient to deal with this question in a separate chapter, and to include the results of State ownership in the survey as part of the control policy.

The statistical evidence on the effects of control dealt with in the last chapter was checked by a great mass of evidence from direct observation supplied by several classes of persons professionally concerned in different ways with the condition of the people, the performance of war work and the state of public order in their own localities, and able to watch on the spot the result of restrictive measures as they were introduced. These witnesses included Government officials representing Direct the Admiralty, the War Office and the Board of Trade, the evidence police, works' managers, medical officers and sanitary staffs, of control, hospitals, health visitors, district nurses and midwives, school teachers, lodging-house inspectors and tenement managers. Their testimony was unbiassed, independent, drawn from different fields of observation and based on personal comparison of conditions before and after the introduction of control; and being pretty nearly unanimous it formed an irresistible consensus of opinion in favour of the restrictions.

I tested it myself by personal inquiry in the three great centres of population in which drunkenness is most prevalent namely, Glasgow, Newcastle and Liverpool. I did not know what I should find and had no interest in finding any particular opinions; I merely wanted to get at the truth. But I did find a really astonishing unanimity, such as I have never met with before in any inquiry, on the beneficial effect of the restrictions. It was shared by workmen and by publicans, some of whom told me that the curtailment of hours was a great boon to them. They did not pretend to like all the regulations or to think them all desirable, but they did agree that on the whole the effect of control was good. Nor did I meet with a single expression of opinion to the contrary, though particular measures were criticised and some allegations of more home drinking were made. I say this because official reports, which generally form the published evidence, are regarded with a certain amount of scepticism, and I wish to put it on record as emphatically as possible that in this case they were fully confirmed by the experience of all the persons in the best position to judge. I lay particular stress, with regard to general effects, on the evidence of health visitors, district nurses and midwives, who know more about home conditions than anyone else; and with regard to work, on that of managers and foremen, who are immediately responsible for getting the work done and were desperately anxious about it in the war. All these people really knew, really cared, had no theories or axes to grind, and were not deceived. Against this crowd of inside witnesses adverse comment from outside, inspired by prejudice and untempered by knowledge, was as the crackling of thorns under a pot.

It is neither possible nor necessary since there was practically nothing to set against it to repeat this evidence in full, but some portions of it must be given to show its character. The following official reports were received in 1916, during the first year of the Control Board's administration, and before there had been any reduction in the supply of drink. They are taken from the Second Eeport of the Board.

The Admiralty. The general effect of the restrictions has been decidedly beneficial. Transport officers are unanimously of the opinion that the restrictions have had a considerable benefit upon the efficiency of the Transport Service, and the principal officer at Southampton has commented on the increased efficiency and good health of all the labour at the docks.

The Army Council. Eeports have now been received from the various Commands, the general effect of which is to show that the orders of the Board have had a beneficial effect on the discipline, training and efficiency of soldiers, and have helped in the recovery of the sick and wounded.

The Board of Trade. Statements from the larger ports with regard to the effects of the Board's Orders are singularly uniform in their testimony to the advantages secured, the beneficial effects being mainly attributed to the shortening of the hours during which intoxicating liquor can be obtained.

Police Reports

London. The figures given (Statistics of Drunkenness) are remarkable. They confirm Police observation that many fewer drunken persons are to be seen in the streets, and they indicate that the measures taken by the Central Control Board have had a very marked effect. I have discussed these figures with the G. O. C. London District, who authorises me to say that upon the reports he has received from the military patrols and from personal observation he feels justified in endorsing the opinion above expressed.

Liverpool. Taking an all-round view of the restrictions, and giving due consideration to the fact that some improvement should be expected through the number of men who have left the city to join H. M. Forces, there can be no two opinions as to the good the restrictions have done. There are fewer arrests for drunkenness, people are generally more sober and go home much earlier. The late hour of opening has been most beneficial to workmen and employers; many men turn up to work in the morning who, if the public-houses had been open, would not have done so, the employers get better labour and the men are better for it. Dock labourers have openly expressed their appreciation of the absence of the temptation to drink.

Newcastle. The restrictions imposed by the Board have worked satisfactorily and appear to have had a marked effect on the drinking habits of the people. Scarcely any drunkenness is observable in the streets after 9 p. m., and I understand that timekeeping at the works is greatly improved. The general effects of the restrictions are better order in the streets, more comfortable houses, better cared-for children and better timekeeping at works.

Sheffield. The convictions for drunkenness since the Order has been in operation have decreased almost 50 per cent. This fact, which must have its attendant beneficial effect upon home life as indicating less excessive drinking, is very gratifying. It seems to me that altered conditions of sale of intoxicating liquor, especially early closing, are more effectual in dealing with intemperance than the ordinary punitive measures.

West Bromivich. I am able to speak in praise of the Order. This town and locality is like living in another, better world. The bulk of the licence-holders do not object to the restrictions and say, generally speaking, the old hours were much too long.

Bristol. The quiet, orderly demeanour of the people, as compared with the time before the Order came in force. The streets are just about as empty at 10 p. m. as they used to be at midnight, and in my opinion this is very satisfactory from every point of view. It certainly would never have been brought about had it not been for the restricted hours of closing.

York (West Biding). The Order made by your Board has had a very beneficial effect upon the public generally. The inconvenience has been very slight indeed, and apart from the ' trade," it has given universal satisfaction. The advantages derived from it are as follows: (1) The general decrease of drunkenness not only in convictions but in the number of people seen drunk on the streets.

(2) It has had a marked and beneficial effect in preventing, to a very great extent, drinking amongst women, more particularly during the morning hours, when separation allowances are usually drawn. The children are now better clothed and fed, and their home surroundings have improved.

(3) The ' no treating ' Order has made great changes in the habits of the people, and has had a very beneficial effect.

(4) The 9.30 p. m. closing of all public-houses and clubs has had the effect of causing workmen to retire early; they are better fitted for their work the next day and as a consequence better time is being kept. The closing of public-houses in the early morning has prevented men on the night shift getting the worse for drink before returning to their homes. This was quite a common occurrence in some districts before the Order came into force.

(5) The restrictions with regard to the supply of spirits in some quarters, coupled with the prohibition of off' sales at the week-end, has been a contributing factor in the general decrease in drunkenness, more particularly in drinking in private houses.

(6) The Order is good so far as it relates to the hona fide traveller, a matter which has always been a vexed question.

(7) I am strongly in favour of the continuance of the Order, and have no hesitation in saying that it has done more to reduce drunkenness than all the various Acts of Parliament put together.

Warwicksjiire. The restrictions are working smoothly and satisfactorily. Employers of labour inform me that their men are keeping better time and turn up more fit for work. There is a very appreciable and general improvement in sobriety throughout the districts affected. More especially is this noticeable on Sundays, the regulations having put a stop to the so-called hona fide travellers who, in most cases, were simply drinking parties.

Edinburgh. I am of opinion that, generally speaking, the Order of the Board has achieved the object for which it was intended. Since the Order became operative a considerable reduction has taken place in the number of persons arrested on charges of drunkenness.

Montrose. The restrictions imposed by the Board's Order of September 7 last have had an excellent effect in my area. I am convinced that drinking in public-houses and clubs has decreased to a large extent, and it has been particularly noticeable that the streets have been cleared of people much earlier than was the case previous to the Order coming into operation.

Paisley. The Regulations made by your Board have been to the advantage of the working classes. Their effect on the munition workers has been attended with marked success. Previous to August last I had from fifty to sixty complaints per week from employers of labour of their employees drinking and keeping bad time. Those complaints have now practically ceased and, in most instances, the loafer and the casual labourer have been converted into fairly steady workmen.

Coatbridge. I consider the restrictions have proved most beneficial as far as this burgh is concerned, and at no time more so than during the New Year holidays, just brought to a close.

Greenock. The police statistics may, I think, be taken as an important guide to the effect of the restrictions generally. They are not the only index, of course, of the effect of the Orders, and, in my opinion, what is almost as important, if not more so, in arriving at a true conclusion, is the effect as seen by observation. Every restriction that has been imposed has had its good effect. The restriction imposed by the Licensing Court considerably reduced drunkenness, and the Order of the Board further reduced it. The most noticeable feature after the Order of the Licensing Court came into force was the desertion of the streets at an earlier hour, and the absence of disorderly scenes. The Order of the Board has had the effect of further reducing drunkenness and its associated offences, and possibly the most marked feature of the Order is to be found in the reduced number of offences committed in the homes; such as assaults, breaches of the peace, and cruelty to and neglect of children. This is due, I should say, largely to hcensed premises being closed until six o'clock in the evening during the first five days of the week and until four o'clock on Saturday, preventing men from taking drink on an empty stomach.

Renfrew. (1) Less workmen are to be seen on the streets during working hours, the reason being that, since licensed premises are not open for sale of intoxicating liquor till twelve o'clock noon, the men have less encouragement to stop from their work.

(2) The very objectionable practice of men standing in the streets and closes after closing time at night, drinking liquor in bottles, is greatly minimised, and is now rarely seen.

(3) The nine o'clock closing is beneficial. The streets are clear the sooner at nights, which means that the workmen go home earlier, have longer time to rest, and in consequence are more able to turn out to their work in the morning.

(4) The restrictions (4 to 9 p. m.) on Saturdays are a welcome and much-needed change. Without fear of contradiction this is the most beneficial part of the Order, which should be adhered to for all time. Men are to be seen walking out with their wives and children now on Saturday afternoons who previously had to be assisted home or carried to the Police Station.

Employers and Works Managers

N. E, Shipyards. The effect of the restrictions on the sale of alcoholic liquors has been, we consider, beneficial to the timekeeping of our workmen, and consequently it has had a good effect upon the amount of work turned out. The men have kept turning in to work more regularly at the beginning of the week than was formerly the case, and while this may be due in some measure to the effect of the Munitions Act and also to the patriotism of the men, we think that at any rate in some cases it is owing to the effect of the restrictions. We are of opinion that the stoppage of the sale of alcoholic liquors in the early morning is generally of great benefit.

Elswich Armstrong, Whitworth's). The restrictions have been a great boon and have effected a decided improvement. In the experience of a shop-manager in charge of 7000 of the roughest class of men, the restrictions have made all the difference in the world. He has less trouble now in a twelvemonth than he used to have previously in a single Friday (pay-day).

J arrow (Palmers). Lost time in the shipyard has been reduced from 21-8 per cent, to 16-5 per cent, since the restrictions came into force.

Iron and Steel Works N. E. Coast). The drinking regulations are having a real effect for the better; the men come to work more steadily and are more efficient. The unanimous verdict seems to be that the measure is working well and beneficially both to the men and to the owners.

N. of Scotland. The output appreciably improved after the restrictions were placed in this district.

Midland Steel Works. When the supply of drink was restricted by the closing of the public-houses in the district, a great improvement in the health and the timekeeping of the workmen was noticed, and was admitted by the men.

Black Country Iron and Steel Works. Of six works' managers, five were unanimous as to the good results which have followed the Board's Order (the dissentient was all for prohibition '). The Orders were held to operate beneficially because (1) the temptation for the men to start drinking before going to work had been removed; (2) the men on the night shift went straight home after work instead of resorting to the public-houses; and (3) there were not the same facilities for getting drink during working hours.

South Wales Steel Works. A great improvement in sobriety. There is no morning drinking now, and the output has greatly increased.

These examples are from localities and industries in which drinking was particularly prevalent, and they may be considered as test cases.

The one important exception to the experience of better work was Glasgow, where employers reported little improvement. It was found that there was much evasion of the Orders, and this was encouraged by trifling penalties for violation and other legal decisions in favour of offenders. A marked increase of drunkenness followed one such decision in September 1915. It was subsequently reversed by a higher Court, and more drastic action taken against ill-conducted premises effected improvement which had some effect in the yards and workshops. But Glasgow remained perceptibly more resistant than other large industrial centres.

Health Staffs. Sheffield. The Medical Officer of Health reported: I have made inquiries among our staff of women sanitary inspectors, as they, in the course of their work, have better means of knowing what is going on in the homes than any other members of my sanitary staff. There is a strong general impression amongst them that there is a considerable improvement since the introduction of the restrictions on the sale of alcoholic liquors. The improvement shows itself in various ways; the women are more in their homes in the morning, and consequently the children are better looked after; there appears to be less drinking during the day, and there is more baking of bread and cooking done in the homes than before; families go to bed earlier, and therefore get more rest.

This expresses very well the experience of the health Benefit in staffs, including nurses and midwives, in other large towtis, " ' and particularly in Liverpool, Newcastle and Glasgow, though there was some division of opinion in the two latter towns. All agreed that the homes and the children were better looked after, and in Glasgow this improvement was visible in the streets, where the spectacle of bare-footed children, generally so common, became rare. The only specific allegation raised in the opposite sense was that home drinking had increased. Home This was at one time rather widely maintained, particularly i "iki g-of women, but no definite evidence was produced to support it, and in Liverpool it was denied by health visitors who took regular observations. They found that women at first took home more bottles under the restrictions, but gradually gave it up, and eventually took fewer than before. In Newcastle, where the same complaint was made, it was alleged mainly of a limited class of women, who were said to be drinking more spirits, and the midwives thought harm had been done. But female drunkenness, which is very prevalent there, showed a large general fall. As to men, there was definite evidence of less home drinking. The manager of the largest lodging house in Newcastle, holding 400 single men, said that the number who indulged in excessive drinking had fallen from 80 to 25 per cent., and that whereas he used to collect three gross of empty bottles in a day, he only got about four dozen under the new order. Compared with the state of things before the restrictions, he led now a ' gentleman's hfe," and the same change held good of other houses in the district. In Glasgow the evidence of home drinking was stronger, and several nurses and midwives held that it had increased; but the general opinion among them and others in a position to judge was not that more women were drinking, but that those who did drink were drinking more, which coincides with the findings of the Committee appointed to investigate the question in Birmingham, as explained in the previous chapter. But none of these witnesses denied that homes were better kept.

Hospital Experience. Two statements, both from London hospitals, will suffice.

' It has been of much interest to note the difference in conditions since liquor restrictions came into force. Shortly summed up, the effect is that we get distinctly fewer cases associated with intoxication, and these cases come to us earlier in the evening and are finished by about 11 p. m. In pre-war times our house staff was generally kept at work till 1 a. m. or later."

The liquor restrictions have had a good effect in diminishing considerably the number of intoxicated persons treated as out-patients as well as of those admitted for serious injuries sustained while under the influence of alcohol. Injuries received in domestic altercation or in street brawls are fewer in number than formerly. I believe that this improvement may be attributed to the beneficent influence of the restrictions, particularly as intoxicated persons are now more liable to sustain street injuries on account of the darkening of the streets."

I submit that these samples of evidence from observation, coming as they do from different classes of observers in a wide range of industrial centres, including the most drunken places in the country, amply suffice, in the absence of any evidence to the contrary, to prove the case in confirmation of the statistics already given.

The next question that arises is what share in this result is to be attributed to the different restrictions imposed by the Hours of Control Board and enumerated in Chapter III. The reduc-ciosing. tion of the hours of opening public-houses was there named as the greatest of the changes made, and it will be noticed that in the police reports given above reference is most frequently made to the beneficial effect of the reduced hours. There can be no doubt that this was the main factor in effecting the improvements ascribed to control. It is the teaching of experience that the hours of closing are the most important of all the conditions governing the conduct of the ordinary public-house trade. Nothing else has had such an immediate and marked effect in the history of liquor legislation in this country from the' Metropolitan Police Act of 1839, which in one year reduced the arrests for drunkenness in London from 12-1 to 7"9 per 1000, onwards through successive enactments.

The importance of hours was recognised by the very first regulations made on the outbreak of war, empowering the naval and military authorities to control the hours of opening in certain places (p. 2). The more uniform and general restrictions imposed by the Control Board effected a three-fold change in the existing conditions. The day was curtailed at both ends, and an interval of closing was introduced in the middle. The hours of opening were not only drastically cut down, but were arranged to coincide with meal times at midday. It is difficult to say which of these three changes had the most effect; their action varied with local conditions and different classes of customers, as has already been indicated in Chapter III (p. 38).

In the largo industrial centres of the North, where men were accustomed to slip into the public-house for spirits on the way to work, the early morning closing was most generally held to be beneficial, and met with unqualified approval; and where female drinking was most prevalent importance was attached to the prevention of the practice of running round to the public-house during the forenoon. The police report from Eenfrew, which includes some of the Clyde shipyards, lays particular stress on the special provision applied to Central Scotland for closing on Saturdays until 4 p. m. (see above).

On the other hand, the closing interval in the afternoon affected a different class of customers, and prevented the practice of hanging on in the public-house continuously ' soaking," which generally ends in intoxication by the evening. It also checked loafing just outside, and was very beneficial to publicans and pubuc-house servants, who get a rest in the interval. But the change that had the most general effect was undoubtedly the early closing at night, particularly in London, where the previous time of closing was much later than elsewhere.

Of the other restrictions it is not possible to speak with Treating. equal certainty, except perhaps the prohibition of treating. This measure aroused a great deal of criticism and no little derision, which was natural enough, but was based on ignorance of the reasons for imposing it. It was thought to be merely a meddlesome and futile interference with a harmless custom and doomed to failure; but it had a definite object and was not applied without expert advice. Treating in general, it is true, is a thing that cannot be stopped by law, for evasion is easy and the impulse will not be denied; but there are different sorts of treating. Prohibition was first applied to the treating of soldiers; it was very necessary and fairly observed. The Control Board's prohibition was directed against a custom which had developed among workmen in certain places into a great abuse and nuisance during the earlier part of 1915, partly through the abundance of money and partly through war excitement. I saw it at work. Four, five, or six workmen would come out from the works in a bunch at the end of their shift and drop into the public-house. One would call for drinks all round, and then each of the others in turn had to do the same as a point of honour. The result was that all had more than they wanted and went out in a muzzy state. The prohibition stopped this open practice and relieved the men themselves of a burdensome convention. There was no more calling for drinks all round, and it presently fell into abeyance; such treating as went on was surreptitious, on a small scale and harmless. The measure was effective where it was needed and of considerable importance in a limited application. That it was rather a nuisance and of no use at all in other circumstances is true enough; but that is a defect common to most general regulations which are directed against abuses by the few but apply also to the many. In the circumstances it was justified by the existing abuse and by the results. The police report from the West Eiding bears witness to it. Dilution The dilution of alcoholic strength was another measure of drink. which Contributed to the decline of drunkenness, particularly in combination with the diminished supply in the later stages of the war; but it is not possible to estimate its value. Similarly with the special restrictions on the sale of spirits for off-consumption and the regulations affecting delivery at customers' houses. The prohibition of credit, on the other hand, had no effect at all; and it is difficult to understand how it came to be entertained. There is no trade in which the terms of spot cash are so rigorously enforced as the hquor trade, except in the village inn, which was of no consequence whatever. Prohibition of the ' long pull' may have relieved some publicans, but it had no other effect and would have died a natural death anyhow from lack of beer. Belief in the harm done by this practice is one of the delusions cherished in some temperance circles.

Abolition of the bona fide traveller's privilege was an obviously necessary corollary of the closing regulations, which would otherwise have been stultified.

It cannot be denied that the restrictions as a whole were Restrictions a severe trial of patience, particularly to those for whom they borne, were not intended, such as travellers and persons staying in hotels, but they were all borne for the sake of the war. Complaints came chiefly from prejudiced or interested quarters, and carried no weight. It was generally recognised that the Control Board had a difficult but necessary task to perform and were not actuated by a mere love of meddling for its own sake; and though some of the restrictions were irksome and others rather finicking, sensible persons saw that they represented a middle course between doing nothing at all and the far more drastic measures urged and contemplated in the spring of 1915. All men of good will acquiesced and assisted in carrying out the orders for the sake of the national cause.

The workmen were in general very good about it, and were encouraged to be so by the trade union leaders. What they complained of was not the restraint on their liberty of action entailed by the Board's regulations, but the quality and price of drink and, most of all, the deficient quantity in the later stages of the war. Public-houses were not infrequently sold tity-out long before closing time, and on some occasions did not open at all as they had nothing to sell. The short supply was an acute grievance. This conclusion, formed from observation in industrial areas, was confirmed by the Commission of Inquiry into Industrial Unrest in 1917. The reports from nearly all the eight districts referred to the question and testified to the absence of resentment against the Control Board's restrictions, but laid stress on the grievances of prices, quality and quantity. Some recommended an increased supply of good beer at a lower price. The case was best summed up in the Report on the West Midlands area: ' The Commission were frankly amazed at the strength of the objections to the liquor restrictions. These came not only from men in the habit of drinking beer but from those who were lifelong teetotallers and yet recognised the need of beer to those working in certain occupations. The question is threefold one of hours, price and scarcity. Of these the last is by far the most galling. The limitation of hours, though unpopular, has been accepted as a war necessity. The increase of price is resented chiefly because it is felt that brewers are making an undue profit, but the real grievance is the difficulty of obtaining the article. We recommend to the Government that the supply should be largely increased. We recognise that this may entail some weakening of the article, but we wish to impress upon the Government that besides supplying beer they must supply the sort that men want and that quantity alone will not meet the case."

In effect, the Commission of Inquiry exonerated the Board from treading too heavily on the workmen's toes, since the supply of beer had nothing to do with them; but in the confused state of mind that prevailed as usual among the public and was shared by the newspapers, everything connected with the liquor trade was put down to the Board. The distinction is important for drawing conclusions from the experience and should be recognised in fairness to the Board, who must be credited with the performance of the delicate and hazardous task entrusted to them with surprisingly little friction. At the same time a tribute is due to the trade, without whose loyal co-operation the Board's administration could not have achieved the success it did. The exceptions were few.

The Carlisle-Gretna Scheme

State ownership, which has continued since the war, differs from the temporary control exercised by the Board, and its working needs separate consideration. Of the three cases of State purchase Enfield, Cromarty, and Gretna-Carlisle the first two can be briefly dismissed for the reasons already given in Chapter V. They were on too small a scale and otherwise too exceptional to yield results of general application. At Enfield, State purchase was adopted to meet the special needs of an isolated Government factory which had been greatly extended with a largely increased staff of workmen, for whom inadequate accommodation was available. It was rather a case of food than of drink, as I have said before, and it served its purpose at the time, though perhaps the need might have been met without taking over the licensed trade. The only lesson that can be drawn from it is that economically the acquisition and reconstruction of premises may prove a hazardous proceeding; for the reduction of the factory and the melting away of the staff after the war so attenuated the custom that it ceased to afford a remunerative return on the capital expended, and in 1923 the properties were disposed of.

The case of Cromarty Firth is also exceptional. It is a remote and thinly populated coastal district in which the trade was taken over for naval reasons. Here too the immediate purpose was served, and the business has been retained by the Home Office in succession to the Control Board; but no information is forthcoming about it, and, if it were, the experience of a place of this character would obviously have little value as a contribution to the general question of the liquor trade.

It is otherwise with the Carlisle-Gretna area, which includes one town of some size. Even this cannot be called typical of our large urban and industrial populations, which constitute the real drink problem; but it is sufficiently comparable to throw some light on the subject. How has State purchase worked in Carlisle?

The changes introduced have been described in Chapter V, Effects of and we are here concerned with the effects. With regard to, 1- T 1 control.

mtemperance the police figures tell an extraordinary tale, which is summarised in the following table:

Cause of rising drunkenness.

Causes of falling drunkenness.

The salient feature is the enormous rise in 1916, which is quite contrary not only to the experience of the country at large, but to every single place outside this particular area. The explanation has already been given in Chapter V. It was due to the huge influx of navvies and others for the construction of the Gretna factory, which was not a factory in the ordinary acceptation of the word, but a tract of country nine miles long, in which many miles of roads and railroads with sidings and other appurtenances had to be built, extensive drainage works carried out, hundreds of buildings erected, water and light supplied and all the appointments of a considerable town provided. On this work there were 22,000 men employed in the summer of 1916. They had begun to arrive in the autumn of 1915 and gradually increased in number until they fairly overwhelmed the whole neighbourhood.

It was then that the drunkenness rose with such extraordinary rapidity, and this was the sufficient cause. Previously the convictions had been falling, it is to be noted. Of the 277 recorded in 1915, 205 occurred in the second half of the year, when the influx was taking place, and only 72 in the first half. Carhsle was in fact behaving like other places before the invasion. And here in passing I would draw attention to the accuracy with which the police returns reflected the course of events. In November 1915 the Board made an Order applying the usual restrictions, fortified by Sunday closing, to the area, and but for this the state of Carlisle would undoubtedly have been much worse than it was; but no measures were able to control the torrent. The monthly convictions, w hich had risen during the autumn of 1915 from 9 in July to 76 in December, fell somewhat at the beginning of 1916, showing that the restrictions were not without effect; but they rose again later up to 139 in June 1916, when the high-water mark was reached. After this the movement was reversed; a sudden and rapid fall set in, which continued with minor fluctuations down to July 1918, when the convictions were at zero.

The fall in 1916 coincided with the inauguration and development of State purchase, and was naturally attributed to it by the friends of that system. But an alternative explanation was furnished by a change in the population, which also coincided with the fall. This was the gradual departure of the navvies and their replacement by workers of a different class. Rivalry between these alternative explanations has led partisans on both sides to some misstatement of the facts. On the one side it is alleged that the Control Board came in only after the navvies had gone, and on the other that the number of workers engaged on the Gretna factory remained stationary after the inauguration of the State purchase until 1917 was well advanced. Both statements are somewhat misleading. I was at considerable pains to ascertain the facts at the time from the resident engineer, and found that the navvies had begun to leave when the new administration started, but that their withdrawal was gradual and it could not be said that they had gone when the Board came in. On the other hand, while it was quite true that the numbers remained stationary, their character had changed. In the summer of 1916 there were 22,000 men employed at Gretna on construction work; a year later there were still 22,000 persons employed there, but only 6000 on construction work, the remaining 16,000 were in the factory, and of these 11,000 were girls.

The conclusion is that the main cause of the fall was the withdrawal of the men who had caused the rise, but that it was assisted by the administration, and notably by the order prohibiting the sale of spirits on Saturdays (market day), which was introduced in February 1917 and was immediately followed by a sharp fall. Saturday, which had been the heaviest pohce day in the week, became the lightest. This is the clearest piece of evidence for the effect of the administration on sobriety.

The subsequent further decline followed the general curve for the whole country, with some minor variations, and must be attributed mainly to the same causes. On the whole it seems that the novel and dramatic character of the transformation under State purchase inclined both those who carried it out and friendly observers to take a too sanguine view of its influence on sobriety and to underrate others. A calm survey of the facts in the hght of after knowledge does not sustain the claims then made for it. But hostile criticisms passed on it by partisans on the other side were still more overstated. It would have been strange if this had not happened, for it is the common experience in all such highly-controversial questions. Financial With regard to the economic aspect of the scheme a similar results. Yfnt less acute conflict of opinion arose and still continues.

The Board itself was rather cautious about the financial results. The Fourth Report, which brought the record down to March 1918 and consequently covered about two years total experience, conservatively estimated' that, after meeting all the usual trading charges, the annual return on the total capital commitments had been on the scale of about 15 per cent., but this estimate was given subject to reserve on account of certain stated considerations. The General Manager of the Carlisle area in his Report for 1918 claimed an unquahfied financial success, and contended that the 15 per cent, profit shown by the accounts really represented more as compared with a private brewery company. The total capital involved in the undertaking at March 31, 1918, amounted to 835,053 3s. 5d., and the surplus accruing to the Exchequer, after meeting all expenses, was 107,329 17s. Sd. He maintained that this surplus represented a much higher rate of interest than the 15 per cent, on the Exchequer issues actually advanced for the undertaking, and pointed out that the profits from the inception of the scheme had sufficed: (1) to meet all ordinary recurrent expenditure and depreciation charged on a severe scale; (2) to defray extraordinary charges for preliminary expenses and reconstruction not estimated to add to realisable properties; (3) to pay interest on the net sums issued from the Exchequer; (4) to replace upwards of one-fifth of the average capital employed in the scheme after allowing for the fact that the accumulation of the capital is gradual. In the Report for 1920 the last one made to the Control Board the profit was put at 16 per cent, on the average capital involved in addition to the interest already provided for, making ' a full return of 19 per cent, on the whole capital engaged," and that without any attempt to ' push the trade ' for the sake of gain.

The criticism offered on behalf of the trade was that in the exceptional circumstances and with the advantages enjoyed by the Board in acquiring the properties any business man could have made an equal or greater success not a very strong argument. The judgment of the Geddes Committee on all the undertakings of the Board, issued in 1922, was distinctly cold, and did not recommend the continuance of the system as economically advantageous to the State.

During the war the State undertook the direct control of the Liquor " traffic " in four areas Carlisle, Gretna, Cromarty Firth and Enfield Lock with the object of maintaining the greatest possible efficiency of the munition workers in those areas. The retail sale of intoxicating liquor was taken over, full compensation being paid to the Trade, so that within the areas there is now a virtual State monopoly of the retail liquor traffic." In the Carlisle area breweries have also been taken over. It appears that the total capital employed was approximately 1,270,000, of which over 1,000,000 represents capital assets, and that during the year 1921 a profit of about 138,000 was made. The total profit made during the period from April 1, 1918, to March 31, 1921, one mainly of good trade, amounts to 464,000, representing approximately 12 per cent, on the average capital employed during that period. This profit is arrived at before making provision for interest on capital provided by the Exchequer, Excess Profits Duty, and Income Tax which would have been payable by a private firm.

The original object for which this trading operation was undertaken no longer exists, and there does not appear to be any reason for its continuance as a State undertaking, except for the purpose of making an experiment in the direct administration of the liquor " traffic." We are informed that the scheme is not intended to be primarily profit-making, but that its present as well as its original aim is the provision of food and drink under model conditions. We do not enter into the political or social reasons for this experiment, but in view of the results so far obtained and of the risk of loss in future years its continuance as a State undertaking would not appear likely to afford any special financial advantage to the taxpayer."

It seems to be a fair conclusion from the facts, taking all considerations into account, that while State ownership was

Carlisle as pioneer.

Scientific investigation of the action of alcohol.

not quite so financially successful as its friends maintained, it was sufficiently so. And when we remember how most war enterprises were carried out by or on behalf of the State, and the prodigious waste that was incurred, it is clear that this transaction, which formed a striking contrast, was conducted with great business ability and sound judgment. If the Board had some advantages they also laboured under some economic disadvantages; and it would not have been surprising if the very extensive transformation effected had resulted in a dead loss.

But beyond the actual achievement, whether in regard to temperance or finance, lies something else. The whole venture has a high experimental value as an essay in new methods. It has shown, in the first place, that the trade can be completely reorganised without loss, and that much waste can thereby be eliminated without seriously inconveniencing consumers. It does not follow that this should be done or should be done precisely in the same way; it might be done, by the trade itself and in such a way as to retain what seems desirable in the light of experience while omitting useless changes. At any rate we know that it can be done.

In the second place the venture has given a great stimulus to a change which has for a good many years been slowly in progress; and that is the creation of a new kind of public-house. The resonance given to the Carlisle scheme has aroused widespread interest in that development, and it happens to have coincided with the evolution of a new public need which it is precisely adapted to meet. But further remarks on this head will come better in the concluding chapter. I am only pointing out here that the direct State administration of the trade had other and wider aspects than its immediate results.

No mention has hitherto been made of a different kind of enterprise undertaken by the Control Board. This was the appointment in November 1916 of a Scientific Advisory Committee ' to consider the conditions affecting the physiological action of alcohol, and more particularly the effects on health and industrial efficiency produced by the consumption of beverages of various alcoholic strengths, with special reference to the recent Orders of the Central Control Board, and further to plan out and direct such investigations as may appear desirable with a view to obtaining more exact data on this and cognate questions." I have omitted this item from my account of the proceedings of the Board partly because it had no direct influence on the actual administration of control, with which I was commissioned to deal, and partly because the subject requires fuller and more critical treatment than it is possible to give it here. I will therefore confine myself to a brief notice.

The Committee produced a Eeport published at the end of 1917 by the Stationery Office, under the title of ' Alcohol: its Action on the Human Organism," in which they reviewed the evidence and formulated certain conclusions. This contains a most useful compendium of information which has hitherto been scattered about in scientific periodicals and other publications. In bringing together the results of previous research in the action of alcohol the Committee performed a valuable service and greatly assisted the further investigation of the question. The conclusions reached may be thus summarised: (1) the main action of alcohol is confined to the nervous system; (2) its action is narcotic not stimulant; (3) the objective effect is a lowering of functional activity; (4) this has a proper utihty under given conditions; (5) alcohol undoubtedly has a food value, but this is limited and accompanied by drawbacks which make it suitable only for special conditions; (6) its habitual use by the worker as a substitute for food, or in the belief that it gives a fillip to energy is physiologically unsound; (7) alcohohc beverages should be taken at intervals sufficient to prevent accumulation in the body, not without food and not in a concentrated form.

The last conclusion has a bearing on the control measures discussed above, in that it affords scientific support for the hours of sale adopted and for the dilution of spirits.

The course of events subsequent to the war has been to some extent anticipated in previous chapters; but it demands separate and further treatment as a whole. The relaxation of war restrictions is not less instructive than their imposition, and a study of post-war changes is indispensable to a clear view of the relation of cause and effect. Changes. The following is a chronological statement of the principal changes introduced after the Armistice up to the Act of 1921.

1918, Noveniber 11. Armistice.

1919, February 5. Output of beer raised by Food Controller from 10,700,000 to 13,400,000 barrels.

1919, February 24. Clearance of spirits raised from 50 per cent, to 75 per cent, of 1916 level.

1919, March 3. Prohibition of spirits in certain areas of Scotland withdrawn.

1919, March 17. Weekday evening hours of sale in England and Wales extended from 3 to 3 hours (6 p. m. to 9.30 P. M.). Supply for consumption with a meal permitted to residents in hotel or club up to 11 p. m. Extension of sale on special occasions permitted up to 11 p. m.

1919, April 1. Beer output increased to 20,000,000 barrels; gravity raised to 1040 degrees; duty raised to 70s. a barrel.

1919, April 21. Evening hours in Scotland made uniform,

"'"'" namely 6 p. m. to 9 p. m. except on Saturdays (4 p. m. to 9 P. M.).

1919, May 1. Duty on spirits raised to SOs.

1919, May 12. Weekday evening hours in England and

Wales extended to 10 p. m. 1919, May 23. Beer output raised to 26,000,000 barrels. 1919, June 3. Prohibition of treating withdrawn.

1919, June 20. Eestriction of beer output ended; gravity-raised to 1044 degrees.

1919, July 22. Extension of hours on special occasions permitted between 10 a. m. and 6 p. m.

1919, August 1. Scale of beer gravities revised and raised.

1919, November 19. All restrictions on clearances of spirits withdrawn.

1920, April 20. Duty on beer raised to 100s. a barrel and on spirits to 72s. Qd. a gallon.

1920, July 5. Sunday evening hours amended for summertime ' to 7 to 10 P. M.

1920, November 26. Sunday evening hours permanently amended as above.

1921, April 25. Spirits permitted to be sold for off-consumption in midday opening time on Saturday.

Sale of spirits in less quantities than quart bottle permitted.

Extension of hours on special occasions permitted later than 11 P. M.

Dilution of spirits without notice limited to 35 degrees u. p. instead of 50 degrees u. p. 1921, June 30. Eestriction of beer gravities ended. 1921, August 17. Licensing Act of 1921, putting an end to the Control Board, passed.

The chief points to notice are that no change was introduced for three months after the Armistice, that the first step taken in unwinding the chain was to increase the supply of liquor, and the second to extend the hours of sale, and that both changes were carried further by degrees during the first six months of 1919, so that in June all restrictions on the output of beer had ceased and the time of closing was an hour later than during the war. These relaxations, with some other minor ones, naturally tended to increased drinking in 1919, and were offset only by the further raising of the already very high duties on both beer and spirits. In 1920 all restrictions on quantities of beer and spirits had been removed, the Sunday hour of closing in England was extended to 10 P. M., and the duties were again raised. In 1921 some further minor relaxations were permitted. What was the effect on sobriety?

If we turn to the drunkenness chart, reproduced for the years 1918-21 from p. 94, we observe that there was practically no change for the first three months after the Armistice. The figure in October 1918 was 2124, and in February 1919 it was only 2316. But after the relaxations had begun it drunkenness. j-Qse rapidly and continued to rise to the end of the year, when

Effects of changes.

Rise of it reached 8730, which is the post-war high-water mark, only once recorded again in March 1920. This high-water mark is almost exactly one-half the figure for July 1914, which was 17,410, After March 1920 a downward tendency set in, became accentuated in the latter part of the year, and was prolonged till June 1921. The two main features are the rise in 1919 and the subsequent fall. The latter coincides with the appearance and development of unemployment, which is undoubtedly the chief cause, though it was appreciably assisted by higher prices following on the raised duties. The 1919 rise is not so simply explained and deserves some studj.

During 1919 three important influences tending to increased drinking were simultaneously at work. These were demobilisation, increased supply of drink, and extended hours of sale. They cannot be altogether separated, but some indication of their relative importance can be gathered. With regard to Demobiusa-the first it is to be noted that, though men were being dis- ' charged and returning home during December, January, and February, no appreciable increase of drunkenness took place until March, when the limitation of output began to be relaxed and the hours of opening were extended. The latter took effect at once from March 17 onwards, when closing time was changed from 9 p. m. to 9.30 p. m., and again from May 12, Lengthened when another half-hour was added; whereas the permit for ' increased output granted in February would not take immediate effect, but would necessarily require some little time to be realised in practice. Now the curve of drunkenness shows a very sharp rise between February and March from 2316 to 3429 and again between May and June from 3836 to 4704 and only a comparatively small advance between March and May. That is to say, the sharpest rises coincided very closely with the successive lengthening of hours. Only once did an equally marked rise occur, and that was in December; it reflected the usual Christmas festivities accentuated by the return of many men from war service to private life.

These facts suggest the conclusion that disbandment of itself had very little effect until the hours had been lengthened and the supply of drink increased, and that of these two influences that of the hours was the more distinctly marked. This is entirely in keeping with the lessons of the reverse movement, when the greatest fall in drunkenness coincided with the reduction of hours. Further confirmation is afforded by two other facts. The first is that by 1920 conditions other than hours of sale were practically the same as in 1914, except for the high price of drink, which was largely offset by the prevailing abundance of money and the festal spirit still enhvening the country. Yet the record of maximum drunkenness was only one-half that of July 1914. The second is the J?"" "? remarkable effect produced in this respect by the Act of 1921. 1921.

It lengthened the hours in the controlled areas and shortened them in the uncontrolled. The following table from the official Licensing Statistics, 1922 (Cmd. 1703), gives the figures for controlled and uncontrolled areas in the four months before and the four months after the passing of the Act.

CONVICTIONS FOR DRUNKENNESS ENGLAND AND WALES
Prices.

It will be seen that a very large increase equal to 39 1 per cent, took place in Greater London (the Metropohtan and City Pohce Areas), where also the hours were most extended, and in particular the permitted closing time was prolonged to U P. M. In other controlled areas, in which closing time remained at 10 p. m., the increase was comparatively slight. Turning to the imcontroued areas, in which there had been no change from the pre-war hours, we find a contrast too marked to be accidental. Here the Act reduced the hours of sale from sixteen or seventeen to eight; that is to say it halved them. And instead of a rise we find a fall of 36'6 per cent. The actual figures are small, because the population concerned is small, and minute comparisons with the other areas cannot properly be made on the strength of them. But the broad contrast is enough to demonstrate a radical difference, and this can be found only in the corresponding contrast between lengthened and shortened hours.

When these items of evidence are put together and added to those pointing to the same conclusion and given in previous chapters they afford a proof, as complete as the nature of the case will admit, of the predominant importance of the hours of sale.

It is not the only factor, of course, as has repeatedly been shown, but it does seem to be the most decisive under normal conditions, that is when the quantity of drink is not artificially curtailed. Its relation to two other factors, also of great importance namely, the price of drink and the state of trade cannot be exactly estimated; but the effect of the Act of 1921, just explained, throws some light upon it. The increased drunkenness in London after the passing of the Act took place in spite of very high prices, falling wages, and growing unemployment. Longer hours were able to counteract them all for the time being.

The Licensing Act of 1921

The foregoing references to the Act of 1921 have been prematurely introduced in order to complete the evidence in regard to hours and make the argument continuous; but it requires further notice. The full text will be found in the Appendix, and only the more salient points are here discussed.

The Act was the eventual outcome of much controversy Post-war and many pro- posals, ranging from prohibition, to which a controversy, great impetus was given by the example of the United States, to complete restoration of pre-war conditions. The war was no sooner over than the clamour broke out and dissatisfaction with the restrictions, repressed for the sake of the war, found free expression. Control had been well borne on the whole, as has already been said, but it had never been liked, and when the emergency had passed a strong movement for abolishing it set in and grew in spite of the relaxations enumerated above; they somewhat modified but by no means put an end to the complaints, which came from different quarters and were inspired by various motives. These complaints were generally focussed into demands for abolishing the Control Board, to whom all the disagreeable conditions were popu- larly attributed not only by the public but by many newspapers, which never took the trouble to distinguish between the respective shares of the Board, the Food Controller, and the Treasury in imposing the obnoxious restraints on the trade. The heavy post- war increases of duties in 1919 and 1920, imposed for revenue, were attributed to the Board and did not tend to diminish discontent.

Li addition to these interested reasons for ending war conditions and especially the Control Board, there was a strong feeling, based on constitutional grounds, in favour of regularising the situation and bringing the conduct of the trade again under Parhamentary control and statutory law in place of the arbitrary system of administra- tive orders. This also imphed the disappearance of the Control Board but for totally different reasons, which had nothing to do with retaining or discarding any war-time restrictions as imposed by the Board. The feeling was that whatever the restrictions might be they ought to be embodied in an Act of Parliament and not be left to any administrative body.

On the other hand, the administration of the Board had never gone far enough to satisfy other people who were interested in the question and had various solutions of their own to propose. Some desired to see State purchase extended and applied to the whole country; others, looking eventually to prohibition, urged local option or continued and more drastic control.

As time went on controversy increased rather than diminished, and in June 1921 the Government, following the course so often taken during the war, appointed a conference of M. P."s representing various interests ' to consider in connection with the law of licensing how best to adapt in times of peace the experience obtained during the period of war." The question could no longer be delayed. The Government had promised a Bill in the King's speech on the Opening of Parliament, and their hand was forced by a private Bill introduced in April by Colonel Gretton and only withdrawn on the understanding that an agreed measure would be passed before the end of the session. The conference was called to give effect to this undertaking, and resulted in the introduction in July of a Ministerial Bill which passed, with some amendments, in August and came into force at the beginning of September. The Act. The principal effects of this Act were to put an end to the

Control Board, to restore full jurisdiction to the justices, to render statutory and uniform the conditions imposed by the Board which it was thought desirable to retain, to abohsh the others, and to hand over the State-owned districts to the. administration of the Home Office. The most important point was the retention of changes in the conduct of the trade introduced by the Board and their application to the whole country.

In this respect the Act effected a compromise between the demand for complete restoration of pre-war conditions which was not seriously pressed in any quarter and complete retention of the war restrictions. The relaxations granted in 1919 and enumerated above were somewhat extended, but the principal changes introduced by the Board were retained.

The weekday hours of sale, reduced by the Board in con- Hours, trolled areas from sixteen, seventeen, and (in London) nineteen and a half per diem to five and a half, and subsequently extended again to six and a half, were further extended to eight and (in London) nine; but the principles of early morn- ing closing and a break in the afternoon were retained. The earliest hour for opening in the forenoon was fixed at 11 (subject to special exceptions), there was to be a break of at least two hours in the afternoon, and the latest hour for closing was to be 11 in the Metropohs and 10 (or 10.30) outside, with an additional hour for liquor supphed with a meal. Sunday hours were left as amended by the Board in 1920: that is to say, they were not to exceed five, but closing time was extended to 10 P. M. Within these limits a certain amount of discretion was allowed to the local justices. Eestrictions on the supply of drink to residents on premises and on the ordering of liquor for delivery were abolished; but house-canvassing for orders, credit for on-consumption, and the ' long pull' remained prohibited. Monmouthshire was added to Wales for Sunday closing, and the bona fide traveller was finally abolished.

The practice of the Board in making registered clubs clubs, subject to the same regulations as licensed houses in regard to hours of sale was continued, except that the discretion to vary hours allowed to the justices in regard to licensed houses was vested in the case of clubs in their own rules. Very little has been said about clubs throughout this book, partly because they were covered by the pubhc-house regulations and partly because their numbers fell off considerably during the war. They had previously been increasing every year, and in 1914 numbered 8902 in England and Wales, but during the next three years they fell to 7972. After the war, however, this fall was rapidly made good by very large annual additions, and in 1921 the total stood at 10,650. Since the year

Effects,

Hours in London.

the number of clubs had increased by 4061 down to 1921, while hcensed houses had diminished by 17,410, and club membership had increased at a greater pace than the number of clubs. The club is therefore a more important factor than ever, and, though subject to the same hours of sale as the pubhc-house, it possesses many privileges. The Ucensing justices have no jurisdiction over it; no permit is required for music, dancing, games, or other entertainments; it is not subject to complete Sunday closing where that is imposed on public-houses; it is less heavily rated, and subject to no levy for compensation.

With regard to the effects of the Act on pubhc sobriety, it has already been shown that it was followed by a rise of police drunkenness, chiefly in the Metropolitan area, in which the greatest extension of hours was granted and, in particular, closing time was later at night. In this connection the discretion allowed to the justices to vary the hours within the statutory limits had certain effects which require notice. The hours of opening laid down by the Act as in force until the justices had had an opportunity of exercising their discretion at the first licensing sessions were as follows: Weekdays in the Metropolitan area, 11.30 a. m. to 3 p. m., and 5.30 p. m. to 11 P. M.; other areas, 11.30 a. m. to 3 p. m., and 5.30 p. m. to 10 P. M.; Sundays uniformly 12.30 p. m. to 2.30 p. m., and 7 p. m. to 10 p. m. The discretion allowed to the justices empowered them to begin and to end the day earher, and to regulate the intermediate hours accordingly, without exceeding the total number allowed. Outside the Metropolis they were also empowered to extend the eight hours to eight and a half, and to make the closing time 10.30 instead of 10 p. m.

Considerable use was made of these discretionary powers at the first licensing sessions in 1921, which were ' transfer ' sessions. In London only a few licensing districts maintained the hours laid down in the Act and stated above. These were Holborn, Strand, St. James's, Hanover Square, and Paddington, all central and west-end districts. The rest made various changes, chiefly in the direction of earher opening (11 A. M.) and earher closing (10 p. m.) on weekdays. There was less change on Sundays, but all the districts south of the

Thames, with Marylebone, St. Pancras, and Finsbury on the north, adopted 12 to 2 and 6 to 9 instead of 12.30 to 2.30 and 7 to 10. It is not necessary to give all the variations, which have since undergone further changes, but the general effect was to establish earlier opening and, still more, earlier closing than the hours stated in the Act. This tendency was rather emphasised at the general licensing sessions in 1922, when Paddington, which lies between Kensington and Marylebone, joined them in closing at 10 p. m. instead of 11 p. m. on weekdays. It appears that the London benches had been strongly impressed by the good effect of earlier closing on pubhc order during the war, and were unwilling to give it up.

In the extra-Metropolitan districts, 351 out of a total of 989 accepted without change the weekday hours laid down provisionally in the Act. In only twenty-eight was advantage taken of the permission to extend the hours of opening from eight to eight and a half, and in only twenty-one was the evening closing hour fixed at 10.30 instead of 10. On the other hand, in sixty-three cases the closing hour was made earher than 10, and in 595 the morning hour of opening was made earlier than 11.30. Broadly, these districts displayed the same tendencies as the Metropohtan ones, and such changes as were made in Sunday hours were also in the direction of earlier opening and earlier closing.

The most noticeable effect of the variation of hours by magisterial discretion was a discrepancy in some adjacent Metropolitan districts, particularly in regard to the time of closing in the evening on weekdays, which was 10 p. m. in the great majority of districts, but 11 p. m. in a few; and where these happened to adjoin, the houses on one side of a street might be open for an hour longer than those on the other side. In Oxford Street, for instance, the hour was 10 p. m. on the north and 11 p. m. on the south side. On the ground of this anomaly considerable efforts were made in 1923 to get 11 p. m. made the uniform closing hour for London, but without success. Ever since the passing of the Act there has been a more or less active agitation for carrying the restoration of pre-war conditions further, particularly in regard to the hours of closing; but hitherto the benches have resisted it, with

Drunkenness in 1922.

Carlisle.

some few exceptions. The requests for a general extension of hours have always come from the trade, not from the public, and it is a fair inference that in resisting them the benches have rightly interpreted the general sense of the community. All the great provincial towns and the great majority of London districts have chosen 10 p. m. for closing time in preference to 10.30 P. M. or 11 P. M.; and this is undoubtedly the result of war experience.

The Licensing Statistics for 1922 were not published in time to permit the inclusion of that year in the chart of convictions for drunkenness, but the figures are given in the Appendix. They do not add materially to our knowledge, but so far as they go they are in keeping with the conclusions already drawn. They show a slight fall for the whole country from 77,789 to 76,347, which is accounted for by the continued depression of trade and unemployment. A clearly marked rise in the summer months reflects the seasonal improvement; and the influence of the trade element is further shown by the fact that in Northern England, which suffers most from unemployment, the decline of drunkenness is much more strongly marked than elsewhere. The fall for the year was 11 "16 per cent., which is in striking contrast with the record for London, where a rise of 12 76 took place. The difference is accounted for partly by the milder incidence of unemployment and partly by the longer hours of opening in London. If the first eight months of 1921, before the hours were lengthened, are compared with the same months in 1922, the influence of the longer hours in London becomes very plain.

There remain to be considered the State-owned areas, which were handed over to the Home Office on the dissolution of the Control Board under the Act of 1921. They were subject to the same post-war relaxations as other areas and to the provisions of the Act of 1921, except in regard to the jurisdiction of the justices; but they differed in being owned and managed by the State in the manner explained in Chapter VI. In this respect the Act of 1921, which substituted the Home Office for the Control Board, made no difference. The previous pohcy was maintained and the trade conducted on the same lines as before. Consequently the post-war experience of these areas affords an opportunity of comparing the State ownership and control with the ordinary system in peace time, when the special conditions created by the war no longer operated as a disturbing factor. For the reasons given in the previous chapter we must confine attention to the Carlisle area, which alone furnishes sufficient data and is fairly comparable with other normal districts. Here also the process of adapting and acquiring licensed property, which had not been completed, was continued; for instance, in 1922 the Mary port brewery was closed down, so that the brewing for the district was further consolidated into a single establishment in place of five in 1915, and other changes initiated by the Board were carried a step further.

Carhsle, then, is a complete example of State ownership and control under peace conditions. The difference between it and other similar places under the ordinary system is that the whole trade has been reorganised, the licensed houses greatly reduced in number, rearranged, reconstructed, improved within and without, supplied with food, and conducted by salaried managers with no interest in the sale of intoxicating liquor, but rather encouraged to sell other things. At the same time competition, both wholesale and retail, has been eliminated, the sale of drink for off-consumption has been separated from the sale of other goods (grocers' licences abolished) and concentrated in a few establishments, the age for the admission of children and for the serving of young persons has been raised, and there has been Sunday closing and the ' spiritless Saturday." In short, all the structural, managerial, and administrative changes urged by temperance reformers have been carried out, while the trade has also been subject to the same statutory conditions in regard to hours, prohibited practices, and police supervision as elsewhere. What has been the experience during the four years that have elapsed since the war?

With regard to sobriety, which is the chief point, the only Dmnkenness. precise evidence is that of the police returns, to which recourse must be had if the question is to be discussed at all. They have been'used above for the country as a whole, and the only caution necessary in applying them to a single rather small

Carlisle compared with
Lancashire towns.

place is that they must be read broadly, and that in making comparisons conclusions must not be drawn from small variations and differences. The convictions for drunkenness in Carhsle for 1918 and the post-war years were:

The first point to notice is that there was no increase in 1919 over 1918, which is quite contrary to the general experience. The convictions both for England and Wales as a wholend for the northern counties almost exactly doubled between 1918 and 1919. So far, then, this looks hke a great triumph for State ownership, under which the war level of sobriety was maintained in spite of the relaxations which were accompanied by a great rise of drunkenness elsewhere. But this conclusion is completely shattered by the figures for 1920, which show a great increase on those for 1919, and still more by the record for 1921, when the population had returned to pre-war level according to the census and drunkenness was still rising, while it was falling not only in the country as a whole, but also in towns fairly comparable with Carlisle. Indeed, the Carlisle record for 1921 stands out as exceptionally unfavourable. It looks as though the upward movement were a year later in Carlisle than elsewhere.

A marked improvement occurred in 1922, but even then Carhsle did not make a very favourable appearance. The table opposite gives the population (1921) of Carlisle and the eight Lancashire boroughs under 100,000, together with the convictions for the years 1913, 1921, and 1922.

These figures for particular towns must not be used for minute comparisons between one place and another or one year and another, because accidental variations play too large a part in small areas, but the eight Lancashire towns taken together afford sufficient material for a broad comparison with Carhsle, which points at least to the negative conclusion that the special conditions of the trade in Carlisle have not produced any distinct or corresponding effect in the improvement of public order. It would not be safe to say that Carlisle is worse than its neighbours, but it is impossible to say in face of these figures that it is any better. The Lancashire towns enumerated have been taken because they are in the next county, but if towns of similar size and character elsewhere be used for comparison the result is much the same. No greater improvement in sobriety and public order over the pre-war standard has been secured in Carlisle by all the changes effected under State ownership than has been secured in other comparable places without them. In other words, the conditions of the trade involved in such changes are not those that influence sobriety and public order; their effect in these respects is imperceptible. They may have other effects, other The appearance of the town is generally held to have been effects, improved, the provision of meals in the new model houses and on other reconstructed premises is a convenience appreciated by those who use them, and there is no evidence of any general desire to go back to the old state of things. Moreover, Carlisle has in some respects set an example which is being followed. All this may be granted, but tried by the same test as other places the test used to prove the beneficial effect of the State system in 1916 Carlisle has in nowise done better than its neighbours in regard to sobriety.

Bootle is a suburb of Liverpool.

Reduced duty on beer.

This, I must admit, has surprised me. I have long known that far too much importance was attached by many people to the number of public-houses in a place, their situation, their external appearance, their internal arrangements, the interest of managers in selling drink, the provision of food, grocers' licences, and other conditions that have all been dealt with in Carlisle. A comparative study of actual conditions in many different places and different countries has convinced me that these are not the things that really matter, and that expectations of diminishing drunkenness based on them are doomed to disappointment. But I did expect that such a complete transformation of conditions that were in many respects open to objection, such a complete reorganisation as has been carried out in Carlisle, would tend to lighten the labours of the police and leave a distinct mark on the public order. But it is not so, and no good is to be got by pretending otherwise.

Since the Act of 1921 one other change has been made, which must be mentioned to complete this survey. In the Budget of 1923 the duty on beer was lowered for the first time since the beginning of the war. All previous changes, which have been already enumerated in their proper place, were rises. Their cumulative effect was to raise the duty on beer from 7s. 9d. to 100s. per standard barrel, with a corresponding rise in the duty on spirits and wines and a corresponding increase of price to consumers. The largest rises were imposed after the war and served the double purpose of checking consumption and raising revenue. The following table shows the quantities consumed and the taxation raised in the years 1918 to 1922:

Revenue from taxation.

CONSUMPTION AND REVENUE UNITED KINGDOM

It will be seen that both consumption and revenue rose rapidly between 1919 and 1920, but that after 1920, when the duties were raised to a maximum, consumption tended to fall while revenue continued to rise. The double object of higher revenue and increased sobriety was attained in 1921; but in 1922 the year of the greatest pressure from unemployment the revenue also fell, showing that the most advantageous financial point had been passed. At the same time popular resentment at the high prices, particularly of beer, had been steadily growing, and demands for reduction were becoming more general and more urgent. The Government were probably influenced by both considerations in deciding to reduce the duty on beer by 20s. a bulk barrel, which by arrangement with the brewers enabled the price to be lowered hj Id. a pint.

The whole experience is very instructive. It cannot be doubted that the high taxation and consequent high prices acted as a drag on consumption after the war, and particularly played an important part in checking the rising tide in 1920 and so contributed to the fall in drunkenness, which set in after March in that year, while at the same time swelling the revenue. But the sequel shows that there is a limit to the use of this instrument, just as the experience of 1917 showed that there was a limit to the curtailment of supply. The people would not stand deprivation beyond a certain point, whether imposed directly by limitation of output or indirectly by prohibitive prices. In both cases the breaking-point was reached in regard to beer, which is the staple drink of the country. So long as beer can be had deprivation of spirits is better tolerated, at least in England. A reference to the table given above will show that a heavy fall in the consumption of spirits between 1920 and 1921 was accompanied by an increased consumption of beer, which was clearly of a compensatory nature. But when the continued depression of trade made beer also too dear for the depleted pockets of the people, which happened in 1922, a revolt set in too strong to be ignored. But it is to be noticed that there are limits also to the safe taxation of spirits. I do not say that they have yet been passed, but the accumulating evidence of methylated spirit drinking both in Scotland and in many parts of England, especially among women, is a warning that they have been approached. The police cases in England rose from 227 in 1920 to 516 in 1922.

It should be noted that the taxation of beer has an indirect effect upon the strength of the liquor supplied. The duty is levied on beer of a given specific gravity (strength); a barrel of such beer is a standard ' barrel. A barrel of beer of lower specific gravity pays less duty in proportion to the difference; or conversely, more beer of lower specific gravity can be brewed for the same tax. The table given above of the number of standard barrels brewed in each year does not therefore represent the actual quantity or the number of bulk barrels brewed, as many were brewed of a lower gravity. The reduction of 20s. in 1923 being made on the bulk barrel would tend to an increased output of beer at a lower gravity. Local A post-war change in the British licensing system, but option. having nothing to do with the war, should be briefly mentioned for the sake of completeness. This was the coming into operation in 1920 of the Scottish Local Option or Local Veto Act passed in 1913, and known as the Temperance (Scotland) Act. The first polls were taken under it in November and December 1920. Out of a total number of 1215 areas into which the country was divided, a poll was taken in 584 with the following results: for no change 508 areas, for limitation of Hcences 35, for no licences 41. The proportion of electors voting was 69 6 per cent, of the whole. Of the votes cast 60 per cent, were for no change, 1 6 per'Jcent. for limitation, and 38 4 per cent, for no licence. On account of irregularities a re-poll was taken in six areas in 1921. In five of these the vote for no licence was reversed in favour of no change (2) and hmitation (3), so that the amended results gave: no change 511, limitation 37, no licence 36. In two other areas polls taken in 1922 resulted in no change.

The facts described and critically examined in the preceding chapters contain some valuable lessons for our guidance in dealing with the problem of alcoholic drink. The war experience has added a special chapter to the long history of the subject and thrown a searchlight upon various aspects of it by applying the test of experiment in a way that would not have been possible under normal conditions. The result is much new material for forming opinion on important points, upon which opinion is greatly divided. Having dealt with that material as fully and fairly as I can, I might leave the reader to draw his own conclusions, and no doubt many will do so. But others will expect some summing up, and I shall endeavour to satisfy that very legitimate expectation by indicating, in a candid spirit, what seem to me the chief lessons to be learnt from the unique experience of the war and its sequel. But in doing so I seek only the truth, and offer my opinion for what it may be worth to those who care to have it. I have not the shghtest desire to impress it upon anyone else or to argue the matter. In so far as it is true it will stand, in so far as it is not, let it perish.

1. The first lesson to which I would draw attention is the Drink in importance of alcoholic liquor as an element in national life. This may seem a truism, but like many other truisms it is imperfectly realised or misunderstood. The war has brought it out as nothing else has ever done. So great was the importance of the liquor trade that it called into existence special legislation and a special organ of Government armed with extraordinary powers; and that not because the war interfered with it as in the case of shipping, transport and food supply, or national life.

Drink and efficiency.

Restriction justified.

because its expansion was necessary for the prosecution of the war as in the case of munitions all of which called for special legislation and special control but for the opposite reason, because it interfered with the war and its restriction was necessary in the interest of national safety. This constitutes a tremendous indictment.

Consider those early months. The war had no sooner begun than the naval and military authorities found themselves confronted by an influence so hostile to the efficiency of their operations and so serious as to constitute a national danger necessitating special measures to counteract it. The danger was recognised immediately, nor was it ever denied. And as the national effort demanded by the war developed, extended and increased in intensity, the same danger extended with it and demanded further counter-active measures. That danger was excessive drinking or the abuse of alcoholic liquors. I have shown in Chapter II that the case was over-stated in the prevailing excitement, and that advantage was taken of it to push extreme measures for their own sake; but that must not blind us to the remarkable demonstration afforded by the war of the real disability involved in the habit of excessive drinking. The war searched out every weak spot in national character and conduct as nothing had ever done before, because the nation had never before been subjected to so great a strain; and this habit of excess was so plainly revealed as a weak spot that extraordinary measures for dealing with it were adopted with general approval and acquiesced in by the community at large. Too many people could not be trusted.

This, then, is the first point. The war proved to demonstration that, though the nation is more sober than it used to be and more sober than some others, the habit of excessive drinking still prevails to such an extent as to constitute a serious national disability. To the two standing grounds that justify the compulsory restraint of individual liberty by society in this matter, namely, public order and public health, a third was added by the supreme emergency of war. This was public safety, and it was held to justify much more drastic measures of restraint than those previously in force.

But it was not held to justify the compulsory suppression No proof all drinking or the attempted suppression. This was li ition. strongly urged and even contemplated by the Government, but was eventually held to be inadvisable, and from what subsequently happened it is quite certain that prohibition would not have been tolerated. The inquiries into industrial discontent in 1917 and the resistance offered to the Food Controller's limitation of output proved conclusively the popular value attached to the customary beverages of the country and the determination to retain the immemorial rights of the people in choosing for themselves. They submitted to limitation and reduced facilities, but deprivation they "" would not tolerate. This is the other side of the lesson afforded by the war on the importance of alcoholic liquor in the national Ufe, and it is not less instructive than the proof of disability caused by excessive drinking. Equal attention should be paid to both.

2. The second conclusion I would draw is that excessive Effects of drinking can be effectively checked and the disabihty caused restrictioui by it proportionately reduced by appropriate measures, which yet leave an amount of liberty sufficient to avoid a widespread revolt against the law or a resort to wholesale evasion. That this was actually achieved in Great Britain is proved by the evidence detailed in preceding chapters. The police returns and the medical statistics confirming each other attest the improvement in public order and public health, in so far as these are affected by drink, and the testimony of the authorities and employers who called for control in the interests of national efficiency proves that the measures taken were effective to that end. The working of control without serious resistance or evasion proves that the object was achieved without provoking a dangerous reaction or creating a new evil worse than the old.

3. The third conclusion is that the principal measures The contributing to this result were (1) curtailment of the hours g suri of sale, (2) limitation of supply and

diminution of strength, (3) raised prices. It has been shown by both positive and negative evidence that each of these had a distinct effect. In combination they reduced the curve of intemperance to the lowest point reached during the war, when the monthly-convictions for England and Wales, which had been 17,410 in July 1914, fell to about 2000 in the latter part of 1918. This fall was fully shared by women. After the war hmitation of quantity was gradually abandoned and hours of sale were lengthened while men were returning to civil life, and these changes were accompanied by a rise of intemperance. But the hours of sale were only extended to one-half the pre-war time of opening and taxation was heavily increased; and to these conditions must be attributed the fact that, in spite of the disbandment of the Forces, the level of intemperance at no time rose to more than half the pre-war height, and since 1920 has been considerably lower. Permanent 4. A fourth conclusion fouows, namely, that under peace improvement, conditions the volume of intemperance can be kept far below the former level by means of shorter hours and higher taxation, which at the same time provides an increased revenue. These measures have proved really efficacious, while others particularly State ownership and control, the reduction of licensed houses, alteration of premises, disinterested management and sifpply of food have failed to exert any perceptible influence on sobriety and public order. Limits of But it has also been shown that, however desirable the restriction. suppression of intemperance may be and however efficacious the methods just indicated, there are limits to their application; they cannot be effectively and safely pushed beyond a certain point. During the war they were carried as far as they could be without provoking reaction, and an attempt to carry them further had to be given up because of the resistance aroused. Nor is the issue merely one between hberty and sobriety; it is also one between increasing and diminishing sobriety.

The assumption that measures which within limits conduce to sobriety by making excess difficult will continue to do so in proportion to their stringency is a fallacy. It has often been put to the test of experience, and always with the same result. When drinking by legahsed channels is made too difficult, recourse is had to illegal ones, and the practice tends to spread with disastrous effects.

This did not happen here during the war, because control Example of was judiciously handled and not carried beyond the limits of ' '-toleration. But it happened in Sweden, and the experience furnishes such a clear illustration of the principle that it is worth recounting. The licensed trade under the Swedish or Gothenburg system is in the hands of a quasi-public body of citizens called the Bolag or Company, which manages the public-houses and the sale of spirits for off as well as for on consumption. In 1914 the Stockholm Bolag was reconstructed and a system of rationing spirits was introduced, by which the monthly allowance was limited to 2 litres a head. In 1917 it was found necessary to restrict distillation as a food measure; the stocks became very low and the ration was reduced to 2 litres a quarter. The following table, giving the annual consumption per head and the convictions for drunkenness, shows what happened:

The table shows a progressively falling consumption of spirits, particularly after 1916, and a corresponding fall of drunkenness down to the year 1917; but in 1918 a remarkable discrepancy is revealed between the two. Consumption Drunkenness continued to fall, but drunkenness showed a very large rise, increased. It appears from the monthly figures that this rise began early in 1918 and continued progressively throughout the year; the number of cases, which had been 195 in January, had risen to 784 in December. And these police figures were confirmed by the cases of dehrium tremens admitted to hospital, which had gradually fallen from 623 in 1913 to 127 in 1917, but during 1918 rose again from a monthly average of 3-3 in the first quarter to 17-3 in the last quarter.

Illicit distillery.

Reasons for failure of suppression.

Judicious control.

The explanation given by M. Bratt, ctiairman of the Bolag, was that so long as the reduced consumption was not carried beyond a certain point it was tolerated by the people and the result was increased sobriety; but the final reduction in 1917 went too far, and caused a reaction. The people took to drinking commercial spirit and to illicit distillation, which increased rapidly during the year, until the Chief Constable declared that it was carried on in every house in Stockholm and the police could not cope with it. So drunkenness and disorder increased, while the legal sale diminished. The cases of drunkenness from methylated spirit rose from 265 in 1917 to 2609 in 1918, although the spirit was ' denatured," showing that denaturation is no effective safeguard.

This experience is one more proof that there are limits to the compulsory suppression of drinking, and that when carried beyond those hmits it defeats its own object by tending to promote more injurious forms of drinking and evasion of the law by common consent. Nor is it possible to counteract those tendencies in a free country for three reasons: namely, the ease with which alcohohc drink can be produced, the lucrativeness of the illicit traflc, and the refusal of society in general to regard drinking as a crime, whatever the law may say.

The result of Prohibition in the United States is precisely what everyone really conversant with the history of the question expected. If the object is to close the open saloons (American euphemism for pot-houses) it has succeeded; if it is to stop drinking it has failed and must fail just where drinking most needs suppression. In attempting to enforce it the authorities are running their heads against a stone wall.

The practical problem is to reduce the evils of excess, which have been once more demonstrated by the war, to the lowest point, and the general lesson from all the experience here set out is that this can best be done by controlling the trade on the lines indicated within the limits of popular toleration. The object has been achieved in this country more successfully by these methods than by any others in any comparable country, and the war-time experience has

CONCLUSIONS 153 led to a great advance in national sobriety along this path. If we are wise we shall keep to it and not be beguiled either into the restoration of former conditions, which are not demanded by the public and are not in the public interest, or, on the other hand, into fanciful measures of control and repression, which are still less demanded and have no evidence of success to recommend them.

It may be desirable to make changes from time to time, Eeasons for but they should be made for sound and definite reasons, for ' S-which purpose the working of the conditions laid down in 1921 should be carefully watched. There is no finahty about them, and if change is clearly demanded in the public interest, it should be made, but not otherwise. For instance, the recent concession in regard to the taxation and price of beer was in my opinion justified by a real demand, and there are signs that the taxation of spirits may have to undergo some modification too, as I have aheady pointed out. On the other hand, there is no such evidence in favour of lengthening the hours of sale, and the persistent agitation carried on in some quarters for gradually creeping back to the old conditions is not in the public interest. The great gain left us by the war is the reduction and the midday interruption of the hours of sale, which had not been changed for forty years and are now seen to have been excessive. It is a gain not only to sobriety but also to public health, and particularly to the health of children, who go to bed earlier and get more sleep.

To go back to the old conditions would be to go back to the old level of drunkenness. Is that desirable? It all depends on what the object is. Alcohohc sobriety is not the be-all and end-all of existence, and it may be too dearly bought. There are worse things than intemperance; it is possible propter vitam vivendi jperdere causas. But the intemperance we had in 1914 was a very bad thing, a great national weakness and burden; and to have reduced it to one-half without any serious drawback is a great gain. It National is sometimes argued that this reduction is due to the general sobriety, tendency of the nation towards increased sobriety, but the argument is based on ignorance of the facts and quite untenable. There is such a tendency, but its working is very gradual and visible only over a long period of years. I am not likely to underrate it, for I was the first to assert and prove it, to the general surprise, about twenty-five years ago, when the assumption of temperance reformers that intemperance was a growing evil, was accepted without examination. My argument to the contrary was at first angrily disputed, but eventually became generally admitted. The improvement, which is due to many influences, is not a continuous movement but one marked by oscillations, which correspond broadly with the state of trade. Good trade is always followed by a rise of drunkenness, bad by a fall, and each continues some little time after the corresponding trade movement has ceased. Drunkenness had been rising for four years while licensed houses were being reduced by over 1000 a year, and was still rising when the war broke out; to attribute the immense war and post-war reduction to a general tendency to sobriety is absurd. The new The war change will, however, leave a permanent mark, standard. because it sets a new standard for a new generation. This is the real character of the general movement towards sobriety. It is due to a number of causes which combine to alter gradually the standard of conduct for successive generations; and it is revealed in both high and low periods. The crest of the wave is not so high as it used to be, the trough is deeper, but no sudden reduction is effected. Now the war has set a new standard, and it is here that the value in particular of the Carlisle experiment lies. It has given both resonance and precision to the movement for raising the status and function of the public-house from a mere drinking bar to a place of family refreshment. This does not take immediate effect in the conduct of adults whose mature habits are not so easily changed. But it will take effect by degrees as the younger generation grows up, accustomed from youth to a different atmosphere and a different rule. This is real temperance, natural, not forced, and therefore lasting. When the Gretna Tavern was opened in 1916, it was observed that the older customers thronged the bar in spite of the comparative discomfort, and avoided the large room with all its advantages, but that the young people appreciated them, and so I found it still in 1922 after six years. By degrees the former will pass away and their places will be taken by the younger generation, who will set a different fashion. And as the movement spreads a gradual change will be accomplished. It is in progress now; brewers have taken up the idea of the new public-house, and the demand created by modern road traffic is a growing economic stimulus to development, which will prevail against the opposition offered by theorists who wish to aboush the public-house and consequently object to its improvement, and by licensing justices who cling to antiquated ideas.

This is the direction in which change will mainly proceed. Classification and it will tend to sobriety. It will probably also tend to an alteration of the law, which has been long overdue. One of the greatest obstacles to practical improvement has long been the lack of discrimination by the law between the different classes of estabhshments at which drink is sold. Places which fulfil entirely different functions are all lumped together by the law and subjected to the same regulations because there is only one licence for all of them. The bar where people only drink, the dining-room where they also eat, and the hotel where they sleep in addition, are all identical in the eye of the law. Could anything be more ridiculous? During the war discrimination was found necessary for practical reasons, and was introduced in the Control Board's orders by way of ' saving provisions." The restrictions on the sale of drink were relaxed for meals and for hotel guests, and these distinctions were continued in the Act of 1921 by the insertion of exemptions. But this is a clumsy way of recognising realities, and it is incomplete. What is really needed to bring the trade into accord with public requirements and actual conditions is a re-classification of licences, of which there should be five: (1) hotel, (2) restaurant, (3) club, (4) bar, (5) off-sale. It would solve the difficulty of different closing hours in contiguous London districts, which is due to the application of the same rule to estabhshments serving different purposes. At present either restaurants must close at 10 o'clock or bars keep open till 11 o'clock, and so the hour is 10 in some districts and 11 in others. But if the hour was uniformly 10 o'clock for bars which is quite late enough and 11 o'clock for restaurants, all districts would be alike and the anomaly would disappear. This illustration shows the absurdity of the present system and the remedy; but the suggested classijcation of licences would permit of other adjustments in the interest both of temperance and of public convenience, such as, for instance, a special treatment of wayside country inns in regard to hours. It is a common-sense reform, which would bring the law into conformity w4th actual conditions, and which will be called for with growing insistence as change proceeds and the conditions of the trade more and more outgrow an obsolete law.

I mention this as a practical measure, but it may be open to objection, and I have no wish to stress it unduly. The thing most needed, in my opinion, at the present juncture is not fresh legislation, but rather co-operation in the conduct of the trade on the lines indicated. If the trade interests, the licensing benches and the temperance societies will recognise that there are principles or laws, deducible from experience, which may serve as a sound guide to effective action; and if they will combine to apply them, real progress w ill be made both in checking excess and raising the whole standard of character and conduct. But if the old antagonisms, which by inciting each other lead on the one hand towards unwise relaxations, and on the other towards vexatious and useless interference, are kept up, the result will be to jeopardise the present gains. Cannot the people concerned agree to drop polemics and give common sense and co-operation at least a trial?

Return to an Order of the Honourable the House of Commons, dated 29 April 1915; for, Copy ' of Report and Statistics of Bad Time kept in Shipbuilding, Munitions, and Transport Areas."

(A.) Admiralty Reports

Percentage of Hours worked by Government Employes in Portsmouth Dockyard during week ending April 24, 1915.

Men working 85 hours a week and upwards 80 75 70 65 60 55 50

Normal (48 hours) Less than normal 6 per cent.

It will be seen from the foregoing that no less than 78 per cent. of the workmen at Portsmouth were working for 60 hours or over in the week ending last Saturday 24th instant i. e., 12 hours or more in excess of the normal working hours of the week.

The above statistics may be taken as typical of all the Admiralty dockyards.

Reports to the First Lord of the Admiralty on the Effect of Excessive Drinking on Output of Work on Shipbuilding, Repairs, and Munitions of War.

First Lord,

THE enclosed statement has been drawn up, showing the effect of excessive drinking on the output of work as regards shipbuilding repairs, and munitions of war being carried out by contract for the Admiralty.

A report by the Director of Transports as to the effect on transport work is also enclosed.

F. C. T. TUDOR,

Third Sea Lord. April 2, 1915.

REPORTS which have been received from the Clyde, Tyne, and Barrow districts recently are in agreement that at the present time the amount of work put in by the workmen is much less than what might reasonably be expected.

Put briefly, the position is that now, while the country is at war, the men are doing less work than would be regarded as an ordinary week's work under normal peace conditions. As instances of this, tables are attached showing the numbers of hours worked in a submarine engine shop and in shipyards on the N. E. Coast.

It will be seen that in the case of the 135 fitters employed on submarine engine work, the number of hours lost during the first week of March amounted to the equivalent of a full week's work of twenty-eight men, i. e., on the average each man did little more than three-quarters of a day's work.

The reports from the N. E. Coast show that over periods of five to seven weeks the time lost at one of the shipyards by riveters equals about 35 per cent, of the normal week's work; platers, 25 per cent.; and the caulkers and drillers about 22 per cent.; the later returns for the same yard show that by far the greater majority of the workmen are absent at starting time 6 a. m.

The figures reported from two other shipyards on the North East Coast are similar, and the reports from the Clyde, though details have not been received, are to the same effect, showing that the large amount of lost time is general throughout the country.

Thus the problem is not how to get the workmen to increase their normal peace output, but how to get them to do an ordinary week's work of 51 or 53 hours, as the case may be.

The reasons for the loss of time are no doubt various, but it is abundantly clear that the most potent is in the facilities which exist for men to obtain beer and spirits, combined with the high rates of wages and abundance of employment. Opinion on this point is practically unanimous.

The matter has been referred to from time to time in letters which the firms have written in regard to progress of work in hand for the Admiralty, as shown by the following extracts:

Clyde.

' We regret to say a number of men are losing a considerable amount of time, mostly, we are afraid, due to their drinking habits, no doubt aggravated by the extra money they are earning by working overtime, and we respectfully submit that if some step could be taken to restrict their opportunities to indulge in intoxicating liquor enormous benefits would result in the progress of this and other naval work we have in hand."

North-East Coast.

' Regret to say considerable number of our workmen absent from duty to-day drinking."

Clyde.

Regret to complain construction of H. M. S. delayed through workmen absenting themselves from work through excessive drinking."

The Captains-Superintendent of the Clyde and Tyne districts, who supervise the warships being built and repaired by contract, are very well placed to form an opinion on this matter.

The Captain-Superintendent on the Tyne (which district includes the north-east coast of England and Barrow) reported on 26th February that the early morning drink was responsible for a great deal of the short time, and that it would be a great help if the public-houses were closed until 10 a. m. In a later report he stated that everyone agrees that if the pubs could be closed until 10 a. m. things would improve, and they should close at 9 p. m., being open say from 5 or 6 P. M. In this district no one in uniform can be served between 1 and 6 p. m., so I would advocate closing altogether for those times and not only in the neighbourhood of the shipyards. I have spoken to some of the foreman class, and they tell me 90 per cent, of the men would approve."

The Captain-Superintendent of the Clyde district considers that the one thing needed to get the full output of work is to prohibit the sale of all spirits.

In a further report, he states that the drinking is on the increase and is causing delay and bad work; and as a remedy he proposes the prohibition of spirits and of the sale of liquor by the bottle by public-house, grocers, c., and the restriction of the hours during which public-houses are open.

The Captain-Superintendent of the torpedo-boat destroyers building in various parts of the country reports that ' the main difficulty that contractors have to contend against is the inability on the part of the men to work full time, and the only way to meet the difficulty appears to be to have some form of enlisted labour, or further restrictions imposed on the licensed houses in the vicinity of shipyards."

An officer, who is overseeing the construction of vessels building by a firm on the North-East Coast, reports: The time-keeping of the men is not at all satisfactory; whole gangs are thrown out owing to the absence of three or four hands. The firm are of opinion that, short of Martial Law, the only thing to stop it is to stop the sale of spirits."

The Director of Naval Equipment's report, after his visit to the Tyne, is appended; a further report has now been received from him after a visit to the Clyde.

In this he states that ' the conditions of labour on the Clyde are such that, except for one or two firms, the abstentions are so great as to cause a serious loss of time, and consequent difficulty in meeting contracts.

When war broke out the opening of public-houses was limited to the hours of 10 a. m. to 10 p. m., and this has had a beneficial result, but does not entirely meet the case, and it is generally considered that much greater restrictions should be imposed in the hours that liquor may be sold, and that such restriction should apply to all classes equally."

The foregoing remarks have reference chiefly to the large shipbuilding yards and engineering works, but amongst these are included some of the largest armament firms, who are manufacturing munitions of war of all sorts. The output of the last is also adversely affected by the drink question. The manager of works on the North-East Coast, where large quantities of shell are manufactured, stated that if the two public-houses just outside the works could be closed his output would be very largely increased.

The question of the extent to which it is desirable or necessary to curtail the sale of intoxicants involves serious national considerations, and is not a matter for one or two Government departments only, but from the point of view of Admiralty work it does not appear that partial measures are likely to be successful, judging from the results of the partial restriction of opening of public-houses which has been in operation on the Clyde during the war.

Total prohibition, with all its attendant objections and disadvantages, would at least have the general effect that all classes would at last realise the existence and seriousness of tlie war, and tliat they were personally involved in its consequences.

A great principle, such as ' prohibition for the war," will probably depend for its success largely on details, such as the convenience of obtaining hot and cold non-alcoholic drinks, both outside and inside the yards and works.

Further, an attractive scheme for saving the large amount of money earned by the men, of which so much is now spent in drink (which might possibly be worked through the Government Insurance organisation), seems well worthy of consideration, but should in no way delay decision and action on the vital question of restricting the sale of intoxicants.

Enclosures (A). Submarine engine-shop. Time lost by fitters. (B). Time lost by ironworkers at shipyard on North-East Coast. (C). Time lost by workmen on repairs of a battleship. (D). Time lost by workmen at shipyards on North-East Coast. (E). Copy of Report from Captain Barttelot (Captain-Superintendent, Clyde district), dated the 25th March, 1915.

(A). Submarine Engine Shop

Lost Time by Fitters working on Submarine Engine Work from 6 A. M. on Monday, March 1, to 12 o'clock noon on Saturday, March 6, 1915.

Monday, March 1, 1915.

Total number of fitters employed. 135

Only 60 of these worked a full day (9 hours). The following statement shows the time worked and lost by the remainder:

Hours. 20 were absent all day, time lost. 190 2 worked 3i hours, time lost. 12 1 worked 5 hours, time lost. 4 52 worked 7 hours, time lost. 130

Total 336J 135 fitters working full time. 1,282 Actual time worked by 135 fitters. 946

Time lost 336J

This represents a total loss on the day's working of 35 men working full time.

Tuesday, March 2, 1915.

Total number of fitters employed. 135

Only 90 of these worked a full day (9 hours). The following statement shows the time worked and lost by the remainder:

Hours. 18 were absent all day, time lost. 171 27 worked 7 hours, time lost. 67J

Total 238J 135 fitters working full time. 1,282J

Actual time worked by 135 fitters. 1,044

Time lost 238J

This represents a total loss on the day's working of 25 men working full time.

Wednesday, March 3, 1915.

Total number of fitters employed. 135

Only 86 of these worked a fuu day (9J hours). The following statement shows the time worked and lost by the remainder:

Hours. 21 were absent all day, time lost. 199J 28 worked 7 hours, time lost

Total 135 fitters working full time. Actual time worked by 135 fitters 269i 1,282J 1,013

Time lost 269J

This represents a total loss on the day's working of 28 men working full time,

Thursday, March 4, 1915.

Total number of fitters employed. 135

Only 77 of these worked a full day (9 hours). The following statement shows the time worked and lost by the remainder:

Hours.

22 were absent all day, time lost. 209 1 worked 2 hours, time lost. 7 1 worked 2 hours, time lost. 7J 33 worked 7 hours, time lost. 82J 1 worked 6 hours, time lost. 3j

Total 309J 135 fitters working full time. 1,282J

Actual time worked by 135 fitters. 973

Time lost 309

This represents a total loss on the day's working of 32 men working full time.

Friday, March 5, 1915.

Total number of fitters employed. 135

Only 91 of these worked a full day (9 hours). The following statement shows the time worked and lost by the remainder:

Hours. 16 were absent all day, time lost. 152 1 worked 3i hours, time lost. 6 27 worked 7 hours, time lost. 67J

Total 135 fitters working full time. Actual time worked by 135 fitters 225i 1,282 1,057

Time lost 225J

This represents a total loss on the day's working of 24 men working full time.

Saturday, March 6, 1915.

Total number of fitters employed. Only 103 of these worked a fuu day 5 hours). The following statement shows the time worked and lost by the remainder:

Hours. 17 were absent all day, time lost. 93 15 worked 3 hours, time lost. 37

Total 135 fitters working full time Actual time worked by 135 fitters 742 611i

Time lost 131

This represents a total loss on the day's working of 24 men working full time.

Summary 135 fitters working full time for one week (53 hours) = 7,155 hours.

Actual hours worked by 135 fitters in one week = 5,644

Time lost by 135 fitters in one week = 1,510J

This represents a total loss on the week's working of 28 men working 53 hours each.

1 3 hours each.

(B). Statement of Lost Time of Ironworkers in a Shipyard on

North-East Coast

Percentage of Absentees in the Ironworkers' Department of same Shipyard, Monday, March 22,

Peecentage of Time Lost by Ironworkers in the same Shipyard,

Monday, March 22, 1915

Analysis of Riveters' Time for week ending February 9, 1915 Total riveters employed, 211, of which 211 men at 51 hours = 10,761 hours; lost time, 3,770 hours = 35 per cent., an increase of 3 per cent, over the preceding two weeks.

(C). Time Lost by Workmen on Repairs of a Battleship (D). Time Lost by Workmen at Shipyards on North-East Coast.

(E.) (No. 425456.) Sir, 3, Clyde View, Partich, Glasgow, March 25, 1915.

IN accordance with the directions contained in your telegram of the 20th March, calling for proposals that will facilitate the completion of H. M. ships, I have the honour to report on the effect of drink on the output of work.

2. From close observation and my opinion is shared by all the managers of shipyards the amount drunk by a section of the men is much greater than it was before the war, and it is on the increase. Those principally concerned are the iron-workers and shipwrights, and on their efficiency the output entirely depends.

3. The sole reason for this heavy drinking is that the men earn more money than they know what to do with.

4. In a shipyard last week where a warship is under repair, work on the inner bottom of the ship was so badly carried out as to suggest at once on inspection that it could not have been done by men who were sober. It was dangerous, and had to be condemned. In the same yard (and it is common in most others) drunken men, nominally at work, have had to be removed. Men are bringing or smuggling liquor into the yards in bottles, and facilities for buying spirits in bulk at public-houses and at licensed grocers must be stopped, 5. All this (and the serious point is that it is getting worse) has a much greater effect on delay than the shortage of labour.

6. I cannot state too forcibly my own opinion that the total prohibition of the sale of spirits would be the most efiective act that could at the present time be taken to win this war. Any measure less drastic will not be a cure; it will keep alive the craving which has been growing after six months indulgence, and some men will endeavour to satisfy it by keeping away from work.

7. The hours I recommend for the public-houses to be open for the sale of drink (not spirits) are from

Noon tni 2 P. M.

and 7 P. M. till 9 P. M.

and drink must be consumed on the premises, a prohibition being placed on the sale of liquor by the bottle by public-houses and by licensed grocers.

8. As to the districts in which restrictions should be enforced, they cannot be too wide. Public-houses here are opened at 10 a. m., and I am informed by the manager of one yard that some of his men have been known to go several miles before coming in to work in the morning in order to obtain drink under the travellers' clause. I would like to see and in this view I am supported by all shipbuilders on the Clyde the whole city of Glasgow, and from there down to Gourock and Dumbarton on either side of the river, included in the restricted areas.

9. If that is not considered possible, then the following districts closely connected with shipyards must be the minimum:

On the North Bank On the South Bank

All Finnieston. All Partick. All Whiteinch. All Scotstoun. All Clydebank. All Dalmuir. All Dumbarton.

From Kinning Park. All Govan. All Renfrew. All Port Glasgow. All Greenock. All Gourock.

I would also submit that a most beneficial efiect would be produced if the men could be told by some leading statesman exactly and very plainly where they are failing their country. They have been flattered and told what splendid fellows they were just at the time when slackness was beginning to set in, and tliis has not had a good result. It is not that the men (I am referring always to the men who drink) are bad at heart or unpatriotic, but they have failed through weakness and opportunity, and they know they have failed and would at heart welcome being corrected and put right.

I have, c. (Signed) BRIAN H. F. BARTTELOT.

Report by Captain Greatorex, R. N., Director of Naval Equipment, dated ith March, 1915, to Third Sea Lord

THE condition of labour is deplorable, and the men are in a most uncertain and undependable state. This is so serious, that at any time the whole of the shipbuilding work on the Tyne may come to a standstill.

Sunday working is of little value, as the money paid for Sunday work leads to abstention from all work for often two days, and a Sunday worker will frequently not return till Wednesday.

The money earned is sufficient to satisfy the men's standard of living, and anything extra beyond ordinary wages encourages abstention to enable loafing in public-houses, instead of doing their honest day's work.

The opening of public-houses at early morning conduces to abstention from work till after breakfast, and then the work is unsatisfactory, due to the amount that has been imbibed.

I was informed by one of the firms that the average non-attendance of workmen amounts to 1 45 days in six days' work, practically 25 per cent, of time is lost.

Unless something drastic in the way of measures is taken, I fear that the state of deliveries of ships and vessels of all kinds will be most seriously afiected; but in the present frame of mind of the men, drastic measures might have the effect of producing a critical situation. On the other hand, further extra grants and bonuses only accentuate the present deplorable indiserence of the workmen to their duty and to attendance to their daily work.

The only approach to a solution that was suggested as being likely to do good was to partially or totally close all public-houses, and that all offers of extra wages were most harmful, and only accentuated the difficulty.

I make the foregoing remarks with a full sense of the fact that it is not my personal duty to inquire into these matters, but these facts were apparent in tte course of my visit of inspection to the ships building in the Tyne district, and as the deliveries of ships are being so influenced by these facts, I consider it my duty to bring them to your notice.

C. GREATOREX, Director of Naval Equipment.

(B.) Report of Deputation to the Government from the Shipbuilding Employers' Federation on 29th March, 1915 (Extract from The Times of the 30th March, 1915)

AN important deputation from the Shipbuilding Employers' Federation was received yesterday at the Treasury by the Chancellor of the Exchequer and the Secretary for Scotland. With Mr. Lloyd George and Mr. Mckinnon Wood were:

Mr. E. S. Montagu, M. P., Mr. Cecil Harmsworth, M. P., Rear-Admiral Tudor, Rear-Admiral Morgan Singer, Captain Greatorex, R. N., Major-General S. B. von Donop, Sir Francis Hopwood, and Sir George Gibb.

The following representatives of the Shipbuilding Employers' Federation were present:

Mr. G. J. Carter (Messrs. Cammell, Laird, and Co., Limited, Birkenhead), Mr. James Marr (Messrs. J. L. Thompson and Co., Limited, Sunderland), Mr. H. B. Rowell (Messrs. R. and W. Hawthorn Leslie and Co., Hebburn-on-Tyne), Mr. H. M. Napier (Messrs. Napier and Miller, Limited, Old Kilpatrick), Colonel R. Saxton White, Mr. F. E. W. Couer, Sir Charles Ottley (Sir W. G. Armstrong, Whitworth, and Co., Limited, Walker-on-Tyne and Newcastle-on-Tyne), Mr. F. N. Henderson (Messrs.

D. and W. Henderson and Co., Limited, Partick, Glasgow), Colonel J. M. Denny (Messrs. William Denny and Brothers, Dumbarton), Mr. A. B. Gowan (Messrs. Palmers Shipbuilding and Iron Company, Limited, Jarrow and Hebburn-on-Tyne), Mr. N. E. Peck (Messrs. Barclay, Curie, and Co., Limited, Whiteinch, Glasgow, and Messrs. Swan, Hunter, and Wigham Richardson, Limited, Neptune and Wallsend-on-Tyne), Mr. George Jones (Sir William Gray and Co., Limited, Hartlepool), Mr. W. Beardmore Stewart (Messrs. Beardmore and Co., Limited, Dalmuir, Glasgow), Mr. J. B. Hutchison (Messrs. Scott's Shipbuilding and Engineering Company, Limited, Greenock), Mr. J. Barr (Messrs. Vickers, Limited, Barrow), Mr. J. Hamilton (The Fairfield

Shipbuilding and Engineering Company, Limited, Govan), and Mr. Thomas Biggart and Mr. James Cameron, joint secretaries.

The deputation, which was representative of the leading shipbuilding firms in the country, was unanimous in urging that, in order to meet the national requirements at the present time, and the urgent necessities of the position, there should be a total prohibition during the period of the war of the sale of excisable liquors. It was represented by them that mere restriction of hours, or even total prohibition, witliin certain war areas, was not sufiicient, as certain classes would be entirely unaffected, and it was felt by the deputation that total prohibition should apply as an emergency war measure not only to public-houses, but to private clubs and other licensed premises, so as to operate equally for all classes of the community. In putting forward these views, those who spoke on behalf of the deputation expressed themselves as satisfied that there was a general consensus of opinion on the part of the workers favourable to total prohibition along the lines indicated.

Less Worlc than Before the War

It was stated that in many cases the number of hours being worked was actually less than before the war, and, in spite of Sunday labour and all other time, the total time worked on the average in almost all yards was below the normal number of hours per week. In spite of working night and day seven days a week, less productiveness was being secured by the men. The deputation was of opinion that this was principally due to the question of drink. There were many men doing splendid and strenuous work, probably as good as the men in the trenches. But so many were not working anything like full hours that the average was thus disastrously reduced. The members of the deputation stated that, speaking with the experience of from twenty-five to forty years, they believed that 80 per cent, of the present avoidable loss of time could be ascribed to no other cause than drink. The figures of weekly takings in public-houses near the yards were convincing evidence of the increased sale of liquor. Allowing for the enhanced price of intoxicants and for the greater number of men now employed in shipbuilding, the takings had in one case under observation risen 20 per cent., in another 40 per cent.

Curtailment, in the opinion of the deputation, resulted in excessive drinking during the shortened hours. The takings of certain public-houses which had had their hours reduced from ten to nine had actually increased, and there had been a considerable growth in the pernicious habit of buying spirits by the bottle and taking it away to drink elsewhere. It was this ' drinking habit' rather than drunkenness that the deputation had to face. The cost of the drink habit was sufficiently illustrated by the case of a battleship coming in for immediate repairs and having these repairs delayed a whole day through the absence of the riveters for the purpose of drink and conviviality. This case was one of hundreds.

This was not the only reason in favour of prohibition as against curtailment. As long as public-houses were open there would be found men to break the rules of the yard and come late to work in order to secure drink beforehand. And the indisposition to work after the consumption of excessive alcohol was too obvious to need elaboration.

Different members of the deputation gave different hours for their week's total of labour, but it was emphasised that the important factor was not the average time worked, but the time worked by certain of the most important branches. In one yard, for example, the riveters had only been working on the average forty hours per week, in another only thirty-six hours.

The deputation drew attention to the example set by Eussia and France, and urged upon the Chancellor of the Exchequer the need of strong and immediate action.

(C.) Summary op Statistical Material submitted to the Government by the Shipbuilding Employers' Federation

Hours actually Worked by Ironworkers

THE Shipbuilding Employers' Federation have laid before the Government detailed figures for the month of March 1915, taken out by 48 representative firms. Of these 48 firms, 15 are in the Clyde district, 27 in the North-East Coast District, and 6 at Birkenhead, Barrow, or Hull.

The figures analysed are not selected or merely illustrative figures. They are the record of the actual number of hours worked by every ' ironworker ' separately tabulated, and the resulting percentages are therefore based on precise and exhaustive facts.

By ironworkers are meant: platers, riveters, holders-on, heaters, angle-iron smiths, caulkers, and drillers. The work of these men determines the output of each shipbuilding yard.

The ordinary working week for ironworkers is 53 or 54 hours a week according to district (excluding overtime). Analysis of the hours now actually being worked shows that in spite of the effort to increase the output by overtime, the hours actually being worked are less than the hours of a normal week in a time of peace. Only a quarter of the ironworkers are working more than this.

Table I

Hours actually Worked by Ironworkers in March 1915 (Standard "Week in Time of Peace 53 or 54 hours (excluding

Overtime).)

The above analysis shows conclusively (a) Only 24 per cent, of the men are working more than a normal week of 53-54 hours.

(b) Of the remaining 76 per cent., 40 per cent, are working between 40 hours a week and the normal week of 53-54 hours; 36 per cent, are working under 40 hours per week.

(c) 493 men out of every 1000 are in time of war working less than 45 hours a week.

Comparison of Districts

This state of things is not peculiar to any one district. The following table shows the comparison between the Clyde and the North-East Coast ironworkers:

Table II Comparisons between Clyde and North-East Coast Ironworkers.

Clyde. North-East Coast

Clyde. North-East Coast

Clyde.

North-East Coast 27 6 per cent, worked over 53-54 hours per week. 1Q'7 39-4 40-5 39-8 40 hours and under 53-54.

under 40 hours per week.

An examination of the detailed statistics increases the significance of the summarised figures. For example, detailed sheets from a very important firm show in the case of every one of their ' drillers ' for four weeks in March how far each man (a) Failed to come to work until after breakfast; or (6) Was absent from work all day.

From these sheets it appeared: 1. The vast majority of the men fail either in (a) or (6).

2. A minority of workmen are absolutely regular in their attend- ance. They keep uniformly good time. There are also a few cases where the only absence throughout the period is an occasional absence before breakfast.

3. Many workmen made it an almost regular habit not to come until after breakfast.

4. When a workman keeps bad time, it is nearly always continued for several days running. Many of them are absent from work altogether for three, four, or five days.

The effect of the detailed sheets about the ' drillers' is shown in the following table. Similar results can be worked out for any other of the ironworkers:

Table III Record of 159 Drillers during 22 Days Sth March-lst April)

It must be remembered tbat these figures represent absences during ordinary working tours.

Another set of figures supplied by the same firm compares the absences from work of men in the Shipyard Department with those of men in (1) the Engine and Boiler Shops and (2) the Kepair Department. The special importance of these figures is that they show that while engineers are not as bad as shipyard workers, they are also keeping very bad time, while the bad time kept in the Repair Department is (having regard to the urgency of repairs) a specially serious matter.

The figures provided show the number of men of each class (platers, joiners, pattern-makers, fitters, c.) who were out all day for each day between the 1st March and the 8th April.

The figures have been extracted for a fortnight and put in summary form in a table as follows:

Table IV Men out all Day

The following points should be specially noted: 1. Monday and Saturday are usually the worst days. (There must have been some special cause influencing the 17th and 18th March.) 2. No Sunday work was being done, so the men had a week-end rest.

3. These figures are limited to all-day absence. No account is taken of failure to work before breakfast.

4. Absences in the Repair Department are particularly serious, and though engineers are not so bad, their figures indicate great delay in construction.

The 2nd to 5th April were holidays. On Tuesday the 6th April, 1798 men of the Shipyard Department failed to turn up; 1431 of the Engine and Boiler Shops, and 666 in the Repair Department; and the absences continued abnormal for some days. On the 7th April, 2916 men were out from work the first quarter of the day, of whom 1670 remained out all day. Even on the 8th, 2500 were out the first quarter, and 1500 remained out all day. The importance of these last figures lies in the fact that three days' holidays had been given to the men in these yards.

7s Drinjs the Cause of this abnormal Loss of Time?

The evidence is really overwhelming that the main cause of this alarming loss of time is the ' lure of drink." The employers say so most emphatically; the Admiralty have received elaborate reports emphasising the same conclusion in the case of shipbuilding, repairs, munitions of war, and transport. The Home Office reports are to the same effect, and the detailed figures summarised above are, in themselves, strong evidence that drink is the cause. A section of each class of workmen keep perfectly good time throughout the week, and therefore the cause is not one which is common to all workmen, or due to any general industrial condition. The worst time is generally kept after wages are paid, and at the beginning of the following week. When absence from work occurs the workman is usually absent for several days together. Staleness and fatigue no doubt must arise from working during long hours over an extended period, but inasmuch as half the men are not in fact working for more than 45 hours a week, the cause must be found elsewhere. The testimony of observers in each district is that drink is by far the most important factor. The facilities for excessive drinking in the immediate vicinity of these works are abundant; the men in many cases work at a long distance from their homes. The restriction of hours in these districts has rather tended to concentrate drinking into a period without diminishing the temptation, or limiting the quantity consumed.

' The contention that the cause of irregular hours is the excessive time worked is completely disposed of by observing that on average the time worked is unfortunately not so great as the standard in time of peace. The figures show, not that workmen who have been working long hours for days together occasionally take a day os, but that while some workmen are working steadily day by day for long hours, those who fail to work even ordinary hours are continually repeating this failure.

In conclusion it may be pointed out the detailed returns which have been furnished by the Shipbuilders' Federation show that during the four weeks of March, 670,000 hours of work have been avoidably lost. This is no less than 25 per cent, of the normal working hours.

(D.) Extract from Letter dated 26th March, 1915, from Admiral Sir John Jellicoe to the First Lord of the Admiralty:

I AM very uneasy about the labour situation on the Clyde and Tyne. I have sent a telegram or two lately about it. You may think I am exceeding my sphere of action in doing so, but the efficiency of this Fleet is so afiected by it that I felt it my duty to wire.

To-day an officer in a responsible position arrived. His account of things on the Clyde was most disquieting. He said that the men refused altogether to work on Saturday afternoon, that they took Wednesday afternoon ofi every week (if not the whole of Wednesday), and worked on Sunday because they got double pay for it. He said also that they only worked in a half-hearted manner. My destroyer dockings and refits are delayed in every case by these labour difficulties, and they take twice as long as they need do. I feel that you ought to know the facts, and so put them before you now.

(E.) Reports from Armament Works

THESE are not as serious as those received from the shipyards. They indicate, however, that much time is avoidably lost in some of the most important works.

For example, this is a report received on the 19th March, 1915, from important works engaged in the manufacture of munitions: ' Some drastic restrictions are absolutely necessary if largest possible output of certain war munitions is to be obtained. Among some shell workers there is a considerable amount of lost time due to their drinking habits. With the better class mechanics the time lost due to drinking is comparatively small, but in the case of labourers and the semi-skilled trade it is a very serious item."

Another most important firm reports: ' Speaking generally, margin of lost time allowed by us before the war has now to be trebled. Conditions much worse in shipyards. Much of this loss of time is attributable to drink."

In another report from these works it is said:

Loss of time from drink most noticeable in shell department, about 10 per cent, of total time worked."

In another important munitions works:

Avoidable loss of time considerable among a minority."

Even in districts least heard of in this connection, and from which fewest complaints are received, all say that work would be considerably improved were there a restriction of facilities for the sale of intoxicating liquor.

The following are particulars of a week's work in April in one of the most important shell shops in England:

Particulars of Times Worked in Week ending April 13,1915

Per thousand.

Working over 80 hours per week 75 up to 80 hours per week

Percentage who have worked 53 hours per week and over Percentage who have worked 40 hours per week and under 53 Percentage who have worked under 40 hours per week

Men.

Note. The percentage of time lost for the corresponding week of last year amounted to 7-8.

Here is a report, dated the 16tli March, 1915, which came from works engaged in the manufacture of high explosives: ' We would also take this opportunity of expressing in the strongest possible manner our opinion that something should be done in this district to curtail the sale of drink. We fear that unless drastic steps are taken to lessen the sale of alcohol, before long we shall find it impossible to deliver anything like the quantities of trinitrotoluene we have imdertaken to supply to your department. Even at the present time we are not tvirning out as much as we could otherwise, owing to various troubles, and this is due to the fact that the men have been making good money and unfortunately wasting most of it in drink. Consequently, they are in such a condition that it is impossible for them to attend to their duties in a proper manner even when they come to the works, which is at odd times and to suit their own convenience."

There are several works engaged in the production of munitions of which this is not in the least true. Here again the great majority of the workmen are above reproach, and their action is praiseworthy.

(jr.) Report of Inquiries made by the Home Office in regard

TO Loss OF Time in the Shipbuilding Trades

THE inquiries were made by 33 investigators, 17 of whom were sent to various places on the Clyde, 6 to Newcastle and the Tyne, 4 to Barrow, and 2 each to Sunderland, Stockton, and West Hartlepool respectively. The inquiries occupied three days, from the 1st to the 3rd April inclusive.

Separate districts were marked out for each investigator. Detailed instructions were given them in which they were asked to ascertain the principal causes which had led to the loss of time among the workers, and the questions put to them were so framed as not to prejudice their judgment.

Each investigator made a separate report of the results of his inquiry without collaboration with his colleagues. A general summary of these reports is attached, followed by a more detailed summary of the reports, arranged according to districts.

The inquiries made by these investigators have been supplemented by reports from three factory inspectors, which are printed in full.

April 12, 1915.

(a) General Summary

Shipbuilding is the main industry of the districts visited, but there are also many engineering works and other factories engaged on Government contracts.

Owing to the demands made by the war on the trades engaged in shipbuilding and the manufacture of munitions, the pressure of work in these districts is unprecedented. The demand for labour is greater than the supply, especially as large numbers of the regular workmen have enlisted in the naval or military forces. Wages are uniformly high, which means a large increase in the spending power of the working classes. Wages of 51. or Ql. a week are common, and it is possible for a skilled and energetic mechanic to earn as much as 101. or 15 a week.

The hours of work are about fifty-four a week, excluding overtime. The day is divided into two shifts of eleven or twelve hours with intervals for meals, but many of the men work overtime. There is also a certain amount of Sunday labour with the attraction of double pay, but this has not proved altogether a success. Steady workmen feel the strain of working seven days a week, while others are disposed to work on Sunday and lose time on other days. An important feature of shipbuilding is the system of working in gangs consisting of two riveters, one holder-up, and one or two boys. While many of the men are working regularly and steadily beyond the normal hours, there is a considerable number, especially among the ' black squad," in the shipbuilding yards who are not working up to the maximum of their capacity. The riveters are mentioned particularly, and some distinction is drawn between them and the mechanics employed in engineering factories.

The reasons given for irregularities of attendance are mainly staleness and fatigue due to long hours over an extended period: unusually high wages leading to idleness: and habits of drinking. It is not altogether possible to isolate these causes, as they are more or less closely connected with one another, but the reports are unanimous in the conclusion that drink is by far the most important factor.

Many of the workmen engaged in these industries are, in normal times, heavy drinkers, partly, no doubt, owing to the nature of the work. Much of it is hard manual labour in severe heat, which creates a desire for stimulant. It is not suggested that all the workmen drink heavily. Many of them are abstemious, and in Scotland especially there is a considerable proportion of teetotallers. To those who are heavy drinkers, the facilities for drinking are unfortunately very great. An instance is given in one street where there were no less than thirty public-houses within a distance of half-a-mile. The yards and works are surrounded by public-houses and drinking-bars, where every possible facility is offered for obtaining drink for consumption both on and off the premises.

The drinking habits of the workmen on the Clyde differ somewhat from those of the English workmen. The popular drink there is half-a-gill of whisky, quickly followed by a schooner of beer (about I pint), and the beer is of a heavier quality than English beer. This particular combination of liquor, though it does not apparently produce much effect on the hardened drinker at the moment, is not calculated to improve the capacity of the men for sustained work. Heavy drinking on Saturday in the public-houses, and on Sundays in clubs, is described as a feature of the life of the workmen on the Clyde, which frequently results in unfitness or loss of time at the beginning of the week. There is also a prevalent practice in Scotland of taking whisky in bottles home in the evening, especially on Saturday night for consumption on Sunday when the public-houses are closed. On the Tyne and in Barrow, spirit drinking is not so common, as the popular drink is beer, and the English workman's drinking appears to be more evenly distributed over the week, though the effect is very much the same in all the districts referred to.

Apart from the public-house great facilities for drinking are offered by clubs, which are open to members and to which visitors can be readily introduced. These places are freely resorted to on Sundays when the public-houses are closed.

Attention is drawn in the reports to the fact that many of the workmen take insufficient food, which not only increases the temptation to drink, but makes the effect of the liquor taken more injurious, so that the result is to incapacitate the workmen for the strain of heavy work. The men whose homes are near the works are able to obtain meals without difficulty, but owing to the lack of housing accommodation many workmen are obliged to travel long distances to get to their work. This is especially the case at Barrow-in-Furness. The usual practice is for the workmen to take cold food with them, which is generally consumed in the public-houses with their liquor. Reference is made in some of the reports to cases where food could not be obtained at the public-houses, and it is evident that the sale of drink is out of all proportion to that of food. The reports emphasise the need for mess-rooms and canteens in the yards where the men could get good meals in comfort without having to resort to the public-houses. Such accommodation is very rarely provided.

The practice of paying the whole wages of a ' black squad ' to the leader is also said to be productive of drinking, as the men go to the public-house to divide the money, and the custom is for each member of the squad to stand drinks all round.

It is stated that some of the worst offenders in the matter of drinking are men who in normal times are not employed in the yards but who now, owing to the scarcity of labour, have been given work. Where a large proportion of the steadiest men have enlisted, and great numbers of inferior men are brought in to meet the pressure, a general increase in drinking is inevitable.

The investigators say that trade union restrictions which might tend to diminish the output have been very generally abrogated to meet the exceptional conditions, though some of the men still display reluctance to undertake different work from that to which they are accustomed.

Much absenteeism is caused by the ' black squad ' system. If one of the members of the squad is absent from idleness, or drinking, the rest of the squad is held up, and where several squads are affected the cumulative result is very marked. To some extent this evil is being met by pooling men, so that if one of a squad is away his place can be taken by another.

The evils of excessive drinking were readily admitted by some of the better work-men, who considered that the action of a minority was bringing unmerited discredit on the workmen as a whole. Others considered that the part played by drinking had been exaggerated, that the workmen had been subjected to too great a pressure and were suffering from the strain, and that the deficiency of output was largely due, especially on the Clyde, to the withdrawal of skilled men, who should be recalled from the colours.

(b) Detailed Summaries

The Clyde

Scotstoun and Clydebank. The investigators who visited Scots-toun and Clydebank came to the conclusion that the falling-o E in output is mainly due to excessive drinking, especially at the weekends. Fatigue and insufficient food are contributory causes. The day-shift men have an interval for dinner from 1.30 to 2.15, when a considerable portion of the workmen indulge in drinking. The day-shift ends at 5.30, when a smaller number of men take a drink before their tea. At 9.45 p. m. the night-shift men have an interval of ten minutes, when some of them get drink.

There are large numbers of drinking bars in the neighbourhood of the works with circular bars designed for quick service. There is, as a rule, no seating accommodation, but they are said to be well conducted.

Although there is a considerable amount of drinking during mealtimes, most of the drinking takes place on Saturdays at the drinking bars. One of the features of these bars is the preparation for drinking after wages have been paid. Three or four hundred glasses of whisky are made ready to meet the rush of customers, and in some cases some of the workmen are taken on to help in the service. These are called ' 5s. helpers." If drinking were limited to Saturdays, and the men took a rest on Sundays, they might recover in time for the work on Monday, but unfortunately men take bottles of whisky home with them, which is frequently consumed the same night. Although the public-houses are closed on Sunday, it is also easy for them to obtain liquor at the various clubs. These places are restricted to members, but they are able to introduce one or more visitors. The clubs are used not only on Sundays, but also on weekdays late at night when the public-houses are closed. The normal drink taken by the men is half a gill of whisky followed by three-quarters of a pint of beer, and the gravity of the beer is said to be higher in Scotland than in England.

The workers admit that the output could be increased, but in their opinion many of them are overtired from working long hours of overtime, and they also allege that their meals are insufficient owing to the want of proper accommodation for getting meals in the yards. Others allege that the want of skilled labour is the chief cause of the falling ofi of output, and those who are employed are working as hard as possible.

It is stated that the trade union restrictions have been set aside in the present emergency, but they still exist to a certain extent, as many workmen will not accept work outside their own particular line.

Renfrew and Govan. In one of the reports a distinction is drawn between the engineers and iron-turners engaged mainly on the production of shell cases, and the men who comprise the ' black squads ' employed in shipbuilding. The former are said to be working strenuously and are very abstemious, many of them being teetotallers. Instances are given of engineers working thirty-six hours at a stretch, with intervals for meals. The ' black squads," on the other hand, are frequently held up by irregularities on the part of members of the gang. Attention is drawn to the practice of paying the ' squads ' a lump sum, which is afterwards divided in the public-house. This leads to treating all round and much heavy drinking, and it is suggested that if each man could be paid his own wages there would be an improvement.

Although the amount of drinking during the day did not appear to be excessive having regard to the character of the work, a large number of men drink to excess at the end of the week. One of the investigators states that in one public-house in Govan between 12.30 and 1.35 p. m. on Saturday he saw 100l. taken. The national drink is a half gill of whisky, price id., followed by a schooner of beer, price 2J(Z. The beer in Scotland is heavier than in England. Bottles of whisky are also sold in large quantities on Saturday night, as the public-houses are closed on Sunday. Drinking goes on very largely on Sunday in clubs, and this is responsible for a lot of time lost on Monday.

Another reason suggested for the deficiency of output is that many skilled men have joined the colours, and their places have been filled by unskilled men. If some of the men who have enlisted could be sent back the output would be materially increased.

The public-houses are large open bars without seating accommodation. They have conspicuous notices affixed," Liberty and sobriety: avoid excess."

Large numbers of bottles, varying in price from 6d. to 2s., are put ready in the public-houses, to be carried away just before closing time for use the next morning, owing to public-houses not opening until 10 A. M. In some cases men wait about in the morning till they do open, preferring the loss of time to going without their morning drink.

In none of the yards on the Clyde, except one at Govan, is there any accommodation for taking meals. Men have to go long distances to and from their homes, and form the habit of taking refreshment by the way. The provision of accommodation for meals inside the works would be greatly appreciated, and would lessen temptation to drink.

Partich, Pointhouse, Old Kilpatrich, Dalmuir, and Whiteinch. There was not much evidence of excessive drinking during the day in this district, though men frequent public-houses at meal-times. In the evening, about 6 o'clock, the men resort to the public-houses and drink freely. Week-end drinking is the principal feature. After being paid on Saturday men adjourn in parties to the public-houses and indulge in drinks all round. The popular drink is half a gill of whisky swallowed at a gulp, followed by a schooner (three-quarters of a pint) of beer. Afterwards many of them adjourn to a football match or other amusement, and then return to the public-houses for the rest of the day. In the evening bottles of whisky are taken home for Sunday drinking, but they are often consumed the same evening. On Sundays drink is freely obtained in clubs, where members can introduce visitors. Liquor is also obtained from the licensed grocers, who deliver whisky or bottled beer to their customers.

The method of working known as the ' black squad ' is said to encourage excessive drinking. A ' black squad ' is composed of one blacksmith, two riveters, one holder-up, and two boys. The wages are paid to the principal of the squad, and the money is divided in a public-house, when the custom of standing drinks all round is observed. One of the investigators states that during the conversations which he had with some of the workers in the ' black squads," they gave him the impression that they could not perform the work of holding and striking hot metal without the aid of stimulants.

The men complain that there are no places in the yards where they can take their meals. The majority of the men are of opinion that the workmen employed are turning out as much as possible, but there is a want of skilled labour, as many of the younger skilled men have enlisted, and their places are filled by inferior workmen. A good deal of time is lost where one member of a ' black squad' fails to turn up and the rest are obliged to stand down for the day. This defect has been remedied to some extent by the system of pooling men, by which men can be found to take the place of absentees.

Dumbarton. Two reports were made on the conditions found at Dumbarton, in which deficiency of output is attributed partly to fatigue on the part of the steadier workmen, principally those who have been working overtime on hard manual work, and partly to excessive drinking by a minority of the workmen. A number of the best workmen have joined the army, and their places have been filled by men who, prior to the war, did little or no work, or existed on what the regular workers would give them. It was suggested that if some of the men who have joined the army were allowed to return to their work it would have a good efiect on the output.

As regards drinking habits, there were not many signs of drunkenness, but the public-houses were well patronised during meal times. In addition to drink consumed on the premises the men were in the habit of purchasing whisky in bottles, which usually contain a ' mutchkin," or just over half a pint. The usual drink in Dumbarton, as in other parts of Scotland, is whisky followed by beer. Many of the men have two or three such drinks on each visit to the public-house. One of the investigators mentions the case of a workman who had been away from work five days drinking, and had spent 1 a day in drink for himself and other persons. He was decidedly shaky, though not drunk. He was expecting to work on the sixth day, but it was obvious that he was not in a condition to stand hard work for any length of time.

The difficulty of working in squads where one of the squad is absent from drink may be obviated to some extent by a new arrangement, which seems likely to be made in the shipbmlding yards at Dumbarton, for pooling the squads. "Where there are several broken squads, complete squads would be formed by allowing a riveter to act as a holder-up, etc. This is against the ordinary trade union rules, but has been agreed to.

Some of the better-class workmen suggest that the drinking problem would be overcome by closing the public-houses outside, and opening canteens inside, the yards. Many of them, who are apparently anxious to do their best to expedite the output, expressed the opinion that some stimulant is necessary for men engaged in some branches of shipbuilding.

The public-houses in Scotland being closed on Sunday, a practice has grown up of purchasing whisky on Saturday night. One of the investigators noticed a barman who had filled about 100 bottles of whisky which he expected to sell between half-past nine and closing time. The result is that the men are able to drink on Sunday and are frequently unfit for work on Monday morning. The question of prohibition has been much discussed in Dumbarton; many of the working men are in favour either of total prohibition or of suspending the sale of liquor for consumption ofe the premises. Total prohibition would meet with considerable opposition from others.

The suggestion made by one investigator is that the public-houses should be closed during meal hours and also from 12 to 3 on Saturdays in order to induce the workman to go to his home with his wages and get proper meals. The practice of taking drink without food has a bad efiect on their physical condition.

Greenock. The men are working more than normally, and loss of time may be due in some cases partly to fatigue and partly to wet weather; but, generally speaking, it is due to the temptation to idleness owing to good wages and heavy drinking among a minority.

Drinking is indulged in especially on Saturdays, Mondays, and Tuesdays, when drunken persons can be seen both m the streets and public-houses. The favourite drink is whisky, followed by beer, and if spirit drinking were stopped there would be less drunkenness. Many of the workmen admitted that drink was the chief cause of the decrease of output, and advocated universal prohibition.

The public-houses are open from 10 a. m. until 9 p. m., so that early and late drinking is prevented; but there is a great deal of liquor taken during the meal-times by men on the day-shift, and in the afternoon by men working on the night-shift.

The system of working in squads also leads to drinking where one of the squad is absent from any cause, and the usual result is that the whole squad goes ofe work and drinks.

While the above statement in regard to excessive drinking is true of a considerable number of the workmen, there are many who are working very hard, and who feel the strain of the prolonged hours. The more respectable workmen are in favour of drastic restriction, and even prohibition, either of spirits or of all liquor, and the belief is that some such steps will be taken. Prohibition on the Clyde or in Scotland alone would lead to trouble; the men say that if prohibition is to come it must apply to the whole country.

There are plenty of facilities for drinking in Greenock. The public-houses have small rooms like cubicles, where several men can sit comfortably round a small table and drink as long as they wish, as they are free from observation. The suggestion was made in the town that the firm should establish canteens in the yards.

Port Glasgow. This small town on the Clyde has a population of about 17,000, almost entirely supported by shipbuilding.

Men work from 6 a. m. to 9 a. m., 9.45 a. m. to 1 p. m., and 2 to 5.30 P. M. On Saturdays work ends at noon. The week's work is fifty-four hours, but there is much lost time as well as insufficiency of labour. The loss of time is attributed mainly to drink, especially in the evenings. The public-houses are open from 10 a. m. to 9 p. m. (instead of 8 a. m. to 10 p. m. before the war). In many cases men prefer to wait until 10 a. m. in order to get a drink before going to work, thereby losing half a day. The popular drink is four pennyworth of whisky followed by a pint of beer. The investigator could find no evidence of men being overtired or idling because of good wages. Most of the men are in ordinary times heavy drinkers, and while further restrictions are needed, prohibition wovdd be resented. The establishment of canteens in the works would be a great safeguard.

The Tyne

Six investigators visited various places on the Tyne, including Newcastle, Walker, Elswick, Hebburn, Wallsend, and North and South Shields. The war has brought great prosperity to all workers on the Tyne generally, with the result that high wages are readily obtained by all who are willing to work. Many of the men attracted by high wages are working steadily and during long hours, and some of the regular workmen become stale and need an occasional holiday. The general impression, however, is that the loss of time, which is considerable, is due to idleness, and especially to drink. It is not alleged that there is a large amount of open drunkenness, though one of the investigators states that at 7.30 a. m. in South Shields he saw fifteen men who had come off the night-shift all under the influence of drink, and several of them hopelessly drunk; but there is plenty of evidence of heavy drinking. The public-houses on the Tyne are generally open from 8 a. m. to 9 p. m., with the exception of South Shields, where the public-houses open at 6 a. m. There is some drinking during the breakfast and dinner hours, but the principal time of drinking is at night, when all the public-houses are crowded. The majority drink beer, not spirits, and the extra halfpenny on beer has not led to a change from beer to spirits, as money is plentiful; but more spirit is drunk than is usual with English workmen, and there is some drinking of spirit and beer mixed. The habit of drinking in batches is a common feature on the Tyne. Four or five men on the same shift will enter a public-house, and each stands drink successively. One investigator saw five men consume five half-pints each in less than ten minutes.

It is said that the payment of double wages for Sunday labour has led to idling on Monday, and no doubt the drinking on Saturday and Sunday has produced the same result. For this reason it is suggested that special restrictions should be made in regard to Monday hours. The earlier opening of public-houses at South Shields not only invites early drinking among workmen from that place, but also attracts men from Jarrow and Hebburn.

Two of the investigators comment on the insufficient food which the men take, partly owing to the difficulty of getting food in the public-houses. It is thought that in this way they are more easily affected by the amount of liquor which they consume, and are consequently unfitted for hard work.

Generally, the effect of the reports from the Tyne is that drinking is a serious evil, largely leading to loss of time, and that fiirther restriction should be placed on the hours during which public-houses are open. Local opinion expects some such restrictions, but would not tolerate total prohibition.

It may be added that shortage of labour has led to the employment of men who would not in ordinary times be given employment, and no doubt they are more likely to take to drink than the regular workman.

One of the investigators, who has had experience of workers in Government establishments, states that he has never seen so much drinking at all times of the day as he witnessed in Newcastle and the surrounding district.

Sunderland

The chief industry is shipbuilding, which employs most of the working population. As in other places, the men work in two shifts covering the twenty-four hours, 6 a. m. to 6 p. m., and 6 p. m. to 5 a. m., with two stoppages of half-an-hour for meals. There is no work between 5 a. m. and 6 a. m. The two investigators who visited Sunderland say that drinking is very prevalent, and that this rather than fatigue is the cause of loss of time. Many men idle because of their good wages, and it is suggested that the temptation to idle from this cause might be met if the employers would bank a portion of the wages until the war is over. It is said that many of the men would willingly agree to this suggestion

The public-houses, of which there are a large number (in one street thirty in the space of half-a-mile), open at 6 a. m. and close at 9 p. m. Thesunday hours are 12.30 to 2.30 p. m. and 6 to 9 p. m. One of the features of the public-houses in Sunderland is the sitting-room where tables and lounges are placed and liquor is brought to the customer. These sitting-rooms are crowded nightly, mostly by the better-class workmen, and they are used by men and women alike. Beer is the popular drink, and it is sold at 2d. per glass of rather under half-a-pint to meet the increase of duty.

The early hour at which the public-houses open seems to be a great incentive to drinking, as the men coming ofi the night-shift loiter about until the public-houses open, and those starting on the day-shift remain drinking and are late at the yards. One of the investigators visited several public-houses between 6 and 7 a. m. and asked for a cup of tea or coffee, but he was told that it could not be supplied, and apparently nothing can be purchased except liquor and cigarettes. There is a great deal of time lost on Monday owing to Sunday drinking.

The drink question is apparently a common topic of conversation among the workmen in Sunderland, and many of them would like to see the public-houses closed altogether during the war, but there are others who say they cannot work without beer, especially where the work is in intense heat, and the opinion is that the case could be met if the public-houses were closed for consimiption of liquor on the premises, but opened for about two hours in the middle of the day for the sale of bottled beer to be consumed os the premises. The suggestion also was put forward that canteens should be provided at the works where food and beer could be obtained.

West Hartlepool

About 12,000 to 15,000 are employed in shipbuilding, engineering, and steel and iron works. The normal hours are, for the day-shift from 6 A. M. to 5 p. m., and for the night-shift from 6 P. M. to 6 A. M., with intervals for meals. Overtime is worked by a good many, but there is very little Sunday work. The two investigators who visited Hartlepool did not think that the men suffered from fatigue and they heard no complaints of the kind: the workmen looked healthy and cheerful. Good wages were causing idleness in some cases, but generally speaking the men were working well. Drink does cause loss of time, but the efiect on output would not be very considerable.

The public-houses open at 8 a. m. and close at 9 p. m., and on Sundays from 12.30 to 2 p. m. and 6 to 9 p. m. The men are unable to obtain liquor on their way to their work, but they drink freely during the intervals for breakfast and dinner. They carry food in their pockets, which they take to the public-houses to eat. The favourite drink is a glass of whisky or rum followed by a pint of beer, which is sometimes repeated. Public-houses are very busy in the evening, and though there is too much heavy drinking, there is comparatively little drunkenness. The consumption of spirits has somewhat increased since the extra tax on beer. There is a good case for restricting fiirther the hours during which the public-houses are open, especially during the breakfast hour, but prohibition would cause a great deal of trouble in the labour world.

Both these investigators thought that the output was affected by trade union re-strictions, For instance, a squad is frequently held up by the absence of one of their number, although the work could proceed with other assistance if it were not for trade union rules, which do not allow one class of job to be done by a man of a different trade.

Stockton-on-Tees

The two investigators who made the inquiries in Stockton-on-Tees came to the conclusion that loss of time was due solely to drinking; although many of the workmen complained that overwork made them stiff and that they were thus unable to keep time. This especially applies to the men working in squads, as frequently one of them fails to turn up and thus prevents the whole squad from working. The public-houses are open from 8 a. m. until 9 p. m. (the hours before the war were 6 a. m. and 11 p. m.), and on Sundays 12 to 12.30 and 6 to 9. The favourite drink is beer, taken in great quantities, and very little spirit is drunk. When the public-houses were opened at 6 a. m. a good trade was done with men on their way to their work. This has now stopped, but there is reason to believe that men take beer home with them in the evening for early morning consumption. Stockton is well supplied with public-houses, many of them close to each other, and these are all crowded in the evenings and on Saturday afternoons with workmen drinking beer. The publicans appear to be taking as much money within the restricted hours as when the hours of opening were longer.

Barrow-in-Furness

Barrow has a population of about 70,000, and of these about 20,000 are employed at Messrs. Vickers, Son, and Maxim, and about 3,000 at the Hematite Steel Works.

The men work in two shifts: Day-shift from 6 a. m. until 5 P. M., with intervals of half-an-hour for breakfast and an hour for dinner. Night-shift, 5 p. m. until 6 a. m., with intervals of two hours for meals. Some of the men, chiefly shell-makers, work two or three hours overtime.

The four reports agree that there was little evidence of drunkenness in the streets, and few cases of drunkenness had been brought into the Courts, but there was evidence to show that during the particular week when the inquiry was made there had been considerably less drinking than recently, owing probably to the fact that the employers had offered double wages on Good Friday and one and a-half wages on Saturday morning to men who had worked regularly all the week, which was a distinct incentive to the workmen to remain sober. It is not clear that the conditions were normal when the inquiries were made.

There was evidence to show that there had been less drinking since the hours of the public-houses had been restricted. They now open from 10.30 a. m. and close at 10 p. m.; on Sundays they are open from 12.30 to 2 and 6.30 to 9. The publicans do not, however, seem to have been hit by the restricted hours, as the men drink more heavily during the shorter period and some take drink away with them.

The men are not spirit drinkers, although the influx of men from Scotland has led to the greater sale of spirits. They are generally drinking at present a rather expensive beer known as ' 6d. and lod.," which is a combination of two beers priced at lod. and Qd. a quart respectively, and sold at 5d. a pint. Prior to the present boom the men could only afiord to drink beer at 3d. a pint, A good deal of beer is consumed in the evening and on Saturday afternoon and evening, but on the whole there was not at the time of the reports very much ground for complaint, though much time had been lost in the past through heavy drinking.

Though the drinking habit may have had serious effects on output, it appears that excessive drinking is not very general. The majority of the men seem to have been keeping good time and working long hours, and there was evidence of fatigue and staleness. The reports indicate that better work could be got out of the men if they were on three shifts of eight hours, but this would be impossible without a large number of extra men, and a great increase in the accommodation.

Accommodation is very diflcult to get, and many of the workmen have to live outside Barrow, at places several miles away. In some cases this increases the temptation to drink, as men have to pass public-houses on their way to and from work. It also appears that the means of travelling are inadequate. It is suggested in one of the reports that increased accommodation could be provided by vessels in the docks.

(2) EEPOKTS OF FACTOEY INSPECTOES

The Clyde

I have had many interviews from time to time with shipbuilders and engineers on the subject of bad timekeeping among workmen, and to-day I have supplemented my information by interviewing the Chief Constable of Govan and a number of publicans in an area surrounding the largest shipbuilding yards.

There does not appear to be any noticeable increase of drinking since the war began. The quantity consumed is about normal, the same men frequent the same premises, and those inclined to drink too much continue as before the war commenced. There is, however, some evidence that small bottles of whisky are purchased and consumed off the premises, especially by men on night-shift work. This, however, is confined to a very few men. For instance, in a yard employing 10.000, three men in one night were found partially intoxicated in the works and expelled.

In fairness to the men it should be noted that irregular time is confined largely to certain specific trades: riveters, caulkers, platers, riggers, and to a very much less extent engineers, are the chief offenders; such tradesmen as pattern-makers, moulders, turners, and time-workers generally keep relatively good time. Broadly speaking, the men engaged in outdoor work, that is, on the construction of the ship itself, usually piece-workers, are responsible for most of the irregular time, and their behaviour has cast a stigma on the general class of workers employed in shipbuilding and marine engineering which is certainly not justified by the facts, and it is undeserved.

Coming to the causes of irregular timekeeping among the outdoor workers, while drinking is an important source of bad timekeeping, it is only one cause, and here again the action of a relatively small proportion will disorganise the work of many others who may be capable and willing to work full time. Riveters and platers work in squads, but if one man fails to turn up at 6 a. m. the squad cannot proceed, and because of the absence of one man four or five will lose a morning's or possibly a whole day's work. Riveting is hard and exhausting work, and it is frequently and necessarily carried on in trying conditions exposure in winter to bitter cold and damp. The temptation to take a morning or a day ofi during very cold or very hot weather is great, as the riveter knows he is indispensable at present, and will not lose his job if he does lie off. Moreover, his pay is sufficient, even with a partial week's work, to keep him and his family in comfort. The machine men working under cover are in a comfortable shop and have not the same temptation to lie off. Again the pay is relatively much less, and being time-workers they cannot make up the lost time by a special spurt. Another important point frequently overlooked is that at present, owing to the extraordinary scarcity of skilled labour, men who in ordinary times would never be employed on account of their irregular habits, are at work in many yards, and materially affect the numbers of those losing time. Briefly, I am convinced that the black squad ' piece-workers have not risen much above the social position of the man earning 30s. a-week, yet their remuneration is equal to that of a professional man. They have not yet been educated to spend their wages wisely, and the money is largely wasted, for they have few interests and little to spend their wages on apart from alcohol.

For some reason, diflcult to define, men do not readily take up riveting and plating, and consequently there is a constant shortage of this class. This shortage has tended to force up wages to such an extent that the present pay is in excess of their needs. The fear of loss of employment is absent, consequently there is no spur to stimulate a man to work regularly such as exists in most callings.

The question of fatigue due to prolonged overtime does not arise to any great extent. The same men do not work overtime week after week, and Sunday work is only done by the same man every second or third Sunday. The general feeling among employers is that Sunday work with double pay is not a success, it is considered that stopping it would improve timekeeping in the rest of the week.

One large works has just taken a vote of their men on the question of further restrictions, and I attach particulars of the questions put to them, and the percentage of men in favour of each alternative.

Per Cent.

1. Are you in favour of total prohibition?. 31 2. Are you in favour of leaving matters as at present?. 44 3. Are you in favour of reducing hours to from 12 noon to 2 P. M. and 7 to 9 p. m., and on Saturday 6 to 10 p. m.? 11 4. Are you in favour of reducing hours to from 7 p. m. to 9 P. M. on week-days, and Saturday from 6 p. m. to 5. Leaving hours as at present, but for sale of beer only. 10

Out of the 2500 men employed about two-thirds voted.

Most of the drink on the Clyde is consumed on licensed premises; it is not the habit to drink much in the homes. A prohibition of the purchase of alcohol for consumption off the premises would possibly improve one class only, namely, those who have to work at night, and now take liquor to their place of employment. One must also, recognise that teetotallers lose time as well as those who do not abstain. Away from shipbuilding pure and simple there does not appear to be any serious irregular timekeeping; it does not exist to any material extent in engineering generally, nor in the iron and steel producing towns in Lanarkshire.

The whole question has arisen because of the action of a few men in the more important shipbuilding yards, and there is a feeling that the mass of workers throughout the country should not be penalised because of the dissipated and unpatriotic behaviour of a small minority of overpaid men in one or two specific callings.

More comfortable working conditions improve timekeeping; for instance, during the last three weeks of fine bright weather distinctly better time has been kept. Again, much time lost by the ' black squad ' is due to wet and windy weather; work outside is difficult and almost impossible under such conditions unless the building berth is a roofed one. To meet this difficulty, sheds are being built over the berths devoted to submarines and small shallow draft craft.

Figures showing the percentage of hours lost by outside workers are valueless unless allowance is made for the periods in which work was impossible owing to weather conditions. It is not uncommon for men to work on piece work until their clothing is wet through, and the experience of employers is that in this condition, if they hang about afterwards, colds and chills supervene, with perhaps the consequent loss of a week or fortnight's employment. These facts I mention so that the men's position can be given full justice.

April 3, 1915. HARRY J. WILSON.

The Tyne

I beg to report that I have taken a deep interest in the subject of lost time since the commencement of the war, and on every possible occasion I have made it a point to discuss the subject with employers, managers, foremen, and with the workers themselves. The following statements show the conclusions I have arrived at: 1. So far as shipyard workers are concerned, there is no doubt whatever, in my mind, that the ' drinking habit' is more responsible than any other cause for the great loss of time amongst the workmen. It is common knowledge to those who know the habits of shipyard workers in this district, that in normal times they usually indulge pretty heavily every week-end, and that Monday is a very bad day as regards the time worked. In the present time of continuous employment, this week-end habit is to some extent broken up, but results in spasmodic indulgence at irregular intervals during the week. The fact that double time is paid for Sunday work, and that consequently the men's earnings are so much more than usual, no doubt tends to foster the habit of frequent indulgence in drink.

As regards engineers and armament workers, and others engaged in emergency work, the drinking habit undoubtedly plays an important part, although to a lesser extent, in the reasons given for lost time. Only yesterday I was informed by an engineering employer that a number of his men occasionally stopped work at 8 P. M. instead of 9 p. m., the usual overtime period. He explained that, when asked the reason for their action, the workmen informed him that ' the " pubs " closed at 9 p. m. and they wanted a few drinks before closing time." He stated further that he had noticed that the men who indulged in this practice formed the majority of the late arrivals next morning.

The ' drinking habit' is not confined to men alone in this district. I have had similar complaints as regards women workers in rope and waggon cover works.

2. The fact that double pay is given for Sunday work no doubt is also a factor in the situation. The men openly state that they can afford to have a ' good time ' (as they call it) occasionally, without reducing their wages below normal. In one large engineering works recently I was shown a statement which one of the directors had prepared. This showed that a large number of men systematically lost time during the week equivalent to nearly a full normal day, so that the Sunday work on double time was of no real value at all to the firm. He also pointed out that a fair percentage of the men good, steady workmen kept excellent time week after week.

I have formed an opinion that Sunday labour can only be made of real value if the sale of alcoholic liquor is entirely prohibited except under doctors' prescription.

3. I do not place a great deal of reliance on fatigue having much to do with lost time. I think the financial aspect combined with the indulgence in drink is solely responsible.

In several works recently I have been informed that the employers intend, as an experiment, to introduce a new system, whereby if a man loses more than a quarter of a day from Monday to Saturday inclusive, he will not be allowed to work on Sunday at all. This is, I think, an excellent plan, as, if the lost time is due to fatigue, it gives the workman a day's rest on Sunday, and if due to a drinking bout, it will reduce the man's wages and make him perhaps more careful the following week. Further, if in a riveting or plating squad one of the men keeps bad time and is not allowed to work on Sunday, it will probably prevent the squad working on Sunday altogether, and consequently the man's mates will put pressure upon him to keep better time.

W. B. LAUDEE.
April 2, 1915.
Barrow-in-Furness

Since tlie outbreak of the war I have paid five visits to the above firm in connection with Emergency Orders, and on each occasion have made inquiries as to loss of time by the workers and the question of drinking. At my second visit, owing to an allegation made that the reasons why Vickers could not obtain sufficient men, and why they were continually losing their men, were that they did not pay them so highly and they had ' a bad name ' amongst the workers, I took the opportunity of going round some of the public-houses in the evening and mixing freely with the men. I then ascertained that the general opinion was that Vickers was an extremely good shop. There was plenty of drinking, though I saw no actual cases of drunkenness up to 9 p. m. The men gave me the impression that they could stand a fair amount of liquor without showing signs of drunkenness.

At subsequent visits I have always noted that the public-houses in Barrow were well patronised during the daytime, and one always saw a number of men in their working clothes in the vicinity of these, with signs that they had had quite as much liquor as they could carry, though I have never seen a workman actually drunk in the town.

1. I think the drinking habit is prevalent in Barrow amongst riveters and platers and the less skilled workers and labourers. At my visit last month several of the foremen whom I interviewed said that drinking had always been rather bad in Barrow, and was now worse than ever. The statement was made that restriction of the hours of public-houses should be uniform throughout the district. Serious complaint was made by several of the managers that though the Barrow public-houses were open only between 9 A. M. and 9 p. m. there were no restrictions at Dalton 6 miles away, and many of the night-shift men took train to Dalton and started drinking there soon after 6 a. m., as the Barrow public-houses were not open. I was unable, for lack of time, to verify this statement personally.

2. I doubt if there is anything like the amount of fatigue among the workers which is considered in some quarters to be prevalent. Much of the manual work in the factories at the present day is not fatiguing: the workmen have simply to stand and watch their machines. The workers at the large shell-forging presses and the heating furnaces are an exception, and also the riveters and platers in the shipyards.

3. I attribute the loss of time in Barrow, which, from figures

I have seen, is serious in some of the departments at Vickers' works, to the fact that many of the workers are earning such good wages that they can maintain their ordinary standard of comfort and living with four or five days' work. Without doubt much is also due to drinking habits. Loss of time through sickness has not been at all pronounced in Barrow during the last winter. In fact, I was assured that the amount of sickness had been below the normal.

W. SYDNEY SMITH.

(G). Eeports on Transport Difficulties

Report hy Director of Transports to the First Lord of the

Admiralty First Lord,

I WISH to call attention to the fact that the transport work is now being conducted under serious difficulties.

The workmen seamen, dock labourers, c. are rapidly becoming absolutely out of hand. The present labour situation on the Clyde and at Liverpool is merely the beginning. Unless effectual measures are taken we shall have strikes at every port in the United Kingdom, and supplies to the Army and the Fleet will be stopped. In the main, we have now to deal, not with the ordinary British workmen, but with what remains after our best men have been recruited for the Army and Navy.

Yesterday the crew of a transport deserted. The same thing happened the day before. The firemen go on board the transports drunk, making it impossible to get up a full head of steam, so greatly reducing the speed and endangering the lives of thousands of troops by making the vessels a target for submarines.

The root cause of the serious congestion at some of the docks is not a shortage of labour, but the fact that the men can earn in two or three days what will keep them in drink for the rest of the week.

What is wanted, in addition to a proper control of the drink traffic, is a well-devised scheme promptly applied for bringing the seamen under naval, and other workmen in Government employ under military, discipline. In many cases it is now taking three times as long to get ships fitted and ready to sail as it did when war broke out. Expedition is a thing of the past, and it is obvious that this may at any moment have a disastrous effect on the naval and military operations.

The following practical instance of the effect of military discipline, even on those totally unused to it, may be of interest:

We sent 250 dock labourers to Havre under capable civilian supervision. They all got drunk and out of hand in the first fortnight. We brought them back and enlisted a similar lot of men imder military discipline. On the first pay-day one got drunk and was given twelve months' hard labour. There has been no trouble since, and the men are working splendidly.

GRAEME THOMSON,

Director of Transports. March 6, 1915.

As an example of a case in which it was deemed urgently necessary to take police court proceedings in this country, the following may be cited:

Seven firemen employed on a certain transport were charged at Southampton on a warrant with unlawfully combining together to neglect duty, and to impede the navigation of the ship, and the progress of the voyage.

All seven pleaded not guilty, but, in answer to a further question from the Magistrate's Clerk, admitted ' signing-on' in the usual way.

Mr C. Lamport, prosecuting, said that he appeared really on behalf of Captain John Roberts, the commander of the transport, and the prosecution, which was supported by the authorities, was of a similar character to that before the Bench a few weeks ago. It was considered by the authorities, as well as the officers, to be a matter of national importance. All these men had signed articles, as they had admitted, and part of their duties were in connection with the transport service. It was necessary for the transport to sail at a certain time, and no man was entitled to be absent without obtaining leave. No leave was asked for and no leave granted, and orders were given that all firemen must be present at a certain time. There were over 1000 troops on board this ship ready to go away, and he must not say more than that the vessel was held up through the absence of these men, and actually had to return to the port, or near it, and the troops had to be transferred to another vessel, for the Bench to see what a terribly serious thing this was. One could scarcely conceive that the legislature had given sufficient power to deal with such offences. As an Englishman and an advocate, he said that it might well be that men who under- took to serve on a transport ought to be under the same liability to severe piinishment as those under military or Admiralty law.

Captain Roberts, the commander of the transport, told the Court that there were over 1000 troops on board, and that the men should have joined the ship not later than 3.30 on the afternoon in question. The sailing hour was 6 o'clock. Two men were brought on board at 7, one of them intoxicated, but the rest did not put in an appearance at all. In consequence of the absence of these men witness was unable to proceed with the ship, which, as a matter of fact, had to return to Southampton. The troops had to be transferred, there was twenty-four hours' delay, and everything was dislocated.

Harold Graham, the chief engineer of the transport, and George Tounson, the second engineer, bore out the evidence of their captain, both stating that they gave no leave whatever.

Asked what they had to say in defence, Carpenter and Payne told the Court that they had no intention of leaving the ship, and, as a matter of fact, did rejoin; Hock and Podesta stjated that their reason for absence was that they were not feeling well; Thompson and Hatton explained that they were detained at the Bargate by the police on charges of drunkenness, and therefore could not join the ship; and Mountain refrained from saying anything. In passing sentence, the presiding magistrate said: ' By the way you have acted by not joining your ship at the proper time you impeded the progress of the ship and affected its destination, and the vessel had to put back and reship its troops. The Bench under these circumstances cannot consider any question but the utmost penalty, and you will all go to prison for twelve weeks with hard labour."

The magistrates having passed sentence as recorded above. Commander Prefect, who said that he represented the Principal Naval Transport Officer, desired to emphasise the seriousness of these cases. Some of the troops, said the Commander, had been travelling for fifty or sixty hours from the north of Scotland and the west of Ireland, and they were detained on board, not by military exigencies, but by the action of these men.

Extract from Report made hy Director of Transports to Admiralty, dated March 27, 1915

Some of the transport workers at most of the large ports are content to earn in three days money which keeps them in drinlc for the rest of the week. It is necessary to secure throughout the country a state of affairs which will make it possible for transport operations to be carried out with speed and efficiency. At present this is impossible, and neither the Fleet nor the Army can get on without transport.

In my opinion measures are necessary to withdraw all licences to sell intoxicating liquors throughout the country.

Extract from letter to the First Lord of the Admiralty from Mr. T. Royden member of Director of Transport's Advisory Committee), dated March 29, 1915 . the labour situation at our seaports is so unsatisfactory that immediate action is imperative. In any remedial steps that may be taken it should be borne in mind that our best men have joined the colours in various capacities, and that in consequence their influence, which under normal conditions exercises a steadying effect on their fellow-workers, is for the time being lost. At the best of times casual labour, and under that category I place dockers and ship-repairers, is unsatisfactory and unreliable, and this characteristic has become still more pronounced with the increased opportunities for employment brought about by the war. The men know they can get work whenever they want it, however indifferent their behaviour may be, and as a result there is an absolute lack of discipline. I am confident that the root of all the trouble is drink, and the high scale of wages now ruling, instead of acting as an inducement to increased effort, tends to produce the opposite effect, inasmuch as it enables the men to earn in a shorter time the amount of money they regard as sufficient for their immediate needs, and they are able to work fewer hours and spend more of their time drinking. I trust that in the national interest, and in the interest of the men themselves, it may be found possible to deal with this great and growing evil by a drastic reduction in the hours during which intoxicants may be sold, or, preferably, by absolute prohibition. If sailors can, and do, abstain from alcoholic refreshment while at sea, it does not seem unreasonable in a time of national urgency that those whose work keeps them at home should do likewise. Pressure should be brought to bear, through the Licensing Justices, on the owners and tenants of licensed premises with a view to largely increasing the facilities for obtaining reasonable refreshment of a non-alcoholic character, as it would be unreasonable to prohibit tlie sale of intoxicants without providing reasonable substitutes. I have discussed the situation with a large number of employers of labour both on the docks and in the repair shops, and so far have failed to discover any who do not endorse my views. I gather from notices that have appeared in the public press that the officials of the Transport Workers' Union are also in sympathy with them.

Yours truly,

T. ROYDEN.

Report from Director of Transports to the Third Sea Lord, dated 1st April, 1915

Third Sea Lord,

I enclose extracts from reports from Naval Transport Officers at various ports in the United Kingdom indicating the extent to which drink is obstructing the progress of transport work.

I can only reiterate that the time now taken to prepare ships for service is a grave danger to the success of the naval and military operations, which depend so largely on efficient sea transport.

To-day I find a transport, required for urgent military service, to prepare for which would normally occupy seven days, will take twenty-two days to complete, in spite of every effort made to accelerate the work.

GRAEME THOMSON, Director of Transports.

I. Report from Divisional Naval Transport Officer (South Coast)

December 12. Seamen under influence of drink; captain and pilot clear ropes away, and take ship out themselves.

January 8. Men on shore all returned drunk; ship unable to put out to sea.

January 20. Men again drunk; much delay in putting out.

November 11. Firemen and seamen on shore return drunk j ship loses the tide.

Comments by Divisional Naval Transport Officer South Coast) 1. Considerable drunkenness: prosecutions not pressed owing to circumlocution of the law and difficulty of obtaining conviction.

2. Recommends as an ' excellent remedy ' Naval Discipline

Act for Transport Service instead of Merchant Shipping Act. Masters ask for this themselves.

3. Cases quoted taken from the twelve transports in port; if details were obtained from the twenty-three transports away, total number of ofiences would be proportionally greater.

This report is from an ofleicer who will never make a complaint if he can possibly help it. Graeme Thomson.

II. Report from Divisional Naval Transport Officer (North-West Coast)

The following points have been arrived at after consultation with the various firms engaged in Transport Service on the North-West Coast:

Restrictions are necessary; delay from drink notorious.

A large Coaling Company say: 1. Some of the men begin to drink on receipt of wages on Saturday, hence Saturday afternoon ' hands' contain a good proportion of men under influence of drink, so choice of men restricted.

2. Men engaged at 4 p. m. on Saturday for work early on Sunday, anticipating well-paid work on Sunday, drink freely in interval, turn up unfit, so ship is undermanned.

3. Every Saturday a certain number of men are dismissed for returning after meals drunk.

4. In event of any inevitable delay men go to public-house, and return long after proper time for resumption.

5. Many regular employees cannot be given important orders Friday or Saturday owing to drink; many stay off on Monday, and do not turn up till Tuesday morning.

III. Report from Divisional Naval Transport Officer (Bristol Channel) 1. Increasingly difficult to get crews for transports owing to laziness, lack of discipline, and drunken habits.

2. Steamship ( ) 21st March, 4 seamen 20 firemen absent; 9 trimmers, she had to stop at to obtain subsidiary labour.

Steamship ( ) sailed 6 men short.

,, ( ) had to take 16 men substitutes.

3. Crews, rather than dock labourers, are usually seen drunk, hence impossible to rely on ships leaving at stated times.

IV. Eeport from Principal Naval Transport Officer (Bristol Channel) 1. Drink question in relation to transport service not so bad here as at other ports.

2. Drunkenness among dock labourers, chiefly amongst night shifts coming out at 6 a. m.

3. British seamen and firemeti of mercantile marine chief ofienders, e. g., crew of steamship ( ) unfit for work, officers have to do crew's work.

15th October to 3rd February

Twenty-six ships delayed through desertions, c., resulting in total delay of thirty-four days six hours almost entirely due to drink. Since February behaviour much improved.

V. Eeport from Divisional Naval Transport Officer (South-East)

Many cases wherein crews have failed to join their ships owing to drunkenness, though the men do not drink to excess in the docks themselves.

VI. Eeport of Principal Naval Transport Officer (South Coast)

Transport work hampered by: 1. Drunken members of crews miss ships, hence ships sail short-handed, or on occasion are prevented from sailing altogether.

2. Firemen return in drunken condition, hence they are unable to keep steam, causing speed to be seriously reduced with obvious dangers resulting constantly occurring.

3. Dock labourers and coal porters, especially latter, knock off work early to get drunk before closing time.

APPENDIX II

Statutory Rules and Orders, 1915 No. 552

DEFENCE OF THE REALM

The Defence of the Realm (Liquor Control) Regulations

At the Court at Buckingham Palace, the 10th day of June, 1915

PRESENT,

The King's Most Excellent Majesty in Council

Whereas by the Defence of the Realm Consolidation Act, 1914, His Majesty in Coimcil has power during the continuance of the present war to issue regulations for securing the public safety and defence of the Realm:

And whereas by the Defence of the Realm (Amendment) (No. 3) Act, 1915, His Majesty in Council has power to issue regulations under the first-mentioned Act, to take efiect in any area to which they are applied under the said Amendment Act, for the purposes of the control by the State of the sale and supply of intoxicating liquor within the area:

And whereas for the purpose of increasing directly or indirectly the efficiency of labour in such areas, and preventing the efficiency of labour in such areas from being impaired by drunkenness, alcoholism, or excess, it is expedient to make such regulations as are hereinafter contained:

Now, therefore, His Majesty is pleased, by and with the advice of His Privy Council, to order, and it is hereby ordered, that in every area to which these Regulations are applied by an Order in Council made under the Defence of the Realm (Amendment) (No 3) Act, 1915, the following provisions shall have efiect: 1. The prescribed Government authority shall be a Board to Constitution be called the Central Control Board (Liquor Traffic) (hereinafter Board, referred to as ' the Board '), consisting of a chairman and such persons as the Minister of Munitions may from time to time appoint. The quorum of the Board shall be such as the Board may determine, and the Board may regulate their own procedure, and no act or proceeding of the Board shall be questioned on account of any vacancy in the Board.

The Board may sue and be sued, and shall have an official seal which shall be officially and judicially noticed, and such seal shall be authenticated by any two members of the Board or the secretary to the Board.

The Board may appoint a secretary and such officers, inspectors and servants for the purpose of these Regulations as the Board, subject to the approval of the Treasury as to number, may determine. Every document purporting to be an order or other instrument issued by the Board and to be sealed with the seal of the Board authenticated in manner provided by these Regulations, or to be signed by the Secretary to the Board or any person authorised by the Board to act on behalf of the Secretary, shall be received in evidence and be deemed to be such an order or instrument without further proof unless the contrary is shown.

Any property acquired by the Board shall be vested in such two or more members of the Board as the Beard may appoint to act as trustees on their behalf for the purpose, and upon the death, resignation, or removal of a trustee the property vested in that trustee shall, without conveyance or assignment, and whether the property is real or personal, vest in the succeeding trustees either solely or together with any surviving or continuing trustees, and, until the appointment of succeeding trustees, shall so vest in the surviving or succeeding trustee only; and in all legal proceedings whatsoever concerning any property vested in the trustees the property may be stated to be the property of the trustees in their proper names as trustees for the Board without further description.

2. For the purposes of the control of the sale and supply of Powers of intoxicating liquor in any area, the Board may by order: co'ivtrol sale (a) direct that any licensed premises or club in the area in which of liquor, intoxicating liquor is sold by retail or supplied shall be closed either for all purposes or for the purpose of such sale or supply; () regulate the hours during which any such premises or clubs are to be or maybe kept open distinguishing, where it is so determined, the hours during which the premises are to be

DEINK IN 1914-1922

Power for Board to prohibit sale of liquor except by themselves.

Power to prohibit treating.

Power to establish refreshment rooms.

or may be kept open for such sale or supply as aforesaid, and the hours during which they are to be or may be kept open for other purposes, and any such order shall have effect notwithstanding anything in the law relating to licensing or the sale of intoxicating liquor; (c) prohibit the sale by retail or supply of any specified class or description of intoxicating liquor in any licensed premises or club in the area; d) provide that the sale by retail or supply of intoxicating liquor in any licensed premises or club in the area shall be subject to such conditions or restrictions as may be imposed by the order; (e) regulate the introduction of intoxicating liquor into the area and the transport of intoxicating liquor within the area; () require the business carried on in any licensed premises in the area to be carried on subject to the supervision of the Board; and any such order may include such incidental and supplemental provisions as appear to the Board necessary for the purpose of giving full effect to the order, and may be made applicable to all licensed premises and clubs within the area or any specified class or description of such premises and clubs, or to any particular premises or club. If any person contravenes the provisions of any such order, or any conditions or restrictions imposed thereby, he shall be guilty of a summary offence against the Defence of the Kealm (Consolidation) Eegulations, 1914.

3. The Board may by order prohibit the sale by retail, or the supply in clubs or licensed premises, of intoxicating liquor within the area, or any part thereof specified in the order, by any person other than the Board, and if any person contravenes or fails to comply with the order he shall, without prejudice to any other penalty, be guilty of a summary offence against the Defence of the Realm (Consolidation) Regulations, 1914.

Provided that the order may except from the provisions thereof any specified class or classes of premises or clubs.

4. The Board may by order make such provisions as they think necessary for the prevention of the practice of treating within the area, and if any person contravenes the provisions of any such order he shall be guilty of a summary offence against the Defence of the Realm (Consolidation) Regulations, 1914.

5. The Board may either themselves or through any agents establish and maintain in the area, or provide for the establishment and maintenance in the area of, refreshment rooms for the sale or supply of refreshments (including, if thought fit, the sale or supply of intoxicating liquor) to the general public, or to any particular class of persons, or to persons employed in any particular industry in the area.

6. Where the Board consider that it is necessary or expedient Power to for the purpose of giving proper efiect to the control of the liquor p g ges supply in the area, they may acquire compulsorily or by agreement, either for the period during which these Eegulations take effect or permanently, any licensed or other premises in the area, or any interest in any such premises:

Provided that the Board may, in lieu of acquiring any interest in such premises, take possession of the premises and any plant used for the purposes of the business carried on therein for all or any part of the period during which these Regulations take effect, and use them for the sale or supply of intoxicating liquor or for the purpose of any of the other powers and duties of the Board.

7. Where the Board determine to acquire compulsorily any Procedure premises or any interest therein, they shall serve on the occupier for of the premises and, if any person other than the occupier will be acm sitioz affected by the acquisition of the interest proposed to be acquired, also on any person who appears to the Board to be so affected, notice of their intention to acquire the premises, or such interest therein as may be specified in the notice, and where such a notice is served, the fee simple in possession of the premises or such interest in the premises as aforesaid shall, at the expiration of ten days from the service of the notice on the occupier, by virtue of these Regulations vest in the trustees for the Board, subject to or freed from any mortgages, rights, and interests affecting the same as the Board may by order direct.

On any premises or any interest therein becoming so vested in the trustees for the Board the trustees may: (a) if the title to the premises is registered under the Land Registry Act, 1862, or the Land Transfer Acts, 1875, and 1897, enter a caveat or caution to prevent their estate or interest from being impaired by any act of the registered proprietor; and (b) if the premises are situate in an area where registration of title is compulsory lodge a caution against registration of the premises; and (c) if the premises are within the jurisdiction of the Acts relating to registration of assurances in Middlesex and Yorkshire register in Middlesex a memorial of the notice, and in Yorkshire an affidavit of vesting against the name of every

DRINK IN 1914-1922

Power to acquire businesses.

Immunity from licensing law.

Provision of entertainment and recreation.

Provision of postal and banking facilities.

person whose estate or interest is affected, and in Middlesex any such notice shall be deemed a conveyance.

A copy of the minutes of the Board to the effect that a notice has been served in accordance with this regulation, certified by the secretary to the Board, or by any person authorised by the Board to act on behalf of the secretary, to be a true copy, shall be evidence that the premises or interest therein mentioned in the minutes have become vested in the trustees for the Board.

8. Where the Board consider that it is necessary or expedient for the purpose of giving proper effect to the control of the liquor traffic in the area they may, by the like procedure, acquire any business (including stock-in-trade) carried on in any premises within the area, whether or not they take possession of or acquire the premises in which such business is carried on, or any interest in the premises.

9. The Board may, without any licence (whether justices' or excise, and whether for the sale of intoxicating liquor or otherwise), carry on in any premises occupied by them any business involving the sale or supply of intoxicating liquor, refreshments or tobacco, and for that purpose shall not be subject to any of the provisions of the law relating to licensing, or to any restrictions imposed by law on persons carrying on such business.

Any person appointed by the Board to conduct any business on their behalf shall have, to such extent as they may be conferred by the Board, the same powers as the Board of carrying on business without a licence, but all such persons shall in all other respects, except in such cases and to such extent as the Board may otherwise order, be subject to the statutory provisions affecting the holders of licences, and the occupiers of premises licensed, for any such business as aforesaid, in like manner as if they were the holders of the appropriate licences, and to any restrictions imposed by law on persons carrying on any such business as aforesaid.

10. The Board shall have power, on any premises in which business is carried on by them or on their behalf, to provide or authorise the provision of such entertainment or recreation for persons frequenting the premises as the Board think fit, and where such provision is made or such authority is given no licence shall be necessary, and no restrictions imposed by law on the provision of the entertainment or recreation in question shall apply, except to such extent, if any, as the Board may direct.

11. Arrangements may be made by the Board with the Postmaster-General and any other person for affording postal and banking facilities on or near premises in

which business is carried on by or on behalf of the Board to persons frequenting such premises.

12. Where, by any conditions or restrictions imposed by the Provision as Board on the sale of spirits, the sale of any spirit is prohibited unless dilution the strength of the spirit is reduced to a number of degrees under proof which falls between such maximum and minimum limits as may be specified, or where by any order of the Board the sale of spirit so reduced is permitted, section six of the Sale of Food and Drugs Act, 1879, shall within the area have effect, as respects that spirit, as if the maximum number of degrees under proof so specified were substituted for the number mentioned in that section.

13. All obligations under covenant, contract, or otherwise, to Suspension which the holder of a licence or the occupier of licensed premises is covenants, subject, and which the provisions of these Regulations or any action of the Board taken thereunder make it impossible for him to fulfil, or which are inconsistent with any conditions or restrictions imposed by the Board, shall be suspended so long as such impossibility or such conditions or restrictions continue, and shall not be binding during that period.

14. Where by virtue of any action taken by the Board under Suspension these Regulations the holder of any licence is temporarily prevented licences. from carrying on his business as the holder of such licence, the licence shall be suspended, and the holder thereof shall be entitled to such repayment or remission of excise duty as he would have been entitled to had the licence been permanently discontinued, and at the expiration of the period during which the disability continues the licence, if a justices' licence, shall revive and have effect as if it had been granted for the then current licensing year, and a person who was the holder of an excise licence which has been suspended shall be entitled to take out an excise licence on payment of such an amount in respect of excise duty as would have been payable by him had he commenced to carry on business at the expiration of that period:

Provided that if during the period for which any licence is so suspended a contingency occurs upon which a transfer of the licence might have been granted but for the suspension, a transfer may be granted either (a) at the time at which, and to a person to whom, a transfer might have been granted had the licence not been suspended; or (6) after the expiration of the period to any person to whom a transfer might have been granted had the contingency occurred immediately after the expiration of the period.

Where a licence for the sale of intoxicating liquor is so suspended,

DEINK IN 1914-1922

Power to grant excise licence on authority of certificate from Board.

Delegation of powers by resolution,

Supplemental powers.

Powers of inspectors.

Prohibition on obstructing inspectors, c.

Attempts to commit ofeences.

the holder of the licence may, during the period of suspension, without further licence continue to carry on in the premises in respect of which the suspended licence was granted any business, other than the sale of intoxicating liquor, which had the suspended licence not been suspended he would have been entitled to carry on by virtue of that licence, but the premises shall be deemed to be duly licensed for the carrying on of such other business.

15. An excise licence may, notwithstanding anything in the law relating to licensing, be granted as respects any premises in the area on the authority of a certificate from the Board, and any excise licence so granted shall be valid in all respects, and, subject to the provisions of these Regulations, the law relating to the holders of justices' licences shall apply to the holders of such certificates as if such a certificate was a justices' licence.

No such conditions need be attached to the grant of any such certificate as must be attached to the grant of a new justices' on-licence.

16. Any powers conferred on the Board by these Regulations may, if the Board by resolution so determine, be exercised on behalf of the Board by any persons whom the Board may appoint for the purpose.

17. In addition to the powers expressly conferred on them by these Regulations, the Board shall have such supplemental and incidental powers as may be necessary for carrying into efeect the purposes of these Regulations.

18. Any inspector or other person authorised by the Board shall have power to enter, if need be by force, and inspect any licensed premises within the area and any club or other premises within the area where he has reason to believe that intoxicating liquor is sold by retail or supplied, to demand the production of and to inspect and take copies of or extracts from any books or documents relating to the business carried on therein, and to take samples of any intoxicating liquor found therein.

19. If any person obstructs or impedes any inspector or other person acting under the instructions or authority of the Board, or refuses to answer any question reasonably put to him by any such inspector or person, or makes or causes to be made any false statement to any such inspector or person, or refuses to produce any document in his possession which he is required by any such inspector or person to produce, he shall be guilty of a summary ofience against the Defence of the Realm (Consolidation) Regulations, 1914.

20. If any person attempts to contravene, or induces or attempts to induce any other person to contravene, any provision of these

Regulations or any order made thereunder, or any conditions or restrictions imposed by the Board, he shall be guilty of a summary ofience against the Defence of the Realm (Consolidation) Regulations, 1914.

21. A person guilty of a summary offence against the Defence Penalties, of the Realm (Consolidation) Regulations, 1914, is liable to be sentenced to imprisonment with or without hard labour for a term not exceeding six months or to a fine not exceeding one hundred pounds or to both such imprisonment and fine, and if the court so orders, to forfeit the goods in respect of which the offence is committed.

22. No person shall be liable to any penalty under the law Exemption relating to licensing or the sale of intoxicating liquor in respect of J: penal-any action taken by him if such action is taken in pursuance of any licensing law. order made or instructions given by the Board.

23. The Board before acquiring any licensed premises or club Notice to be or an interest therein, or taking possession of any licensed premises njmmis- or club, shall

give notice of their intention to the Commissioners of sioners of Customs and Excise, and where the Board carry on, or appoint or Customs and authorise any person to carry on, any business involving the sale or supply of intoxicating liquor they shall furnish to the Commissioners of Customs and Excise particulars as to the nature of the business to be carried on by him, and as to any person so appointed or authorised, and any other particulars required by the Commissioners.

24. It shall be the duty of the police to enforce these Regula- Enforcement tions, and any orders of the Board made thereunder. police.

25. These Regulations shall apply to Scotland subject to the Application following modifications: ' Scotland.

References to real or personal property shall be construed as references to heritable and moveable property respectively: ' intoxicating liquor ' shall mean ' exciseable liquor ': ' fee simple in possession' shall mean ' estate of the proprietor or lessor ': ' mortgage ' shall mean ' heritable security ': and a reference to a justices' licence shall be construed as a reference to a certificate as defined in Part VII. of the Licensing (Scotland) Act, 1903.

In any case where under these Regulations the Board acquire or determine to acquire compulsorily any premises or any interest therein, a person transacting on the faith of any register of sasines with the proprietor or lessor of such premises or with any other person whose title is recorded in such register shall (notwithstanding anything in these regulations contained) not be affected by any notice served by the Board or any vesting

DRINK IN 1914-1922 following thereon unless a certified copy of such notice has been recorded in the register of inhibitions prior to the completion of such transaction.

For the purpose of enabling the trustees for the Board to complete a title if thought fit to any heritable property or estate compulsorily acquired by the Board and vested in the trustees by virtue of these Regulations, by expeding a notarial instrument or otherwise, these Regulations shall be deemed to be and (without prejudice to any other method of completion of title) may be used as a general disposition or assignation of such property or estate in favour of the trustees.

Application 26. In the application of these Regulations to Ireland, the to Ireland. expression ' excise licence ' includes any licence for the sale of intoxicating liquor granted by an officer of excise, and the expression ' justices' licence ' includes any certificate of a recorder, justice, or justices required for the grant of an excise licence.

Definitions. 27. For the purposes of these Regulations

The expression ' sale by retail' means sale other than sale to a trader for the purposes of his trade.

The expression ' supply' in relation to intoxicating liquor means supply otherwise than by way of sale.

The expression ' licensed premises ' includes any premises or place where the sale of intoxicating liquor is carried on under a licence.

Short title. 28. The Regulations may be cited as the Defence of the Realm (Liquor Control) Regulations, 1915.

Almeric Fitzroy.
APPENDIX III

THE ORDERS APPLIED TO SCHEDULED AREAS

The Orders of the Board applied to scheduled areas have all been framed on the same general lines. They are not in all respects identical, some modifications and improvements having been introduced from time to time.

It will be convenient to set out side by side one of the latest Orders (made on the 17th February, 1916), and explanatory notes of its chief provisions.

Text of the Okder

Explanatory Notes

Limits of Area 1. The area to which this Order applies is the Southern Military and Transport Area, being the area comprising the Town and County of Poole, and the County of Dorset (excepting the Boroughs of Bridport and Lyme Regis and the Petty Sessional Division of Bridport); the City of Salisbury and the County of Wilts; the City of Winchester, the County Boroughs of Bournemouth, Portsmouth and Southampton and the County of Southampton (including the Isle of Wight); the County Borough of Beading, and the Boroughs of Maidenhead and Windsor, and the Petty Sessional Divisions of Maidenhead, Reading (excepting the Parishes of Ashampstead, Bassildon and Streatley), Windsor, and Wokingham, in the County of Berks; the Parishes of Maple Durham, Kidmore End, Eye and Dunsden, and Shiplake, in the County of Oxford; the Petty Sessional Division of Stoke, and the Parishes of Farnham Royal, Burnham, Taplow, Hitcham, Dorney and Boveny, in the County of Buckingham; the Boroughs of Guildford and Godajming, and the Petty Sessional Divisions of Chertsey, Farn-

The definition of the area which is embodied in the first Article of every Order is repeated verbatim from the Order in Council by which the area has previously been scheduled. The delimitation of the area is fixed after careful deliberation and local inquiry, and conference with the local Naval, Military, and Civil Authorities. Ihe boundaries selected are arranged in consultation with the Police, to meet frontier difficulties, and to observe local government divisions so far as possible.

DEINK IN 1914-1922

Text of the Order ham, Guildford, and Woking, in the County of Surrey; the City of Chichester, and the Petty Sessional Divisions of Chichester, Arundel, Petworth, and Midhurst, in the County of Sussex.

Hours during which intoxicating liquor may be sold

A. For Consumption ON the Premises 2. (1) The hours during which intoxicating liquor may be sold or supplied in any licensed premises or club for consumption on the premises shall be restricted and be as follows: On Weekdays: The hours between 12 noon and 2.30 P. M., and between 6 p. m. and 9 p. m. On Su7idays: The hours between 12.30 p. m. and 2.30 P. M., and between 6 p. m. and 9 p. m. Except between the aforesaid hours no person shall (a) Either by himself or by any servant or agent sell or supply to any person in any licensed premises or club any intoxicating liquor to be consumed on the premises; or (b) Consume in any such premises or club any intoxicating liquor; or (c) Permit any person to consume in any such premises or club any intoxicating liquor.

E XPLANATORY NOTES

Weekday hours for ON-consumftion

Article 2 (1) specifies the hours during which intoxicating liquor may be sold or supplied in any licensed premises or club, for consumption on the premises.

Before making any Orders the Board considered very carefully what principles they should act upon in the restriction of hours. The general conclusions they came to were that there should be no inducement either to men or to women to frequent places where intoxicating liquor could be obtained during the usual morning and afternoon hours of work, and that a considerable interval should be allowed in the middle of the day owing to the varying meal hour. Hence a uniform rule has been adopted that the mid-day period during which intoxicating liquor can be obtained shall be a period of two and a half hours, a period which in practice extends either from 12 noon to 2.30 P. M. or from 11.30 a. m. to

The Board also decided, as a general rule, that in the evening the hours should be limited to three, and should terminate not later than 9 or 9.30 P. M. In certain Jlilitary and Transport areas in England it has been found necessary on Naval or Military grounds to limit the evening hours to two, namely, from 6 to 8 p. m-In Scotland, in the East and West Centra areas, the same mid-day hours have been prescribed from Monday tiu Friday, but on Saturday, on strong local representation, the midday and evening hours for the sale of intoxicants have been combined, and have been fixed at 4 p. m. to 9 P. M. In the Northern area of Scotland, owing to the special circumstances of different parts of the area.

Text of the Oedee Explanatoey Notes the evening hours have been considerably varied on the representations of the Naval or Military Authorities. In most cases the evening closing hours have followed those previously fixed by these Authorities. The alteration of the general rule on Saturdays was made in order that wage-earners paid at mid-day should have no inducement to spend their money on intoxicating liquor instead of taking it home. Evidence showed that some men frequently went straight to licensed premises with their pay and spent a large portion of it drinking there with friends before reaching home.

In general, the arrangement of hours for on-consumption is designed to meet the special dangers to national efficiency which are involved at the present time in early morning or in late evening drinking, while affording sufficient facilities for reasonable refreshment.

Sunday hours for ON-consumption

On Sundays the hours have been limited to four and a half or five in most areas two in the middle of the day and two and a half or three in the evening. Here again there is some variation in the evening hours, caused by local circumstances which the Board felt it necessary to respect.

In Scotland and Wales the Board's Orders extend to clubs the principle of Sunday closing which is already applicable by the general law to licensed premises. The question of the bo7ia fide traveller is also dealt with (see the Note to Article 11 (b)). In the Western Border area, part of which is in Scotland and part in England, the Board found it necessary to provide that there should be no Sunday opening at all in that portion of Cumberland which is near the border and within easy reach of an important munition factory.

. For Consumption OFF the Premises (2) The hours during which intoxi For consumption off the premises eating liquor may be sold or supphed of intoxicants other than spirits the in any licensed premises or club for hours have in general been practic- consumption off the premises shall ally the same as for on-consumption,

DEINK IN 1914-1922

Text of the Order (subject to the additional restrictions as regards spirits) be restricted and be as follows: Oil Weekdays: The hours between 12 noon and 2.30 P. M., and between 6 p. m. and 8 p. m. On Sundays: The hours between 12.30 p. m. and 2.30 p. m., and between 6 P. M. and 8 p. m. Except between the aforesaid hours no person shall (o) Either by himself or by any servant or agent sell or supply to any person in any licensed premises or club for consumption off the premises or (except as hereinafter expressly provided) dispatch therefrom any intoxicating liquor; or (6) Take from any such premises or club any intoxicating liquor; or (c) Permit any person to take from any such premises or club any intoxicating liquor.

Explanatory Notes except that in most of the Orders the off-sales have been required to cease one hour earlier in the evening than the on-sales. This provision has been pressed upon the Board in order to prevent the practice of drinking in the public-houses until closing time and then carrying away intoxicants in order to resume drinking immediately at home.

Additional restrictions as to spirits 3. In addition to the above general restrictions as to hours during which intoxicating liquor may be sold or supplied, the sale and supply of spirits in licensed premises and clubs shall be subject to the following special restrictions, that is to say: (a) No orders for spirits to be consumed off the premises shall be given by or accepted from any person actually present in any licensed premises or club, except on Mondays, Tuesdays, Wednesdays, Thursdays, and Fridays and during the hours between 12 noon and 2.30 p. m. Spirits to be consumed off the premises must not (except as hereinafter expressly provided) be dispatched from any licensed premises or club, nor must they be taken therefrom by the person to whom they are sold or supplied or by any person acting on his behalf, except on the days and during the hours aforesaid.

The effect of paragraphs (a) and (6) of Article 3 is that the off-sale of spirits is only permitted from Mondays to Fridays in the mid-day period, so that no spirits can be obtained for off-consumption during the evening opening hours on any day, or at any time on Saturdays or Sundays.

This provision was determined upon by the Board in order to diminish the excessive consumption of spirits, and to restrict home drinking, particularly the week-end drinking which results in bad timekeeping on Mondays.

APPENDIX

Text of the Order (c) Spirits to be consumed off the premises shall not be sold or supplied in or taken from any licensed premises or club in any bottle or other vessel not bearing a label showing the name and situation of the premises or club, or in any vessel of a capacity less than one reputed quart, or in any less quantity than one reputed quart, or in any open vessel d) No spirits to be consumed off the premises shall be sold or supplied in or taken from any refreshment room in any railway station.

Explanatory Notes

In the more recent Orders an additional restriction on the off-sales of spirits ' the quart bottle minimum ' has been inserted, by which the least quantity that can be obtained for off-consumption is one reputed quart bottle, thus applying generally the provision which has been in operation with regard to English off-licences since their institution in 1861. The reason for this provision, and for the further prohibition of the sale of spirits in open vessels (i. e., open at the time of sale), was the rapidly increasing trade in small flasks of spirits purchased at public-houses and taken off the premises into works, railway carriages, ships, and other places, and also into the homes, both by men and women. Many Naval and Military authorities were strongly in favour of these provisions, and have also particularly advocated the prohibition of the off-sale of spirits in Railway Refreshment Rooms (Article 3 (d)).

From evidence which they have received the Board are satisfied that the quart bottle provision has done much to reduce the evils at which it is aimed, but in view of allegations that it has encouraged some persons to purchase more than they would otherwise have done, its operation is being carefully watched.

Conditions as to distribution 4. No person shall either by himself or any servant or agent (a) Sell, supply, distribute or deliver any intoxicating liquor from any van, barrow, basket or other vehicle or receptacle unless before the liquor is dispatched it has been ordered and the quantity, description and price thereof together with the name and address of the person to whom it is to be supplied has been entered in a delivery book or invoice, which shall be carried by the person delivering the liquor, and in a day book which shall be kept on the premises from which the liquor is dispatched.

In order to anticipate the increased home-drinking which it might be expected would follow the imposition of restrictions on the sale and supply of intoxicants in licensed premises or clubs, a clause has been inserted in English and "Welsh Orders designed to make more difficult the ' pushing ' of intoxicants into private houses. In the earlier Orders this clause followed the precedent contained in the Scotch Licensing Act, but it was soon found that, notwithstanding this clause, the evil which had been anticipated developed, and in order to check it, the Board's more recent Orders have contained an additional provision prohibiting the system of payment for intoxicants on delivery and the collection of pay-

Text of the Order Explanatory Notes (6) Carry or convey in any van, barrow, basket or other vehicle or receptacle while in use for the distribution or delivery of intoxicating liquor, any such liquor not entered in such delivery book or invoice and day book.

(c) Distribute or deliver any intoxi- cating liquor at any address not specified in such delivery book or invoice and day book.

(d) Refuse to allow any constable to examine such van, barrow, basket or other vehicle or receptacle or such delivery book or invoice.

(e) Authorise or permit any person employed to deliver, distribute or take or solicit orders for intoxicating liquor to receive or make any payment in respect of intoxicating liquor, or, being a person so employed, receive or make any such payment on behalf of any other person, or, being so engaged on his own behalf, receive any such payment. Provided that nothing in this paragraph shall affect the receipt of money paid at the licensed premises.

ments by the canvasser or vanman. This provision was not contained in the Board's earlier Orders, including the Mersey District Order, and in November last the Board received the follo ving resolution: ' That the Liverpool Licensing ' Committee, while expressing ' satisfaction at the result of the ' Order of the Central Control ' Board (Liquor Trafiic) in Liver-' pool, view with concern the ' increasing trade in the delivery ' of beer at the homes of the ' people, and request the Board ' to consider the matter with a ' view to checking this growing ' evu." Continued evidence of the existence and development of this type of trade has led the Board to make a General Order operative as from the 17th April) wmch provides as follows: ' In each of the Orders of the Board now in force in the respective areas to which the Defence of the Realm (Liquor Control) Regulations, 1915, and any Regulations amending the same have been applied the following Article shall be inserted ' No person shall, either by himself or by any servant or agent (i) Solicit or canvass for orders for, or collect or receive payment for, intoxicating liquor except at the licensed premises; or (ii) Send or cause to be sent or leave or cause to be left to or at any premises, or to or with any person, any order form for intoxicating liquor; or (iii) Cause or permit any payment for intoxicating liquor to be made on his behalf by any person in the service or employment of the vendor of the liquor, or, being a person in such service or employment, make any such payment as the agent or on behalf of the purchaser of the liquor. And each of the said Orders shall be read as if this Article

APPENDIX

Text of the Order

Explanatory Notes were inserted therein, and in the case of all the said Orders made on or after the 11th day of November, 1915, as if it were substituted for the provisions of paragraph (e) of Article 4 entitled " Conditions as to Distribution." '

Hours of opening for the supply of food and non-intoxicants 5. Notwithstanding any provisions of this Order or of the Law relating to licensing or the sale of intoxicating liquor: (a) Licensed premises may be opened for the supply of food and non-intoxicating liquor at the hour of 5.30 in the morning on all days and be kept open for this purpose from that hour until the evening closing hour prescribed by the general provisions of the Licensing Acts; and. Refreshment houses may be kept open for this purpose at any time during which they may be kept open under the general provisions of the said Acts.

The limitation of hours during which intoxicating liquor may be sold does not affect the hours during which licensed premises or clubs may be kept open for other purposes, and there is a clause in each Order specifically stating this. Further, in order to meet cases where food and non-intoxicants are wanted before the ordinary morning opening hour there is a provision that they may open at 5.30 a. m. (in the London area at 5 a. m.) for this purpose. This provision applies to Sundays as well as to weekdays.

Saving provisions 6. Nothing in the foregoing provisions of this Order shall be deemed to prohibit, in cases where the same is otherwise lawful: (a) The consumption of intoxicating liquor by any person in any licensed premises or club where he is residing; or (6) The consumption of intoxicating liquor at a meal by any person in any licensed premises or club at any time within half an hour after the conclusion of the afternoon and evening hours during which the sale or supply of intoxicating liquor is permitted by this Order; Provided that the liquor was sold or supplied and served during such hours at the

This ' saving provision' does not apply to sale or supply, but only to consumption.

This provision was the result of representations which reached the Board from many quarters that the meal business at bond fide hotels and restaurants had been unreasonably interfered with, in that large numbers of persons had not finished their midday or evening meal by the afternoon or evening closing hour respectively.

Text of the Obder Explanatory Notes same time as the meal and for consumption at tlie meal; or (c) The sale or supply of spirits to any person producing a certificate in writing dated and signed by a duly qualified medical practitioner that the spirits are immediately required for medicinal purposes and specifying the quantity of spirits required; Provided that the quantity sold or supplied shall not exceed the quantity specilied in such certificate; or d) The dispatch from licensed premises for delivery at a place more than five miles distant of any spirits or other intoxicating liquor in the forenoon of any day on which the sale of the same for consumption off the premises, i8 permitted by Article 2 (2) and Article 3 of this Order as the case may be.

Treating prohibited 7. No person shall either by him This clause is contained in all the self or by any servant or agent sell Board's Orders and has been uni- or supply any intoxicating liquor to versally approved. It is well known any person in any licensed premises that many persons were practically or in any club for consumption on compelled to drink more than they the premises unless the same is desired owing to the extent to which ordered and paid for by the person the practice of treating had de- so supplied; nor shall any person veloped. An exception is made in order or pay for or lend or advance favour of treating with a meal, but money to pay for any intoxicating it is easily seen that to open the door liquor wherewith any other person wider as for instance even to allow has been or is to be supplied for con a man to treat his wife would lead sumption on the premises; nor shall to an ever-increasing circle of evasions any person consume in any licensed and abuses. The special difficulty premises or club any intoxicating which arises in clubs through the liquor which any other person has illegality of allowing a non-member ordered or paid for or agreed to pay to pay for liquor has been met in for or lent or advanced money to some cases by the admission of the pay for: wife to membership.

Provided always that if such intoxicating liquor is supplied or served for consumption at a meal supplied at the same time and is consumed at such meal the provisions of this regulation shall not be deemed to be contravened if the person who pays for such meal also pays for such intoxicating liquor.

APPENDIX

Text of the Order

For the purposes of this regulation consumption on the premises includes consumption of intoxicating liquor in or on any highway open ground or railway station adjoining or near to the licensed premises or club in which the liquor was sold or supplied; and any person consuming intoxicating liquor in or on any such highway open ground or railway station shall be deemed to consume the liquor in such licensed premises or club as the case may be.

Explanatory Notes

Experience showed the necessity of this additional provision, which was not contained in the Board's earlier Orders.

Credit prohibited 8. No person shall (1) (a) Either by himself or by any servant or agent sell or supply in any licensed premises or club or dispatch therefrom any intoxicating liquor to be consumed either on or off the premises; or (6) Consume any intoxicating liquor in or take it from such premises or club; unless it is paid for before or at the time when it is supplied or dispatched or taken away. Provided always that if the liquor is sold for consumption at a meal supplied at the same time and is consumed at such meal, this provision shall not be deemed to be contravened if the price of the liquor is paid together with the price of such meal and before the person partaking thereof quits the premises.

(2) Introduce or cause to be introduced into the area any intoxicating liquor unless it is paid for before it is so introduced.

The giving of ' credit' for intoxicants is prohibited in all the Board's Orders. Like the treating prohibition this has received general approval, almost the only objection being raised by Beer and Wine Merchants trading with a limited portion of the community. It must, however, be clear that to make special exemptions, even were it possible, for persons who conduct trade with the well-to-do classes would justify the suggestion that the Board's Orders savoured of class legislation.

The prohibition on dispatching intoxicating liquor before receiving payment is designed to prevent the practice referred to in the note to Article 4. It is not contained in Orders made before the 11th November, 1915, but it is incorporated in them by Article 2 of the General Order mentioned in that note.

Long Pull Prohibited 9. No person shall either by himself or by any servant or agent in any licensed premises or club sell or supply to any person as the measure of intoxicating liquor for which he asks an amount exceeding that measure.

In the later Orders of the Board, in consequence of representations received from many quarters, a provision has been inserted which prohibits that form of illegitimate competition known as the ' long pull," in terms taken from a clause of the Licensing Bill of 1908 which had been generally treated as non-contentious. The practice has been condemned as much by members of the trade as by licensing authorities.

DEINK IN 1914-1922

Text of the Okder

EXPLAKATORY NOTES

Dilution of spirits 10. The sale of whisky, brandy and rum reduced to a number of degrees under proof which falls between 25 and 50, and of gin reduced to a number of degrees under proof which falls between 35 and 50, is hereby permitted, and accordingly, in determining whether an offence has been committed under the Sale of Food and Drugs Acts by selling to the prejudice of the purchaser whisky, brandy, rum or gin not adulterated otherwise than by the admixture of water it shall be a good defence to prove that such admixture has not reduced the spirit more than 50 degrees under proof.

By the Sale of Food and Drugs Acts, 1875 and 1879, the legal maximum dilution of spirits, other than gin, without notice to the purchaser, is 25 degrees under proof, and of gin, 35 degrees under proof. From the point of view of efficiency, it is desirable that licence-holders should not be obliged to sell a more intoxicating drink than their own interests or the wishes and interests of their customers demand. In their earlier Orders, therefore, the Board permitted dilution of whisky, brandy, and rum, up to 35 degrees under proof. This permission was not readily taken advantage of at first, but it is believed that dilution is now freely practised. No doubt this is partly due to the substantial rise in the price of spirits and to their scarcity. The permissive dilution has been progressively extended, and the Board have recently authorised dilution to 50 degrees under proof in all scheduled areas.

Note. Proof spirit is composed of 49-28 alcohol and 50-72 water (by weight).

Spirit 25 degrees u. p. contains 75 proof spirit, or 35-91 pure alcohol. Spirit 35 degrees u. p. contains 30-85 pure alcohol. Spirit 50 degrees u. p. contains 23-49 pure alcohol.

Explanatory Provisions (a) Nothing in this Order authorises any licensed premises to be kept open for the sale of intoxicating liquor except during the hours permitted under the general provisions of the Licensing Acts.

(b) The prohibition under this

Order of the sale supply and consumption of intoxicating liquor except during certain hours is not subject to the exceptions provided for in the Licensing Acts with respect to bond fide travellers and the supply of intoxicating liquor at railway

As is well known, the misuse of the bond fide traveller enactment has led to wide evasion of the Licensing Act, and while inconvenience may sometimes be caused now that the enactment is superseded in the scheduled areas, its abolition is of the greatest importance in securing the proper observance of the Board's Orders.

Text op the Order Explanatory Notes stations or any other provisions in those Acts enabling intoxicating liquor to be supplied during closing hours in special cases.

(c) The expression ' licensed premises' includes any premises or place where the sale of intoxicating liquor is carried on under a licence.

(d) This Order does not affect the sale or dispatch of intoxicating liquor to a trader for the purposes of his trade or to a registered club for the purposes of the club.

(e) This Order does not affect the sale or supply of intoxicating liquor to or in any canteen where the sale of intoxicating liquor is carried on under the authority of a Secretary of State or of the Admiralty,

Exhibition of the Order 13. The secretary of every club to The copies required for exhibition which this Order applies and every are supplied to clubs and licensed holder of a licence for the sale of in- premises by the police, toxicating liquor shall keep permanently affixed in some conspicuous place in the club or in each public room in the licensed premises a copy of this Order and any notice required by the Board to be aflsxed.:

Commencement of Order 14. This Order shall come into A period of about ten days is force on the twenty-eighth day of generally allowed between the making February, 1916. of an Order and the date at which it comes into force.

APPENDIX IV

CHAPTER 42

A. D. 1921. An Act to amend the law relating to the sale and supply of intoxicating liquor, and for purposes in connection therewith.

nth August, 1921.

BE it enacted by the King's most Excellent Majesty, by and with tbe advice and consent of the Lords Spiritual and Temporal, and Commons, in tbis present Parliament assembled, and by the authority of the same, as follows:

Part I

Conditions of Sale, c., of Intoxicating Liquor

Permitted.(j) The hours during which intoxicating liquor may be sold weekdays supplied on weekdays in any licensed premises or club, for consumption either on or off the premises, shall be as follows, that is to say: eight hours, beginning not earlier than eleven in the morning and ending not later than ten at night, with a break of at least two hours after twelve (noon):

Provided that (a) in the application of this provision to the metropolis ' nine ' shall be substituted for ' eight," and ' eleven at night' shall be substituted for ' ten at night'; and (6) the licensing justices for any licensing district outside the metropolis may by order, if satisfied that the special requirements of the district render it desirable, make, as respects their district, either or both of the following directions (i) that this provision shall have effect as though ' eight and a half ' were substituted for ' eight' and ' half-past ten at night' were substituted for ' ten at night'; (ii) that this provision shall have effect as though 224 some hour specified in the order earlier than eleven, but a. d. 1921. not earlier than nine, in the morning were substituted for ' eleven in the morning."

(2) Subject to the foregoing provisions, the permitted hours on weekdays shall be such as may be fixed, in the case of licensed premises by order of the licensing justices of the licensing district, and in the case of a club in accordance with the rules of the club:

Provided that, pending any decision under this sub-section, the permitted hours on weekdays shall be (a) in the metropolis, the hours between half-past eleven in the morning and three in the afternoon, and between half-past five in the afternoon and eleven at night; and (h) elsewhere, the hours between half-past eleven in the morning and three in the afternoon, and between half-past five in the afternoon and ten at night.

2. (1) The hours during which intoxicating liquor may be sold Permitted or supplied on Sundays, Christmas Day and Good Friday in any ours on licensed premises or club, for consumption either on or off the premises, shall be as follows, that is to say, five hours, of which not more than two shall be between twelve (noon) and three in the afternoon, and not more than three between six and ten in the evening:

Provided that in Wales and Monmouthshire there shall be no permitted hours for licensed premises on Sundays, or on Christmas Day when it falls on a Sunday.

(2) Subject to the foregoing provisions, the permitted hours on Sundays shall be such as may be fixed, in the case of licensed premises by order of the licensing justices of the licensing district, and in the case of a club in accordance with the rules of the club:

Provided that, pending any decision under this subsection, the permitted hours on Sundays, Christmas Day and Good Friday, shall be the hours between half-past twelve and half-past two in the afternoon, and the hours between seven and ten in the evening.

3. (1) The provisions of this Act as to permitted hours on Special pro-weekdays shall, as respects licensed premises or clubs to which this gj f section applies, have effect, if the holder of the licence or the com permitted mittee of the club so elects, as though one hour were added at the hours in the end of the permitted hours in the evening: certain pre-

Provided that any intoxicating liquor sold or supplied during mises.

DEINK IN 1914-1922

AD. 1921.

that hour shall be sold or supplied only for consumption at a meal supplied at the same time in such portion of the premises as is usually set apart for the service of meals, and no person shall consume or be permitted to consume any intoxicating liquor on the premises during that hour except at such meal, and any drinking bar in the said premises shall be closed during that hour.

(2) This section applies to any licensed premises or clubs if and so long as the licensing justices are satisfied that they are structurally adapted and ho7ia fide used or intended to be used for the purpose of habitually providing, for the accommodation of persons frequenting the premises, substantial refreshment, to which the sale and supply of intoxicating liquor is ancillary.

(3) The holder of the licence, or the secretary of the club, shall give not less than fourteen days' previous notice in writing to the superintendent of the police of the district wherein the premises are situate of the date on which he intends to begin to avail himself of the provisions of this section; and on and after that date shall affix and keep permanently affixed in some conspicuous place in the premises a notice to the effect that the provisions of this section apply to the premises; and the said provisions shall apply accordingly for the period of the current licensing year, and shall continue to apply unless the holder of the licence or secretary gives not less than fourteen days' notice in writing before the expiration of any licensing year to the superintendent of the police aforesaid that he intends to cease to avail himself of the provisions of this section, in which case the said provisions shall cease to apply at the end of that year.

4. Subject to the provisions of this Part of this Act, no person shall, except during the permitted hours (a) either by himself, or by any servant or agent, sell or supply to any person in any licensed premises or club any intoxicating liquor to be consumed either on or off the premises; or (6) consume in or take from any such premises or club any intoxicating liquor.

Exemptions- Nothing in the foregoing provisions of this Part of this Act and saving shall be deemed to prohibit or restrict provisions.

(a) the sale or supply to, or consumption by, any person of intoxicating liquor in any licensed premises or club where he is residing; or

Effect of restricted hours.

(6) the ordering of intoxicating liquor to be consumed off the a. d. 1921. premises, or the dispatch by the vendor of liquor so ordered; or (c) the supply of intoxicating liquor for consumption on licensed premises to any private friends of the holder of the licence bona fide entertained by him at his own expense, or the consumption of intoxicating liquor by persons so supplied; or (d) the consumption of intoxicating liquor with a meal by any person in any licensed premises or club at any time within

half an hour after the conclusion of the permitted hours, provided that the liquor was supplied during permitted hours and served at the same time as the meal and for consumption at the meal; or (e) the sale of intoxicating liquor to a trader for the purposes of his trade, or to a club for the purposes of the club; or () the sale or supply of intoxicating liquor to or in any canteen where the sale of intoxicating liquor is carried on under the authority of a Secretary of State or the Admiralty, or to any authorised mess of officers or non-commissioned officers of His Majesty's naval, military or air forces.

6. (1) The foregoing provisions of this Act shall have effect in Application lieu of section fifty-four of, and the Sixth Schedule to, the Licensing adapta-(Consolidation) Act, 1910, but (subject as hereinafter provided in Licensing this Act), all the other provisions of that Act with respect to closing Act. hours shall continue in force. g (2) The provisions of the Licensing (Consolidation) Act, 1910, ' specified in Part I. of the First Schedule to this Act shall be repealed, and the provisions of that Act specified in Part IL of that Schedule shall have effect subject to the modifications provided for in that Part of that Schedule.

7. (1) No person shall either by himself or by any servant or Conditions agent butk.?" ""

(a) sell, supply, distribute, or deliver, or induce any person to sell, supply, distribute or deliver any intoxicating liquor from any van, barrow, basket or other vehicle or receptacle, unless before the liquor is dispatched it has been ordered and the quantity, description and price thereof, together with the name and address of the person to whom it is to be supplied, has been entered in a delivery book or invoice, which shall be carried by the person delivering the liquor,

DRINK IN 1914-1922

AD. 1921

Restriction on credit for on-Balee.

and in a day book which shall be kept on the premises from which the liquor is dispatched; or (6) carry or convey in any van, barrow, basket or other vehicle or receptacle, while in use for the distribution or delivery of intoxicating liquor, any such liquor not entered in such delivery book or invoice and day book; or (c) distribute or deliver any intoxicating liquor at any address not specified in such delivery book or invoice and day book; or d) refuse to allow any constable to examine such van, barrow, basket or other vehicle or receptacle, or such delivery book or invoice:

Provided that the holder of a licence shall not be liable to any penalty under this section in respect of an offence committed by his servant or agent if he proves that such ofience was committed without his knowledge or consent.

(2) Nothing in this section shall be deemed to prohibit or restrict the sale, supply, distribution, or delivery of intoxicating liquor to a trader for the purposes of his trade, or to a club for the purposes of the club.

8. (1) No person shall (a) either by himself or by any servant or agent sell or supply in any licensed premises or club any intoxicating liquor to be consumed on the premises; or (h) consume any intoxicating liquor in such premises or club; unless it is paid for before or at the time when it is sold or supplied:

Provided always that, if the liquor is sold or supplied for consumption with a meal supplied at the same time and is consumed with such meal, this provision shall not be deemed to be contravened if the price of the liquor is paid together with the price of such meal.

(2) Nothing in this section shall be deemed to prohibit or restrict the sale or supply of intoxicating liquor to or in any canteen where the sale of intoxicating liquor is carried on under the authority of a Secretary of State or the Admiralty or to any authorised mess of officers or non-commissioned officers of His Majesty's naval, military or air forces.

Long pull prohibited.

9. No person shall, either by himself or by any servant or agent in any licensed premises or club, sell or supply to any person, as the measure of intoxicating liquor for which he asks, an amount exceeding that measure.

10. In determining whether an ofience has been committed a. d. 1921. under the enactments relating to the sale of food and drugs by selling to the prejudice of the purchaser whisky, brandy, rum or Strength of gin not adulterated otherwise than by any admixture of water, it shall be a good defence to prove that such admixture has not reduced the spirit more than thirty-five degrees under proof, and section 42 43 Vict.

six of the Sale of Food and Drugs Act, 1879, is hereby repealed.- 11. If, under the laws relating to the excise for the time being Certain in force, any liquor, being liquor to which this section applies, may g" ga ted be sold, whether wholesale or by retail, without an excise licence, as an intoxi-that liquor shall not be deemed to be beer or an intoxicating liquor eating liquor within the meaning of the Licensing (Consolidation) Act, 1910, or to ucence not be beer or an exciseable liquor within the meaning of the Licensing required for (Scotland) Act, 1903. ' f-

The liquor to which this section applies is any liquor which, (. 25. whether made on the licensed premises of a brewer of beer for sale or elsewhere, is found, on analysis of a sample thereof at any time, to be of an original gravity not exceeding one thousand and sixteen degrees and to contain not more than two per cent, of proof spirit, 12. (1) The powers of the licensing justices under this Part of Supplemen-this Act may be exercised by them, in accordance with such pro- 7 P""

VISIOIIS IS cedure as may be prescribed by rules made by the Secretary of to orders of State, at their general annual licensing meeting, or at any transfer licensing sessions held before the first general annual licensing meeting held " ' after the passing of this Act.

(2) Subject to the provisions of this Act, and of the Licensing (Consolidation) Act, 1910, an order of licensing justices under this Part of this Act (a) shall apply to all licensed premises and, if applicable to clubs, to all clubs in their district; and (6) may be varied by a subsequent order; and (c) shall be published in such manner as the Secretary of State may prescribe.

(3) A document purporting to be issued by licensing justices Statement to under this Part of this Act shall be evidence of the contents thereof, j cj b rules 13. The rules of every club contained in the register required to be kept under section ninety-two of the Licensing (Consolidation) Act, 1910, shall include a statement of the permitted hours applicable to that club.

DEINK IN 1914-1922

A. D. 1921.

Penalties.

14. If any person contravenes or fails to comply with any provision of this Part of this Act, he shall be guilty of an offence against this Act, and any person guilty of an offence against this Act shall be liable on summary conviction to a fine not exceeding thirty pounds.

Repeal of war provisions and abolition of Central Control Board (Liquor Traffic).

4 5 Geo. 5. c. 77.

5 6 Geo. 5. c. 42.

State management districts.

Pakt II Winding-up of Central Control Board Liquor Traffic) 15. (1) The Intoxicating Liquor (Temporary Restriction) Act, 1914, and the Defence of the Realm (Amendment) (No. 3) Act, 1915, are hereby repealed, and (subject as hereinafter provided) any regulations or orders made thereunder shall cease to have effect, and the Central Control Board (Liquor Traffic) (hereinafter referred to as the Board) is hereby abolished.

(2) Any property (whether real or personal) vested at the time of the commencement of this Part of this Act in the Board or their trustees is hereby transferred to and vested in the Secretary of State as respects property in England, and in the Secretary for Scotland as respects property in Scotland.

(3) If the Secretary of State or the Secretary for Scotland is satisfied that any property vested in him by this Act is no longer required, he may sell or otherwise dispose of it in such manner as he may think fit.

16. (1) Until Parliament otherwise determines, the schemes of State management of the liquor trade established by the Board mdet the Defence of the Realm (Liquor Control) Regulations, 1915, in the districts defined in the Second Schedule to this Act (in this Act referred to as State Management Districts) may be continued, by the Secretary of State as respects districts in England, and by the Secretary for Scotland as respects districts in Scotland. For this purpose, such of the said regulations as are contained in the extract therefrom which is set out in the Third Schedule to this Act are hereby continued in force in their application to those districts, and shall, to that extent, have effect as if enacted in this Act:

Provided that references to the Secretary of State or the Secretary for Scotland, as the case may require, shall be substituted for references to the Board, and a reference to an offence against this Act shall be substituted for the reference to a summary offence against the Defence of the Realm (Consolidation) Regulations, 1914:

Provided also that the power to acquire premises compulsorily a. d. 1921. shall apply only in the Carlisle district.

(2) The powers of the Board to carry on business shall, so far as concerns any premises in which the Board was carrying on business at the date of the passing of this Act, be transferred to the Secretary of State or the Secretary for Scotland, as the case may require, and exercisable by him accordingly.

(3) The Secretary of State and Secretary for Scotland shall appoint such persons as they think fit to act as local advisory committees for the purpose of assisting them in the

management of the State Management Districts, and pending any such appointment the persons acting as local advisory committees in those districts at the date of the passing of this Act, shall be the local advisory committees.

(4) The Secretary of State and the Secretary for Scotland shall cause such accounts to be kept, in relation to the State Management Districts, as the Treasury may direct, and shall cause an annual report to be presented to Parliament as to their procedure in connection with the management of those districts.

(5) In connection with any transfer effected by this Part of this Act, the provisions set out in the Fourth Schedule to this Act shall have effect.

17. This Part of this Act shall come into operation at the Commence expiration of two months from the passing of this Act:

Provided that (a) subject as hereinafter provided, any orders made by the Board under the Defence of the Realm (Liquor Control) Regulations, 1915, and in force at the date of the passing of this Act, shall cease to have effect as from the commencement of Part I. of this Act; and (6) the Defence of the Realm (Liquor Control) Regulations, 1915, shall continue in force until the expiration of the said two months whether or not the war previously terminates; and (c) any order made by the Board under which the sale or supply of intoxicating liquor in any licensed premises or club in any area is permitted at hours other than those applicable to licensed premises and clubs generally in that area shall continue in force until the expiration of the said period of two months; and ment of Part II.

DEINK IN 1914-1922

A. O. 1921.

d) any certificate of the Board by virtue of which any person was, at the date of the passing of this Act, entitled to sell or supply intoxicating liquor shall remain in force until the expiration of such time as will enable an application by that person for a justices' licence to be made and dealt with.

Licensed premises to which Act applies.

Repeal of part of s. 13 of 8 9 Vict. 109.

Definitions.

Application to Scotland and Ireland.

Part III

General 18. The provisions of this Act with respect to licensed premises apply to any premises or place where intoxicating liquors are sold by retail under a licence, and apply to any premises where the Secretary of State or Secretary for Scotland carries on business as the successor of the Board as though such premises were licensed premises.

19. In section thirteen of the Gaming Act, 1845 (which relates to the time when billiard playing is allowed), the following words shall be repealed, that is to say, ' and every person holding a victualler's licence who shall allow any person to play at such table, board, or instrument kept on the premises specified in such victualler's licence at any time when such premises are not by law allowed to be open for the sale of wine, spirits, or beer, or other fermented or distilled liquors."

20. For the purposes of this Act

The expression ' club ' means registered club;

The expression ' Metropolis' means the administrative county of London, with the addition of any area which, though not within the administrative county of London, is within the four-mile radius from Charing Cross;

The expression' permitted hours ' means as respects any licensed premises or club the hours on any day during which intoxicating liquor may be sold or supplied therein; and

The expression ' conclusion of the permitted hours ' means the end of the period in the afternoon or evening (as the case may be) during which the sale or supply of intoxicating liquor for any purpose is permitted.

21. (1) This Act shall apply to Scotland subject to the following modifications: (a) The Secretary for Scotland shall, unless the context otherwise requires, be substituted for the Secretary of State; ' real' shall mean ' heritable'; ' personal' shall mean ' movable'; a. d. 1921. ' intoxicating liquor ' shall mean ' exciseable liquor '; ' licence ' and ' justices' licence ' shall mean a certificate as defined in Part VII. of the Licensing (Scotland) Act, 1903; ' licensing justices ' shall mean ' licensing court'; a reference to a licensing district shall be construed as a reference to any burgh, county, or district for which there is a separate licensing court; references to the annual general licensing meeting and to transfer sessions shall be construed respectively as references to the April and the October half-yearly meetings of a licensing court; and references to the Licensing (Scotland) Acts, 1903 to 1913, shall be substituted for references to the Licensing (Consolidation) Act, 1910; (6) The section of this Act whereof the marginal note is ' Permitted hours on Sundays ' shall not apply except as regards clubs; (c) The sections of this Act whereof the marginal notes are ' Application and adaptation of Licensing Act," ' Statement to be included in club rules," and ' Penalties," shall not apply; d) The provisions of this Act as to the hours during which exciseable liquor may be sold, supplied or consumed in licensed premises on weekdays shall be substituted for the provisions of the Licensing (Scotland) Acts, 1903 to 1913, as to the hours during which such sale, supply, or con-simiption is permitted on weekdays, provided that the hour which the licensing court may direct to be substituted for eleven in the morning shall be not earlier than ten; and any reference in the said Acts to the hours when such sale, supply, or consumption is lawful or unlawful, or to hours of opening or closing, shall be construed accordingly; (e) Subject to the provisions of sections forty and fifty-five of the Licensing (Scotland) Act, 1903, as amended by any subsequent enactment, it shall, notwithstanding the terms of any certificate for the sale by retail of exciseable liquors in force at the passing of this Act, not be lawful for the holder thereof to sell or supply, or permit to be consumed, exciseable liquor on weekdays, except in accordance with the provisions of this Act as to the hours during which such sale, supply, or consumption is permitted; () If any person being the holder of a certificate for the sale by retail of exciseable liquors shall contravene or fail to

DEINK IN 1914-1922

AD. 1921.

3 4 Geo. 5. c. 33.

Short title, construction and commencement.

comply with any of the provisions of this Act, he shall be deemed guilty of a breach of his certificate, and if any other person shall contravene or fail to comply with any of the said provisions, he shall be guilty of an ofience and shall be liable to a penalty of ten pounds; (g) In order that any club may be eligible to be registered under the Licensing (Scotland) Acts, 1903 to 1913, the rules shall include a statement of the permitted hours applicable to the club; (h) The proviso to section thirty-five, and sections fifty-six and sixty-three of the Licensing (Scotland) Act, 1903, and section seven of the Temperance (Scotland) Act, 1913, are hereby repealed; (i) The Secretary for Scotland may by order make such adaptations in the forms contained in the Sixth Schedule to the Licensing (Scotland) Act, 1903, as may seem to him necessary to make those forms conform with the provisions of this Act.

(2) This Act shall not apply to Ireland.

22. (1) This Act may be cited as the Licensing Act, 1921.

(2) This Act shall be construed as one with the Licensing (Consolidation) Act, 1910, and that Act and this Act may be cited together as the Licensing Acts, 1910 and 1921.

(3) This Act as it applies to Scotland shall be construed as one with the Licensing (Scotland) Acts, 1903 to 1913, and those Acts and this Act as it so applies may be cited together as the Licensing (Scotland) Acts, 1903 to 1921.

(4) Save as otherwise expressly provided, this Act shall come into operation at the expiration of fourteen days after the passing thereof.

APPENDIX V

Delirium Tremens (Cases of Delirium Tremens treated in representative areas)

Liverpool Poor Law Unions

Males Females

August 1914 to January 1915. 150 106

August 1915 to January 1916. 72 46

East London and Woolwich Poor Law Unions (excluding West Ham)

Males Females

December 1914 to April 1915. 47 18

December 1915 to April 1916. 26 9

West Ham Union

December 1914 to November 1915 December 1915 to November 1916

Males 62 30

Bradford Union Workhouse

Males December 1914 to May 1915. 11

December 1915 to May 1916. 8

Glasgow and Govan Parishes

Males August 16, 1914, to September 15, 1915 87 August 16, 1915, to September 15, 1916 59

Females 33 22

Females

Females 21 12

In Prisons of Six Scheduled Areas

Males Females During five months before Restrictions.15 8

During five months after Restrictions. 3 3

Total

Printed in England at THE BALLANTYNE PRESS SPOTTISWOODE, BALLANTTfnE CO. LTD.

Lightning Source UK Ltd.
Milton Keynes UK
12 January 2011

165559UK00003B/47/P